The Root of All Evil

This is a courageous book by a group of women of valor, who dared to cross a bridge that others shy away from. The book shows in a very convincing manner how one can fight the demonization of the "Other". Their answer is that through intimate dialog and unique collaboration, one can see the different shades of truth. This book serves as a guide to answer the "God is on My side" argument that has been prevalent since 9/11. These women share humanistic values, and look into the deeper roots of mankind's tendency to repeat past mistakes and go on forever on a march of folly.

David Michaelis, Founder LINK TV

The Root of All Evil is a profound exploration of how the repression of the feminine has caused great imbalances in our world. Few contemporary narratives have showcased with such clarity the conscious denial of the feminine over the course of time, and portrayed how urgent is the need to rediscover, draw out and strengthen the feminine in our world today. As we seek to address the critical problems facing the world community, a key factor will be our ability to reclaim the feminine energies that have long been repressed. As the authors of this important book have shown, this feminine power, present in both men and women, is essential for helping us progress toward a more balanced, loving and compassionate world community.

Dena Merriam, Founder and Convener
The Global Peace Initiative of Women

Compelling, deeply felt and personal — The Root of All Evil demonstrates as much as describes radical solutions for the problems caused by fear-based violence and exclusion in our world. Exemplifying the struggle between diverse points of view, yet demonstrating that cooperation is possible, this book "walks its talk." It is a must-read for those concerned about the deeper roots of fundamentalism, both religious and secular.

Saadi Shakur Chishti (Neil Douglas-Klotz)
co-author, The Tent of Abraham; *author,* The Sufi Book of Life

The Root of All Evil is not bedside reading. It will provoke every one of its readers and will infuriate many of them. It takes on patriarchal societies, governments, and religions, documenting the malevolence of prejudice and gender imbalance from the Hindu caste system to the excesses of the Taliban. However, the book ends on a hopeful note, allowing the authors to tell their stories, accounts of how they transcended their cultural conditioning to bring love, harmony, and egalitarianism into their corners of this tattered, male-dominated, world.

Stanley Krippner, PhD, co-editor, The Psychological Effects
of War Trauma on Civilians: An International Perspective

Perfect timing for a book that carries us to the realm of heart, while exposing the root causes that separate us, as one human family. This highly informative text is masterfully blended between feminine perspective and cultural prejudice; patriarchy and politics; faith and fundamentalism; spirituality and science. The uniqueness of the book is manifested through its epilogue which offers a forum to the authors of diverse cultures and faiths to honestly reflect on their personal selves and upbringings that shaped their world views. Their agreement to disagree with each other on critical issues of concern has added a fascinating and healing dimension.

Sharmin Ahmad (Reepi), author, The Rainbow in a Heart
Consultant: Peace Education, and Interfaith Dialogue

The Root of All Evil

An Exposition of Prejudice, Fundamentalism
and Gender Imbalance

Sharon G. Mijares, Aliaa Rafea,
Rachel Falik and Jenny Eda Schipper

imprint-academic.com

Published in the UK by
Imprint Academic, PO Box 200, Exeter EX5 5YX, UK

Published in the USA by
Imprint Academic, Philosophy Documentation Center
PO Box 7147, Charlottesville, VA 22906-7147, USA

ISBN: 9781845400675

A CIP catalogue record for this book is available from the
British Library and US Library of Congress

Cover design by
Gabo Carabes and Paco Aguayo
www.haiku.com.mx   info@haiku.com.mx
in association with Steve Kelly
stevek@conceptstudio.co.uk

This book is dedicated to
all the innocent peoples of the world
who suffer because of patriarchal injustice.

It is our hope
that we can come together as one human family
and create a world of peace.

Contents

Authors

Sharon G. Mijares, PhD teaches Comparative Religions at the California Institute of Human Science and various Psychology courses at Chapman University. She has been a student of Christian mysticism for over 36 years and has spent the last 16 years studying Jesus' original Aramaic teachings. She is a member of the Sufi Ruhaniat International, and is ordained in its Universal Worship Service — honoring all the world's religious traditions. www.sharonmijares.com

Aliaa Rafea, PhD is a noted Islamic and Egyptian scholar and faculty member at Ain Shams University. She was a visiting professor at RMWC in 2002. She comes from a long line of Sufi guides and is a descendent of the Prophet Muhammad. Her doctoral degree is in Anthropology. She authored and co-authored several books in Arabic and English, the latest of which is *The Book of Essential Islam* (Book Foundation 2005). She is a fellow of Society of Applied Anthropology, and a member in several international academic institutions. She is also a member in several NGOs in Egypt.

Rachel Falik holds an MS. in Organizational Psychology, and has a special interest in intercultural dynamics. She was born and raised in Israel and served as a Lieutenant in the Israeli Air Force. She subsequently had a managerial career as a human resources specialist and currently lives in the US.

Jenny Eda Schipper holds a Master's Degree in Guidance and Counseling from Duquesne University. She is a yoga teacher, a massage therapist and an artist, and is currently co-editing *The Jewish Woman Muslim Woman in the 21st Century: Transcending Differences*.

Acknowledgments

This book would not be complete without acknowledging the specific persons who have contributed in some way to this project. We were each inspired by a variety of people. The following allows for our individual and our shared appreciation.

Sharon: I want to acknowledge my teacher and best friend Saadi Neil Douglas-Klotz, and express my deeply felt gratitude for his untiring efforts for peace both in the Middle East and in the world. His modeling has inspired my own work in this area. My son Raphael Mijares pointed out many of the follies of the current political regime, and also suggested I investigate the prejudicial stance found in the Rig Veda and the Old Testament. Likewise, personal conversations with Jonathan Granoff of the Global Security Institute led to much learning. The threads of the resulting research are woven throughout the text. I would also like to thank the Rev. Hal Lingerman who suggested I study the *Nag Hammadi Library, The Other Bible*, and research specific to Judeo-Christian history. Dr Nahid Angha and Dr Ali Kianfar, co-founders of the International Association of Sufism, enabled me to meet Jonathan Granoff, Aliaa Rafea, and many other fine Sufis and Christian ministers devoted to interfaith work. They also inspired this work. I am also most appreciative of Heather Hurford for introducing me to LinkTV, where I could really learn what was happening throughout this world. My friend Dania Brett read through the first draft and provided many well-thought out editorial suggestions. And, most significantly, I express my heart-felt gratitude to my co-authors, who trusted my vision, agreed with it, and dedicated their efforts to this endeavor — even though it was difficult at times.

Aliaa: I am indebted to my brother and my spiritual guide Master Ali Rafea who has shown me how to listen to my heart, and use my intellect and struggle to make belief and living one and the same thing. Without his guidance and continuous empowerment, I would not have been able to accomplish such a challenging work where I had to get over many of the "taken for granted" notions in my culture, and reconsider them in order to expose aspects of fundamentalism and prejudice. I would also like to thank Ms Aisha Rafea who reviewed some parts of the work, for our discussions enabled me to see things more clearly. Dr Malika Martini, with whom I have shared previous work, read the Introduction, and I greatly appreciated her insightful comments. I would like to express my gratitude to Dr. Ali Kianfar and Dr Nahid Angha for their genuine efforts to gather Sufis from around the world. Through their respected International Association of Sufism, I got to know Dr. Sharon Mijares, otherwise I would never have been part of this project. I would like also to thank Shaykh Ahmed Abdur Rashid for his important notices and discussion about its themes. How can I thank Sharon, I do not find words for appreciation. She opened a wide door for me to accomplish what I have already started; since I have been trying to find ways through my academic and spiritual work to help remove false cultural barriers from human communications, and I very much appreciate that she thought of me to join in this project. I learnt a great deal from her vision of diagnosing the root of separation and enmity. It was very inspiring to work with her. Although I have not met Rachel and Jenny in person, I cherish our relationship, and it was a great pleasure to co-author the book with them. Last, but not least, I would like to thank my family for their continuous support.

Rachel: I am especially grateful to Sima and Moshe (Zigi) Zigdon, my unconditionally loving parents, followers of Ze'ev Jabotinsky's legacy, who always respected my independent thinking and taught me that compassion and tolerance are the highest virtues. A special thanks to the sociologist and philosopher Tom Semm, whose immense political knowledge, critical eye, and unbiased perspective led me beyond the readings of Kierkegaard- Buber and Zinn-Chomsky-Roy to find my distinct voice. And, most importantly, I cherish Sharon's visionary leadership. This book could never have been written without her inspiration. Bringing us all together made this journey of discovery possible for successful journeys are always taken with others.

Jenny: I'd like to greatly acknowledge Sharon Mijares for inviting me into this project, giving me an immense opportunity to grow in a new direction. I am forever grateful to her for this gift and her vision to see how I fit into this book. I want to deeply thank my husband, John Kingsmill, for his unwavering support and encouragement around my participation in this book. I also want to acknowledge my parents, Lewis and Rose Schipper, who taught me to embrace all people as equal and to work for a world that exemplifies this truth. I am also grateful to my brother Henry for promising not to disown me, no matter what I wrote.

We are all especially appreciative of our publisher, *Imprint Academic*, and for all the support of Anthony Freeman, its managing editor. Anthony believed in this book from the onset. He is truly a kindred spirit. We are also grateful to his wife Jacqueline for creating the Index, the editorial staff at Imprint Academic, our reviewers, and our cover designers, Gabo and Paco, who worked long and hard to come up with the right image for the cover of this book. In summary, we cannot thank Dr. Ismail Serageldin enough for the time he gave to read our work and write such an appreciative Foreword, considering his very busy schedule. Our gratitude likewise includes Sr. Joan Chittister for her beautifully expressed Preface. We thank everyone who made some contribution to this book.

Ismail Serageldin

Foreword

Our times are times of paradox. Great wealth coexists with extreme poverty. Exceptional educational and scientific achievements coexist with prejudice and quackery. Unprecedented recognition of human rights coexists with discrimination. In these times, where hatred is being actively nurtured, where the clash of civilizations is advocated as an inevitability, and where those who see threats in every difference are increasingly vocal, it is not only refreshing but also inspiring to see this work by four women who have little in common except their well-attuned consciousness of their common humanity, and their willingness to speak out. They speak out in defense of values they hold dear and to condemn approaches and practices that they recognize as corrosive and destructive.

The work of Sharon Mijares, Aliaa Rafea, Rachel Falik and Jenny Eda Schipper is a collective journey into being human. They hold up mirrors to themselves and recognize where they have come from to be where they are. They open windows through which they see not just landscapes, but other human beings. They recognize the distorting lenses of bias and bigotry, and call out for a candid and courageous rejection of prejudice, fundamentalism, excessive concern with the outward appearance of religiosity, and to work for gender equity and the dignity of the human person. They demand that we speak truth to power, and that we have the courage of our convictions and act upon them.

The four authors come from very different backgrounds. A Muslim from Egypt, a Christian mystic from America, a Jew from the US and a Jew from Israel (but currently living in the US), they have been able to transcend their differences in the search for common ground. This book is therefore very much a labor of love, and a journey of self discovery and of understanding the other. They demonstrate by their words and deeds that the essence of love and tolerance at the core of all religions, of all great traditions, is universal.

They follow their hearts and their minds to a conclusion that much of what is wrong with the world around us is due to fundamentalism, prejudice and gender imbalance. They find common ground despite their differing backgrounds, and can make common cause against the forces that they consider the roots of evil in the world. Theirs is very much a religious quest, but their perspective is open and encompassing. As they point out, it is primarily spiritual, rather than religious in the sense of accepting the authority of any religious group or structure.

They are deeply committed to ensuring that the patriarchal viewpoint that dominates so much of the world today does not obscure women's rights as human rights. Their book rings with honesty and a desire to learn from the past to create a new future. All of us who are unhappy at the state of the world today, can appreciate their taking the time and trouble to share their caring and compassion, their journey of discovery of the self and the other. The world needs many more like these four courageous authors.

Ismail Serageldin
Director, Library of Alexandria
Alexandria, October 2006

Joan Chittister, OSB

Preface

We live in an era when over two-thirds of the US population says that this country is going in the wrong direction. And with good reason. We now have over 10,000,000 children in this country without health insurance, Social Security is at risk, the national deficit is higher than at any other time in US history, and billions of dollars have been spent recklessly and lavishly on a war waged without reason, fought without success, and, in the end, managed to do more to create terrorism than to end it .

The situation seems clear: it is, indeed, time for a change. But of what? Simply the administration that has been so clearly and foolishly committed to such a situation? Or is there something far deeper than present policies that demands attention?

The truth is that at least half of the US public found the current Iraqi war quite palpable at its beginning. The Congress of the United States, said to be the representative of the people, the watchdogs of the system, the balance beam meant to curb errant presidential power, acceded to the presidential proposals designed to make the war possible — to every one of them — with not so much as a whimper, either Democrat or Republican.

As a result, they refused to pass universal health care. They cut back on social programs that might give at least some support to the children of the poor. They accepted the military budget that will become the biggest debt the country has ever known and blithely passed it on to their own children and grandchildren. And most of all, they agreed to the so-called Bush Doctrine of Preemptive War, the notion

The Root of All Evil

that a US president can order the invasion of any country he wants on the grounds that even though they have not yet attacked us, they might. And they made us a terror and torture state ourselves.

The whole sad system comes right out of an Alice-in-Wonderland script where down is up and up is down. It is a frightening excuse for political science, an arrogant and overbearing way to go through the world. It is a kind of drunken imperialism run amok.

A kind of despair has settled over the country. How could the "land of the free, the home of the brave" have come to this? How is it that the US has become an occupying army in a foreign nation, kills thousands and thousands of innocent people and buries its own soldier sons and daughters for nothing? For no clear purpose; for no great and noble goal; for no defensible reason.

What's worse: How is it that any government could bring a rational people to accept such a thing, to participate in such a thing, to applaud such a thing? But we did. And in large numbers.

It seems, then, that the problem may lie as much with the national population as it does with the national politicians who allowed a national president to run rough-shod over American ideals. And in a most messianic way.

We set out, the government told us, to defend ourselves from weapons of mass destruction. But the truth is that the only weapons of mass destruction there were our own. Then they told us that our real purpose was to implant American democracy around the world. But planting democracy at the point of a gun is at least an oxymoron. Our messianism, it seems, is highly defective, grossly deformed, largely bogus.

So the creeping suspicion remains that what we really wanted were military bases implanted in the Middle East that could secure for us the flow of oil from countries whose own officials no longer guaranteed them to be client states of the New American Empire.

How can such goals — any of them — even be thinkable in a nation that talks about democracy and freedom and human rights?

An old Sufi tale may come closest to the answer:

Ali-Shah, the Sufi saint, tells us that Khidr, the Teacher of Moses, gave humankind a warning. On a certain date, he said, all the water in the world that had not been stored would disappear. Then different water would flow and those who drank it would go mad. Only those who stored up water for the time would be saved.

But only one woman listened. She collected water from an old well, stored it and waited.

Sure enough, one day the old streams stopped running, and the wells went dry. So the woman drank the water she'd stored. But when it seemed that water had begun to flow again, she went out about the people. The problem was that they were different now. They were thinking differently and talking differently and acting differently.

And, worst of all, they had no memory of what things had once been like. She could see in their eyes that when she tried to talk to them about past ideals, past practices, past principles they'd held amongst themselves they thought she was mad.

Finally, sick with the loneliness of being different, of thinking differently from everyone else, she took a sip of this, a swallow of that. And little by little, people began to look at her as a maniac become mild again, as once absurd but now miraculously sane again.

How do we explain the differences between what we say we are as a people and what we do? The explanation is a simple one: We can do no wrong, we were told. And we drank the water.

We are a people now drunk on new water: the water of power, and the water of war, the water of vengeance and the water of victimage. We are sick to the center of our souls with the symptoms of it. Hate and anger, pain and revenge, despair and disunity are everywhere.

The question that eats away at the soul of us is clear: Why do we do those things? Is there any answer to it? Or is this simply "the way things are"?

This book, *The Root of All Evil*, exposes the problem under the problem. It says, in brief, that the world is being consumed by a fundamentalism that strikes at the heart of every major religious tradition on earth.

It says, too, that societies, in league with religious fundamentalism, have repressed the gifts and advancement of women—and so the feminine qualities that moderate violence.

And it says finally that the gender imbalance that marks every major human institution as a result of the repression of women and the gifts of women must be righted if the human race is ever to become fully human. If the human race is to survive its own violence, racism, fear and prejudices.

What's more, *The Root of All Evil* brings theology, history, psychology, anthropology, systems theory and the models of the great religious prophets themselves to the bar of the questions.

It is a stunning overview of ideals supported by science, embodied in history and ignored by groups and leaders, institutions and nations everywhere in the race to power, greed and human destruction.

There is an answer to why we do it, there is a solution at hand. The only obstacle now is ourselves. Knowing all of this, will we do what we can to change the world one heart at a time, beginning with our own?

What can people like us, women, who understand struggle and conflict and powerlessness like few others—but who also know better than most that violence has never solved violence and never will—do about it?

The Sufi, Ali-Shah, was right. If, isolated and lonely, we find ourselves sipping the wrong water, we must, at the very least, never forget that it is madness to lose the way of talking kindly and behaving caringly and thinking respectfully of one another.

No matter who tells us otherwise, if we want to stay sane, if we want our children to grow up to be sound of mind and whole of body, if we want our countries to thrive, we must not drink the water of division. We must not drink the water of violence.

And we must cry out till the rest of the world hears us: Do not drink the water, Do not drink the water. Whatever you do—in the name of God, the most merciful, the most compassionate—do not drink the water of hate.

This book, *The Root of All Evil*, is a gift to us all. It takes us to the mountain top to look back to what our great religious traditions have called us to do. It asks us to realize what we have done to those mandates and why. It shows us that we are not trapped into a biology of hate and destruction. It shows us the way out of these patriarchal pyramids of power-mongering.

This book waters the soul and enables it to grow again.

Joan Chittister, OSB
Erie, PA, USA

Picture his fall from heaven – Lucifer, Son of the Morning – what a title and what a birthright! To be born of the morning implies to be a creature formed of translucent light undefiled, with all the warm rose of a million orbs of day coloring his bright essence, and all the luster of fiery planets flaming in his eyes. Splendid and supreme, at the right hand of Deity itself he stood, this majestic Archangel, and before his unwearied vision rolled the grandest creative splendors of God's thoughts and dreams.

All at once he perceived in the vista of embryonic things a new small world, and on it a being forming itself slowly as it were into the Angelic likeness, a being weak yet strong, sublime yet foolish, a strange paradox, destined to work its way through all the phases of life, still imbibing the very breath and soul of the Creator it should touch Conscious Immortality – Eternal Joy.

Then Lucifer, full of wrath, turned on the Master of the Spheres, and flung forth his reckless defiance, crying aloud – "Wilt thou make of this slight poor creature an Angel even as I? I do protest against thee and condemn! Lo, if thou makest Man in Our Image I will destroy him utterly, as unfit to share with me the splendors of Thy Wisdom – the glory of Thy love!"

And the Voice Supreme, in accents terrible and beautiful replied – "Lucifer, Son of the Morning, full well dost thou know that never can an idle or wasted word be spoken before Me. For Free-will is the gift of the Immortals; therefore what thou sayest, thou must needs do! Fall, proud Spirit from thy high estate – thou and thy companions with thee – and return no more till Man himself redeem thee! Each human soul that yields unto thy tempting shall be a new barrier set between thee and heaven; each one that of its own choice doth repel and overcome thee, shall lift thee nearer thy lost home! When the world rejects thee, I will pardon and again receive thee, but not till then."

M. Corelli, *The Sorrows of Satan*, pp. 65–66

Introduction

What force prompts human beings to destroy other people, nations and our environment — ignoring the results and knowledge gleaned from thousands of years of evolution? Our history reveals that religious, political and economic institutions have continuously conspired to denigrate, demonize and destroy *the other*, despite the fact that all of the world's religions teach love and respect for one another, and that our legal institutions were created to assure ethical standards for social relationships.

If we are to survive as a human family, we have to become more accountable for our actions and eliminate religious, racial, ethnic and gender prejudice, selfishly motivated political power and economic greed. This effort requires an in-depth examination of the various forces that motivate human behaviors. The author of I Timothy 6:10 warns readers that, "the love of money is the root of all evil ..." But, if we examine the behaviors associated with greed, it appears that the root motivation behind the desire for wealth and possessions assures that one is as good as or better than others, and, therefore, in a superior class. Superiority is justified for a variety of rationalized reasons; it is validated through religious affiliation, class distinctions and affected by ethnocentric and racist approaches to life. Therefore, this book proposes that the root manifestation of evil is any calculated act intended to demean or harm another human being, and that the inherent gender imbalance found within patriarchal hierarchal systems perpetuates this crime.

The theory and title for *The Root of All Evil* resulted from a contemplation of Lucifer's fall from heaven, a story of prejudice and pride.[1] This creation narrative is a meaningful story found in the monotheistic traditions. It relates Lucifer's rage at God's conception of Adam, the archetypal human being. Lucifer declared that angels were superior to humans. The story metaphorically suggests that prejudice against another creation closes the heart to the divine (hence the "fall from heaven"). It is also a metaphor alluding to the evil trait of prejudicial behaviors that arise from hierarchical pride. It is well worth further exploration, for research into the rise of patriarchal dominance suggests that prejudice is an inherent manifestation of hierarchical pride resulting from gender-imbalance.

Historically, patriarchal influence in religion, culture and family requires hierarchical ordering. Hierarchy is at the core of patriarchy. An individual, a race, nation or religion always has to be better than its counterpart — even spirit is deemed to be superior to form (matter) whereas both are a manifestation of divine creation. Patriarchy is a primary example of prejudice and disregard for others; for, as this book will reveal, patriarchal systems have initiated a continuous pattern of violence and dominance over others. Wars are continuously fought in order to assure one's position as the superior government or empire, and to control the earth's resources. One race is deemed to be superior to another. The inferior race is maltreated, and oftentimes endangered.

Every race has its own prejudice, and, in particular, women have been relegated to lesser positions. Females are considered to be less significant than males in patriarchy. In fact, ongoing violence has been enacted by males against both women and children throughout recorded history. This is not to say that patriarchy is evil itself, but that its focus on hierarchal order and domination have opened it to a multitude of sins. It is inherently flawed as evidenced by its ongoing destruction of *the other*.

---

[1]   Lucifer was later called Satan. In Islam he is known as Iblis.

It is believed that around the fifth millennium BCE,[2] Indo-Europeans (also known as Aryans) began a wide spread campaign of violence across Europe and Asia. This included a conquering of the Dravidians, the people of India. The early Semitic peoples known as Hebrews were also nomadic invaders (Eisler, 1987). As patriarchy established itself, it organized its religious beliefs accordingly. The reign of the conqueror Manu, and associated mythologies, initiated the caste system of India. Likewise, the new monotheistic religion, that would eventually become Judaism, claimed a patriarchal lineage precluding all others.[3] According to these narratives, all history had just begun.

The world's religions have been narrated by a patriarchal mindset claiming to speak for God. Other religions are more often than not denounced as Godless or inferior in order to proclaim one's religion as ultimate. This attitude has encouraged the development of radical fundamentalism, and it represents a significant and increasing threat to humanity's future.

The 2005 Human Rights Watch report indicates that during the last ten years there have been religious wars in Ireland, Cyprus, the Balkans, Rwanda, Burma, Sri Lanka, Nigeria, Sudan, Israel-Palestine, the Philippines (Mindanao), and Indonesia. More recent bombings and killings between Shiite and Sunni Muslims in Iraq can also be added to this list. Abortion clinics have been terrorized by radical Christians in the US Suicide bombings, hostage taking and beheadings have been instigated by fundamentalist fervor.

We have only to look at these many examples of widespread violence against our brothers and sisters to realize that we have neither integrated nor heeded the higher values given to us through our Prophets, sacred texts and the great ethical exemplars of our historical past. It is highly

---

[2] The authors will use CE (Common Era) and BCE (Before the Common Era) when listing dates rather than BC and AD, which is based upon the birth and death of Jesus Christ. This is done in respect for readers of differing religions. Both forms relate to the Gregorian calendar.

[3] Jewish law states that a child born through a Jewish mother is deemed Jewish.

probable that the inability to integrate and apply these higher values is a result of gender imbalance. A woman, by virtue of her mothering characteristics, has inherent relational qualities. She is more concerned with the impact of ideas and beliefs upon people and the environment. Therefore, a gender-balanced humanity will shift and eventually resolve many of our present dilemmas.

Differences and Commonalities

Four women coordinated the authoring of this book. Each is from a different cultural background and religion. We have been able to move beyond the political stands of our governments, American, Israeli and Egyptian, and demonstrate respectful and caring dialogue in co-authoring this document. As women, we realized our knowledge and caring would not allow us to stand aside and witness human destruction on such mass scales. Also, we have each personally observed and/or been victims of the evil known as prejudice, and hope to make a helpful contribution given the critical nature of the current world situation. *Sharon Mijares* is an American with a background in Christian mysticism (and Sufism). *Aliaa Rafea* is an Egyptian scholar and Muslim (living in Egypt). *Rachel Falik* is an Israeli Jew, currently residing in the US. *Jenny Eda Schipper* is a naturalized American Jew whose extended family was almost entirely decimated by the Nazis. A short biographical sketch is provided below so that the reader can understand the background influences and motivations that led us to combine our efforts and write this book.

Sharon Mijares

As a child I attended a variety of protestant churches. The chosen church depended upon location, rather than denomination. My parents were not religious, so I was free to attend the church of my choice. During my early teens I became increasingly aware of the many forms of prejudice pervading each of these churches. For example, one denomination believed it was superior to another if it denounced card playing; if its parishioners danced or didn't dance; or if the members attended church on a Saturday or a Sunday. I realized these minor differences had little, if anything, to do with true spirituality.

My family of origin was also very prejudiced. Perhaps my early rebellion against this inhumanity led me to form friendships with people of differing nationalities and races; but I was also motivated by my love for other human beings. In high school I developed many Hispanic friendships. Terms such as "mi casa es su casa" (my house is your house) spoke of welcoming and warmth. However, a few years later when visiting a family in Mexico, I heard them speak against the "Indios" (basically because they were either darker in skin color or poorer). I also heard references against African-Americans. I heard that it was not unusual for homosexuals to be targeted and attacked — even killed. As a teenager I learned that within each race, ethnic group and religion there is usually some form of prejudice against another group.

My opposition to parental and cultural prejudicial influences also evidenced itself in my partner relationships. For example, my first child was of Hispanic descent, and was born one month before my 17th birthday. My parents refused to talk to me upon the birth of this child. I could return to their home, but only without the "half-breed." I chose to wait three months in juvenile hall for a foster home that would receive us both.

During the birth of my third child, I was profoundly affected by the words of a thoughtless medical doctor during the final hour of labor. The doctor knew that the baby's absent father was African-American. Shortly before the delivery he asked me if I had considered adopting out the child. I was overwhelmed with heaviness and immense pain as I realized the societal prejudice embedded in his words. I soon held my beloved son in my arms, but from that moment on I carried the heart-rending awareness of the power of prejudice along with the desire to protect my child from its dagger.

At age 27 I met a significant spiritual teacher and began an intensive training in Christian mysticism. Later, after many years of religious and relationship training, I began to question my beliefs. Was any religion truly superior? Was a Buddhist view of Nirvana any less valid than the Catholic view of heaven (or vice versa)? Was it possible that each religious perspective differed according to the consciousness of its interpreter? Perhaps each religion represented a unique view and expression of the divine (Khan, 1984). I refused to participate any longer in the insanity of believing that any one religion was superior to another, and chose instead, to recognize that most people found the religion that was right for them. How can we limit the immensity of the Creator?

The above experiences have led to a life-long awareness and study of the devastating consequences of hatred and ignorance. Prejudice appears to be rooted in the fear of anything unfamiliar or unknown, and to be motivated by pride — based upon a false claim of superiority and a lack of love for the rest of the human family. At times I feel pain for the way African-Americans have been treated in this society. I often have African-American students in my undergraduate and graduate courses. I feel mixed admiration and compassion for the struggle these students have endured in order to receive the same benefits that other races take for granted.

At times I also find it difficult to admit I am a Christian because Jesus' teachings have been so poorly represented. The Beatitudes clearly depict a peaceful, simple and compassionate way of life that stands in sharp contrast to a Christian ideology supporting war and large corporations wherein the rich get richer while the poor get poorer. Jesus never said "take from the poor and give to the rich," a policy encouraged by the religious right. The experience of contributing to this book has restored my dedication to Jesus' original teachings — as evidenced in his healing ways that demonstrate compassion and acceptance of all.

Aliaa Rafea

I grew up as a daughter of a Sufi Master in Egypt and was surrounded with enormous energy of love and light. My parents had a very special way of treating their children. They were keen on protecting our dignity, freedom and privacy. For example, my father had never ordered me to pray or demanded that I do anything. Instead, he spent time with us, discussing various issues in religion, culture, politics, literature and other significant matters. In response, I developed a way to respect prayers, but not to consider them as an imposition. Through our talks, my approach to life was developed and my common sense was founded. *No compulsion in religion* was among those premises that were not to be doubted. The fact that no one should be judged according to religious affiliation was another value instilled at an early age, and these values became part of my way of relating to the world. This upbringing had a great impact on my choice of study and my attitudes towards other cultures.

During my teens Egypt was free from fundamentalism. We had an Egyptian Jewish family as our neighbor, and we played together as friends. The head of that family co-owned a business with an Egyptian Muslim. Many large businesses were owned by Jews, and they were praised for their honesty and good service. The foundation of the Israeli state was criticized from a political perspective. Our generation understood the clear distinction between Zionism and Judaism. We sympathized with Palestinians who were expelled from their lands, and we despaired at the atrocities occurring in the holy land. Liberating Palestine was an Arab dream, not only an Egyptian one. As children, we were not thinking of the issue in regards to its numerous complications, we simply considered that retaining the rights of the Palestinian people was similar to retaining one's stolen home. In time, and as a result of new facts concerning the occupied land of Palestine, it has become clearer and clearer in our minds that there must be a solution where the two nations — the Palestinians and Jews — could live and enjoy the right of self determination. With great joy and enthusiasm, I translated Noam Chomsky's book *The Fateful Triangle* into Arabic. I have developed a great respect for this Jewish intellectual, whose religious identity has not veiled his ability to see with fairness and to ask for equal human rights for both Israelis and Palestinians.

I chose to study philosophy and psychology, aiming at opening my heart and mind to other ways of thinking. Later on I developed an interest in anthropology. Because Anthropology by definition deals with living cultures, I learned that the relationships between people are not only based on personal characteristics, but also on how one's perspective is shaped by cultural norms and values. That approach brought me down to earth in that human interactions were even more complex than I had previously believed.

During my stay in Wales, early in the seventies, my husband and I took every opportunity to learn about other religions. We attended Baha'i gatherings, opened our doors to Jehovah's Witnesses, to Mormon preachers, and were curious to know about other religious groups. Guided by my father's teachings, we sought to know more about our own religion by exposing ourselves to other people's points of view. We were sure that there was a common ground among all religions. Inexperienced as we were, it was striking to us to realize that the others were convinced that there was one correct way, and were not ready to enter into serious discussions. They simply wanted to convert us to their beliefs. Deceived by our openness and tolerance, they thought we were an easy catch. That was my first encounter with fanaticism, or what we call idiomatically fundamentalism. I got to realize that it is more common to see how such people are imprisoned in their mental frame of reference, and ignoring their inner guidance. They are rarely able to listen to another point of view, and their words are spiritually empty. Allah was present in my life with tremendous force through my father's teachings, but I never thought that there was only one way to God. Therefore, I was amazed to see prejudiced attitudes overwhelming "religious" people, including Muslims. After six years of staying in the United Kingdom, I was back to Egypt to find another Egypt, not the one that I left.

In the late seventies, as a result of Sadat's policy which encouraged what was called at that time "Islamic Groups" to participate in the political sphere, there was a growing trend of fundamentalism. That trend emphasized the form at the expense of meaning. I found that there was a growing interest in what to do in order to be Muslim-rather than how to approach life. I saw that "veiling" among students was a phenomenon which deserved investigation. I wanted to know if religiousness for these veiled women meant only to attach oneself to certain costumes, or if there was more to understand about their interest in following certain, so called, religious rules. Religion, as I had learned it, had more to do with the believer's heart than what s/he wore.

Unfortunately, this artificial trend of religiousness finds great popularity among Egyptians today. I am not against wearing head scarves as an expression of modesty, because I have learned to respect others and honor their freedom of choice. I am against the rigidity and the imposition of one's way of thinking on others.

I have come to realize that the world in which I lived as a child and young woman is vanishing. The blight of prejudice is strong; it has roots reaching back into the history of humankind. It requires great efforts to remove these historically accumulated and limited perspectives. It became my major interest to remove those false barriers that separate our human family, and to build ties of love between humans everywhere. In response to this conviction, I wrote articles and co-authored books that addressed that goal. My experience as a visiting professor at Randolph-Macon Women's College[4] proved that that such a goal is possible to achieve. RMWC is a private liberal school in Lynchburg, Virginia. The college invites professors from various world cultures to offer courses educating American students about "the others." I was chosen to teach about Islam. I taught two interrelated courses; one about Islam and the

---

[4]   For more information, see the following address:
      http://www.rmwc.edu/academics/quillian.asp

modern world, and the other about Egypt and its continuous spiritual message. The interactive process in that teaching experience built a bridge of understanding between my
students who came from different American cultural backgrounds as well as from over seas and myself as an Egyptian Muslim. We need to remove false barriers by changing
the way we work with our goals and examining the meanings we give to life — thus following the authentic guidance
found at the heart of all religions.

Rachel Falik

I am Jewish, and an Israeli. In my country, every newborn
baby leaves the hospital with a birth certificate and an
infant's gas mask. Mothers fear the moment the child
becomes eighteen as he or she will then enter mandatory
military service. The average citizen's life is based upon fear
and protection. There was a bomb shelter in every apartment building in the town in which I lived, and all single-
houses included a safe room reinforced with concrete and
steel doors. The threat of violence has been constant in my
life.

I endured two wars before the age of seven, thus the
memory of the wailing sirens and the frightened expression
on my mother's face are forever embedded in my memory.
At the age of six, I was trained to watch every backpack at
school in which there might be a hidden bomb. Public trans-
portation was always a dangerous experience. I was taught
the rules for riding a bus. Everyone riding the bus had the
obligation to be vigilant about packages and if unclaimed
luggage was found, all passengers knew to immediately
vacate the bus.

My family experienced first-hand life in the Diaspora,
namely in the scattered colonies of Jews outside Israel.
They, as the majority of the Jewish people after the Babylo-
nian exile, grew up far from their ancestral homeland. Some
of my family came to Israel from Arab countries where they
were a hated minority. Some lucky family members fled to
Israel from Europe after witnessing their relatives mur-

dered by the Nazis. Hearing the stories of my family conditioned me to believe that I was obligated to defend, in all manner necessary, the existence of Israel. At age eighteen, I wore a uniform, carried a weapon, and responded to social pressure to 'fulfill my potential' by becoming an air force officer. As many other soldiers, I experienced a dissonance in being aware of my deadly power and the humanity of my enemies. I was conditioned to believe that there was no other way except mandatory military service to secure the existence of the Jewish people in the Land of Israel. However, despite the threat of violence, despite the constant fear, and despite the conditioning, I was never comfortable responding with hatred. The settlement I grew up in bordered a Palestinian village. We were neighbors with a history of coexistence. At this time a concrete wall has been built between the two villages. This, certainly, will not promote understanding and peace, neither will it guarantee security. Instead, both parties are trapped in a vicious cycle of alienation, dread, and hostility.

I live in America now and this has given me a new perspective. I meet Palestinians and have come to know them as human beings, whereas in Israel I would have been suspicious or afraid of them. Ironically, I have experienced more prejudice in America than I expected. I frequently hear remarks such as *Jews control the media* or *Jews brought the terror over*. These remarks are followed by lengthy explanations that generalize and stereotype Jewish people. Living in America has allowed me to experience the *other* as a human being, and myself as the *other*.

Bullet shells are still targeting Palestinian villages and bombs are still blowing up in crowded Jewish market places, but at this time in my life, I no longer accept the easy answers I was conditioned to accept. The answer to violence and fear cannot be continued violence.

My perception of the *other* as a human being allows me to hope that there will be increasing communication between various nations and religions rather than continued fear, bloodshed and violence. In this global chaos, it is up to us to touch the *other*, it is our personal responsibility to transform this chaotic condition with open hearts and open minds. Our transformational strategy should be to become closer to one another and to share our commonalities with our words, our art, our bliss, and our devotion to life.

In my country, as in the rest of the world, missiles can cruise a longer distance now; atomic bombs can be dumped with a greater aloofness. Killing and destruction are easier as human beings are growing apart from each other, and the enemy is unfamiliar and invisible. But hatred becomes more difficult, and killing becomes unbearable, when we actually know our rivals, when we see them face-to-face, and understand their personal despair.

Jenny Eda Schipper

My life was challenged right from conception. During World War II my parents escaped the Nazi holocaust by fleeing to Palestine. Following the war, they returned to Europe to look for their families. There was no one left. They were staying in Bergen-Belsen, a former concentration death camp, when I was conceived. My parents spent a few months there before moving to another displaced persons camp in Upjever, West Germany, awaiting an opportunity to come to America. I was born in 1950, and six months later we moved to the United States.

During the next two years we moved from place to place as my parents adjusted to their new world. My brother was born in Virginia in 1952. Six months later my mother took us back to Vienna. She hoped to finish her medical studies which had been disrupted by the war. The Nazi influence was still present, discouraging her from pursuing her goal. In the meantime, my father was hired by Ford Motors in Detroit. Two years later we joined him.

I grew up knowing that things were terribly wrong. My home life was very unhappy, because my parents fought bitterly and endlessly. No matter what success my father achieved, he could never enjoy it. Everything was always in his words "too late". He venomously spit out the words as though they were poison. Even at a young age, I caught his bitterness and despair. My father's ever-present anger, with its silent simmering or unexpected outbursts, created an atmosphere of fear and dread in our home. Something was always wrong.

My mother, following a patriarchal female pattern, repressed her own needs in her attempt to please my father. She became a continual victim, while he became the emotional aggressor. They became locked into these roles, inadvertently replaying the war within our own home. In addition, because I shared some of my father's moody behaviors, she displaced her aggression on me. I knew she loved me, yet I suffered deeply from her merciless words. There seemed to be no place for happiness in our family. It wasn't until I had grown up that I understood that we lived within the shadow of the holocaust. Both of my parents, either consciously or unconsciously, had survivor's guilt. The fact that they never spoke about the war or the deaths of their whole families reflected this.

Yet on the other hand, my parents, as socialists, conveyed a humanist ideology to their children. They had shed the trappings of religion and as secular intellectuals embraced the ideal of social justice. I absorbed their ideals, and over time made them my own.

As a child, I grew up wondering why there was so much hatred of one group of people for another. It was obvious to me that what we shared in being human was much greater than the differences caused by religious or racial identity. Why wasn't this apparent to everyone? Why didn't people love each other more? Why did they mask themselves and hide behind roles? These questions often filled my mind. As I embraced both my own pain, and the despair I saw around me, I understood that people were afraid of their own hearts.

As a Jew growing up in a Christian culture, I felt the sting of prejudice. I often felt left out of what others shared. I was flabbergasted upon learning that Jesus was a Jew! How could Christians worship a Jew and at the same time hate his origin, the source of their own religion? I was struck by the fact that Christians did not practice the brotherly love that they preached. How could they hate blacks, Jews and other races and call themselves Christians? If they indeed practiced what Jesus taught, every human life would be embraced, valued, and cared for.

I decided early on that I would trust my own heart. As a result, my life has been dedicated to helping people trust their own hearts and encouraging them to bring forth the creative potential inherent within us all. Despite my concern for current world conditions, I am able to strengthen and heal myself and others through my poetry, dancing, and painting. My healing practice includes body work and teaching yoga for health, healing and wholeness.

The four authors come from different places and embrace different religions; however, we all experienced prejudice for who we are and what we believe. We have been the *other*, not only because two of us are from conflicting Middle-Eastern countries, but also because we are women. We are also deeply concerned about the wellbeing of our human family. This caring led us to pay serious attention to the historical antecedents leading to our current plight.

Human perception (both limited and expanded) plays an essential role in one's interpretation of the physical world. Qualities such as prejudice are fruits of ignorance formed by limited perception, fear, and the outdated, testosterone-driven belief that aggression assures survival. Oftentimes, prejudice takes hold when people do not understand (by choice or circumstance) the *other*. As women of conscience, we are called upon to see the common humanity in the face of all peoples, irrespective of faith, color, or creed. Regardless of differing views based upon our own cultural upbringing, each of us agreed that any prejudice against those who differed because of religion, class, ethnicity, race or sexual behavior (for example, homosexuality, polygamy, and so on) violated the respect each human being deserves.

If we ever want to come to common terms with others and see one another as part of one human family, we have to pay respect to all. Our behaviors have to match our ideals.

We are also women concerned with healing the human family and making the world a safer place for our children and future generations. By being from different cultural and religious backgrounds, the authors of this book break the myth of religious, cultural and ethnic prejudice. We have been able to communicate beyond cultural limitation, political dilemma, or religious bias. We hope to provide an example for others as we explore the dominating influences of patriarchy in each of our own religions and political structures.

Spirituality versus Religiousness

The clash of religious ideologies hangs over us like a dark cloud. Religious fundamentalists are emerging in every religion. Their opposition to one another threatens the well-being and safety of us all. They have forgotten the very meaning of their own religious teachings. There has been much friction defining the meaning of religion. The British philosopher Bertrand Russell noted that "All the great religions that have dominated large populations have involved a greater or lesser amount of dogma, but 'religion' is a word of which the meaning is not very definite" (Russell, 1999, p. 48). For example, on the one hand religion has the potential to open the heart in recognition of the divine; on the other it can be used as a tool for social and political control of the masses. Certainly, the latter is the case with patriarchal influence whereupon obedience to a higher authority (outside oneself) is stressed.

Continued patriarchal influence has resulted in extreme religious fundamentalism. Fundamentalists, irregardless of creed, depict religion as constant concepts that resist any changes and live outside the stream of history. Religious historian Karen Armstrong has traced the common features of fundamentalists in her book *The Battle for God*, noting that they all have the same structure of mind. For instance, each believes in the inerrancy of its ideologies.

The authors present a definition of religion that goes beyond fundamentalism. We are concerned with erroneous religious beliefs and related behaviors. Our understanding of religion is the revelation that all human beings, in fact, all life, are a manifestation of Divine Creation. Therefore all life is sacred. At the deepest level, all prophets and sacred texts represent a message of this unity and guidance to help rediscover it within the universe. In fact, the idea of the "monotheistic religions" (Judaism, Christianity and Islam) is a falsity for each religious tradition bows to an ultimate being — an Absolute.

This universality is the base upon which each "religion" was originally expressed. This core truth makes it possible to find a common spiritual ground despite the particularities of cultures. When people submerge in the social particularity, they fail to see the universality which is shared beyond diversities of expression and symbolism. It must be noticed that patriarchy is a socially created relationship, and is not part of the natural order as claimed by fundamentalists.

To be sure, the process of searching and finding answers to questions about meanings and purpose of existence, as well as experiencing the existence of this divine unity is a continuous and repeated phenomenon in the history of humankind. Both men and women share this experience without distinction. Unfortunately, history has primarily documented the male experience, ignoring the female one.

Human history shows that the tendency to search for the core meaning of existence has re-occurred in different cultures, and there are also shared similarities of spiritual experience. The enlightenment of the Buddha is likewise reflected in Leo Tolstoy's religious experience.[5] The various experiences of Prophets such as Abraham and Muhammad have also been known by others. Our great Prophets did not simply submit to the common values, ideas, and beliefs of their era; rather they asked the perennial questions of existence and manifested an inner knowing. They then provided followers with methods, enabling each to discover and listen to the inner self. Islam called this method "primordial" because it is shared by all humans. From that perspective "religion" is a way, a process, a path where human

---

[5]   See in this respect Tolstoy's *A Confession and Other Religious Writings*.

beings are always in a spiritual transformation. That process of continuous transformation is only fulfilled when the self is free from gender, race, color, class biases.

Because religion has been linked to patriarchally-structured religious institutions, people who are following this primordial path prefer to be called spiritual.[6] Unlike being religious, being spiritual is more often associated with a higher level of interest in mysticism, and increased interest in *experiencing* beliefs, rather than being subordinate to certain religious authority. Religiousness has been associated with following prescribed scriptural readings, and regular participation in traditional forms of worship. This form has been rejected by many because it oftentimes prevents a living awareness of the divine presence because of its emphasis on both hierarchical leadership and conformity of followers.

We have a spiritual core residing deep within. The 13th century mystic philosopher Meister Eckhart called it the "divine spark." Some Christians call it the "indwelling God," or "Christ within." Hindus call this indwelling principle, "Atman" or "Purusha". It is the awakening of a living divine presence within each one of us. Jesus taught that "the kingdom of heaven is within", but this teaching has been ignored by conservative religious followers.

This differentiation between religion and spirituality indicates how far practicing religion has strayed from the original teachings meant to spiritually empower all human

[6]   "Before the twentieth century the terms religious and spiritual were used more or less interchangeably. But a number of modern intellectual and cultural forces have accentuated differences between the 'private' and 'public' spheres of life. The increasing prestige of the sciences, the insights of modern biblical scholarship, and greater awareness of cultural relativism all made it more difficult for educated American to sustain unqualified loyalty to religious institutions. Many began to associate genuine faith with the 'private' realm of personal experience rather than with the 'public' realm of institutions, creeds, and rituals. The word *spiritual* gradually came to be associated with a private realm of thought and experience while the word *religious* came to be connected with the public realm of membership in religious institutions, participation in formal rituals, and adherence to official denominational doctrines" (Fuller, 2002, p. 5).

beings — black and white, male and female. Authentic religion is egalitarian at its core. The spiritual path was meant to be the same as the religious path. Those who adhere to patriarchal social institutions, tend to emphasize outer behaviors, while overlooking what resides in the heart. Instead they believe that a person should be satisfied by going to a church or a mosque or a temple, for these social habits are considered to be proof of religious commitment.

The dichotomy between religion and spirituality is paradoxical. All revelations are intended to guide humankind to the spiritual aspects of their lives by pointing to the encompassing great spiritual power that has been called by different names according to different cultures. A hard line should not be drawn between "religion" and "spirituality." However there is a justification for those who make this distinction because they see that religion became a synonym for patriarchal religious institutions, and controlling dogma. By emphasizing the spiritual aspects of religiousness, the authors are not denying the diversities of expressions denoted to each religion; rather they respect all and each way of expressing that spiritual core within humanity, and all life. This process differs from the tendency of groups, affiliated by birth or conversion to a particular creed, to claim that their creed represents the absolute truth or that they alone have a direct line to the divine. They fail to see that Allah, God, Brahma, the Great Spirit, Tao are symbols for the same reality.

This book examines how patriarchal ideologies have influenced and supported the idea of superiority to *the other*. Claiming to be the best among humankind is a recurring phenomenon in Prophetic and non-Prophetic religions alike. This claim is also based on the belief that one group is privileged by holding the absolute reality, and the best value system. This attitude explains the continuous fights between Hindus and Muslims in India, Jews and Arabs and also Christians and Muslims in the Middle East, Muslims and Christians in Sudan, Indonesia and other places in the world. Another similarity is reflected in gender bias whereupon women are generally considered subordinate to men.

This subordination is claimed to be an expression of an eternal and absolute reality.

However, if we accept that we all share a common humanity, human rights would be an area where our commonality would be mostly recognized. It appears that accepting diversities may go hand in hand with searching for commonalities on one hand, and learning from one another on the other. But the recognition of this commonality has been largely disregarded, and, as a result, we now stand at the brink of possible destruction. In fact, at a recent gathering of spiritual progressives, a prominent speaker noted "We may well be the first generation to make the decision as to whether we will be the last generation."

Human Rights and Losses

The following examples recorded by the Human Rights Watch organization, UN High Commissioner for Human Rights, Amnesty International, the International Criminal Court, and other agencies and organizations demonstrate a need for a major paradigm shift. Vast numbers of massacres and destruction have been perpetrated in the name of religious, racial and ethnic prejudice (often fueled by patriarchal governmental policies and economic greed). These examples clearly support our argument that something is seriously wrong; that disregard for human life is wide-spread indeed. We believe that these statistical examples support the premise that gender imbalance has brought us to the brink of self-destruction.

An examination of these human rights violations reveals that no area is free from the devastation resulting from racial and religious prejudice. Statistics taken throughout 2004, 2005 and 2006 revealed that human rights violations continued with increasing numbers of refugees and displaced persons. Ethnic, political and economic differences significantly exacerbated murder and violence in the name of religious pride. Patriarchal beliefs and standards have gone awry.

The list of human violence appears to be endless as we survey our planet. In the advent of the twenty-first century, every continent has been infected by religious prejudice and political corruption in varying degrees. Genocides continue in Darfur, which particularly portrays a gruesome tale of human atrocities. The International Criminal Court reports that approximately 300,000 people have been killed and two million others displaced in the Darfur region of Western Sudan. Human Rights Watch has since noted the escalating violence in Darfur and consequences for Chad. African Union forces have been unable to protect civilians, who are in continual danger from government-backed militia. Women are beaten and raped.

Mass graves, assumed to be filled with bodies of ethnic Albanians, continue to be found in the Balkans. (The enmity between Serbs and Albanians has historical roots that were primarily due to religious differences.) There have been terrorist bombings in numerous nations; militants kidnapping and murdering innocent citizens in Russia, Iraq and other countries; and tales of torture in Iraq's Abu Ghraib prison and Guantanamo. News reports around the world during the last few years continually highlight these horrors. Meanwhile, tensions in the Middle East have continued to rise, and there are few, if any, signs of hope for the Palestinian-Israel aggressions.

According to Amnesty International's 2005 Report,

> Increasing numbers of Palestinians were killed and homes destroyed by the Israeli army in the Palestinian Occupied Territories. Some 700 Palestinians died, including about 150 children. Most were killed unlawfully, in reckless shootings, shellings or air strikes on refugee camps and other densely populated areas throughout the West Bank and Gaza Strip ... Some 109 Israelis, most of them civilians and including eight children, were killed by Palestinian armed groups in suicide bombings, shootings and mortar attacks inside Israel and in the Occupied Territories ... In May [2004] the Israeli army destroyed some 300 homes and damaged about 270 others in a refugee camp in Rafah, leaving close to 4,000 Palestinians homeless ... The fence/wall and hundreds of Israeli army checkpoints and blockades throughout the Occupied Territories continued to hinder

or prevent Palestinians' access to their land, their workplaces and to education, health and other crucial services.

There is a complex history contributing to these violations; however the inability to support unique religious and ethnic differences adds to the problems. The recent Israeli pull out of the West Bank has not lessened the violence. Militant Palestinians are shooting missiles into Israeli territories. The Israeli military continues to assassinate militant leaders and arrests those running for Palestinian political offices. The election of Hamas further complicated the relationship. Amnesty International reported the implementation of two new laws in July 2005 that increased discriminating against Palestinians.

> In a single day, 27 July 2005, the Israeli parliament (Knesset) passed two new laws, the *Civil Wrongs/Civil Torts (Liability of the State) Law* and the *Citizenship and Entry into Israel Law*, whose effect is to take discrimination against Palestinians to a new level.
>
> In their current form both laws violate Israel's obligations under international law, including human rights treaties to which Israel is a state party and which it is bound to uphold.
>
> According to the new *Civil Torts (Liability of the State) Law*, some three and a half million Palestinians who live under Israeli military occupation in the West Bank and Gaza Strip are considered "residents of a conflict zone". As such, they are denied the right to claim compensation for death, injury, or damage to property inflicted on them by Israeli forces.

The so-called war on terror shows no signs of decline with frightening acts occurring on all sides of the war. Amnesty International reports that during bombings of Fallujah, Najaf and Samarra, untold innocent Iraqi civilians were killed unlawfully by US led forces. Armed groups and suicide bombers have also killed numerous innocent civilians. Over 2,700 US soldiers have been killed since the war began in March 2003. Untold numbers of Iraqis, many of them children, have died because of this ill-conceived act of aggression. According to the tallies of Antiwar.com, somewhere between 43,799 and 48,639 Iraqis are reported dead, but the site also notes that the British medical journal the *Lancet* reported an estimated 100,000 civilians have lost their lives (a figure raised to 655,000 by an epidemiologists' report in the *Lancet* in October 2006). Government personnel and professionals, journalists, security contractors, Iraqi police and military live in constant danger with no end in sight, and many of these have lost their lives.

The multi-faceted face of Asia has likewise witnessed devastation in the name of religion. In 2002, in a politically organized pogrom in the west India state of Gujarat, several thousand Muslims were killed, and 100,000 Muslims were forced out of Hindu-dominated communities. The Bharatiya Janata Party right-wing government claimed to believe in secularism but came to power by affirming Hindu pride. This stance led to killing members of the Muslim minority. Meanwhile in China, North Korea and Vietnam, religious minorities were arrested or killed and mosques, temples and seminaries closed down in an attempt to control the presence of Catholics, Muslims and Falun Gong adherents. Despite constitutional provisions protecting religious freedom, Buddhists with socio-political control in Myanmar (formerly Burma) and Laos have denied minorities basic rights of worship.

During the last decade, acts of violence have been steadily rising in the United States; for example school shootings, children being kidnapped and/or murdered and gang warfare are on the rise. There have been thousands of allegations regarding police brutality. Since 9/11 the United States has experienced a rise in a new form of discrimination, namely against Arabs who are US immigrants or US citizens.

Slavery remains a human rights issue. Contemporary slavery appears in many forms. The United Nations High Commissioner for Human Rights reports that slavery-like practices include the sale of children, child prostitution, exploitation of children in labor and the use of children in armed conflict among other acts of victimization. The International Labour Organization provides an estimate of over 100 million children being exploited for labor. They work in sweat shops, rarely, if ever, experiencing the love, joy and playtime a child needs for healthy development.

Gender has been and continues to be an area of oppression that has manifested itself throughout many cultures and religions. Misogyny has allowed for ongoing and widespread violence, murder and control of women. Illogical and irrational interpretations of religious texts have allowed men to claim dominance over women. Although women's rights activists have brought about considerable improvements in the treatment and equality of women, Amnesty International reports that violence against women is rampant in all parts of the world. This list includes rape and abuse of women in custody, acid burning and dowry deaths, genital mutilation, and women being killed to protect the "honor" of the family. In some cases a young woman may have been raped by a family member and then killed for dishonoring it. Domestic violence is pandemic. Amnesty International estimates that in the United States alone, a woman is battered very 15 seconds and raped every six minutes; and that during this next year over 15,000 women will be sold into sexual slavery in China, 200 women will be burned with acid in Bangladesh for spurning suitors or husbands, and dowry deaths will claim more than 7,000 in India. Over 225 women were killed in Guatemala in the first five months of 2005. The death toll amounts to more than one murder per day, for no other reason than being a woman.

In addition, women often lack the political power to implement effective and meaningful change. For example, in the United States only 13.8% of legislative representatives are women, only 1.1% of Fortune 1000 companies are led by women, and the wage gap between women and men has actually widened in the last decade. The Convention on the Elimination of All Forms of Discrimination Against Women (CEDAW) is the only comprehensive global treaty exclusively addressing the rights of women. Despite the fact that the treaty was adopted by the United Nations in 1979, refusal of countries like the United States to ratify

CEDAW assists in perpetuating the continual abuse of women's basic rights.

Terror of the more powerful over masses is shocking. According to J. Rummel,[7] during the first eighty-eight years of the twentieth century, almost 170,000,000 men, women, and children have been shot, beaten, tortured, knifed, burned, starved, frozen, crushed, worked to death, buried alive, drowned, hung, bombed, or killed in any other of the myriad ways governments have inflicted death on unarmed, helpless citizens or foreigners. The dead even could conceivably be near 360,000,000 people. Our species has been devastated by a modern Black Plague — a plague of *power* rather than germs.

The above descriptions represent a small example of thousands of years of well-documented human brutality. History has evidenced senseless, repetitive patterns of destruction based upon religious, tribal, racial, gender and economic differences; but do we listen and apply its lessons? What justification can we find for the ongoing massacres of whole nations? Often the only honest justification we can offer is that these other nations, religions, genders, ethnic and racial groups are different than ourselves. Based on this, the dominant culture generally attempts to either eradicate those perceived as a threat or to relegate them to controlled positions and environments (for example, slavery, reservations, colonization, prisons, and occupation).

Building a Better World

Our book documents and examines a variety of prejudicial behaviors against *the other*, initiated by the dark desire for superiority associated with patriarchal principles. As we examine our oral and written history it becomes obvious that despite our religious and political ideals, we have failed to make our world a better place. Was Darwin right? Is it the survival of the fittest (strongest and most dominant) that assures success for a small segment of humanity? Manifest Destiny has been a motivating force behind the growth

---

[7]   http://www.hawaii.edu/powerkills/DBG.CHAP1.HTM

of the United States as it spread westward, and now proposes a *new world order*. Colonialism, backed by ethnocentric religious views, has done much damage and its influence is evidenced in many of the world's battle grounds. The drive for superiority has created much despair.

Research supports female leadership in that the character and particular qualities inherent in the female are less prone to corruption and more concerned with egalitarianism and the wellbeing of the entire human family. Religion and political governance are on the brink of a dramatic shift — and women will be at the helm of change.

The post-modern era of easy travel and technological advances has changed the course of history. We no longer live as isolated races, religions and ethnic groups. There are increasing movements recognizing that diversity can be honored — rather than destroyed. We can learn to enjoy and even celebrate our differences. It is time to examine improved ways of interpreting and utilizing spiritual teachings while integrating influences of science and religion. Our human dilemma can be resolved as we recognize our unity, discover common themes and learn to live in harmony with one other.

It has been over one hundred years since the Czar of Russia and the Queen of the Netherlands called the first world peace congress; there is still a great need to promote coexistence. Of the over thirty conflicts worldwide, many are rooted in an inadequate understanding of the political, legal, ethical, moral, and economic dimensions of maintaining social harmony. Now, more than ever, we need to cultivate peace within ourselves, our institutions, and our global community. A critical analysis of the core issues that separate us combats prejudice rooted in ignorance and resulting in oppression. An expose of cultural prejudices is an invaluable tool that can contribute to social reform.

In this book we ask our readers to envision a humanity that respects all life. This is not a book about a specific religious, racial, ethnic or gender group; rather it is a book about the condition of the human heart. As we examine the results of our beliefs and behaviors, we can learn from our past and create a new future—one that assures a better world for future generations.

Heaven lies under the steps of mothers.

Hadith of the Prophet Muhammad
(Angha, 1995, p. 45)

Chapter One

In the Beginning: Stories of Good and Evil

Since the beginning of its recorded history, humanity has organized itself through the metaphors expressed in its allegorical stories. These parables and myths enable human beings to find balance and harmony with the forces of nature, and with one another. They help us to express the conflicts existing among the contradictory powers within the human psyche, as well as those within the universe. These stories have also been used to promote new ideologies, such as the advancement of patriarchal ideals.

Our intention in this chapter is to examine the shift in mythologies occurring at the onset of the patriarchal religions in order to better understand our historical past and thereby improve our future. Literal translations of sacred texts, while ignoring the historical context, have wrought serious consequences. For example, persons with fixed mindsets, influenced by dogmatic translations of scripture, have used these metaphors to emphasize superiority and prejudice. Therefore it is of paramount importance to examine the historical context and the underlying messages within our shared mythologies in order to achieve harmony, rather than continued conflict, between cultures. It would greatly benefit us to examine the lessons of the past and create a more promising future — one based upon an egalitarian relationship with all. We cannot continue to threaten one another and our environment with military might and nuclear weaponry without reaping the destructive results of this evil lack of concern for *the other*. Although we cannot return to idealized, less complicated lifestyles of the past, we can still learn from those who have gone before us to create a healthier future. Their stories were brought forward through the oral tradition; and their history was recorded in the book of nature, to be read by modern anthropologists and archeologists. One result is that we now know that early nomadic hunter-gatherer societies were primarily egalitarian.

Social inequality is actually a recent development in human evolution — one that began with the rise of patriarchal governance. Some anthropologists have suggested that the emergent developments of surplus agriculture, and storage allowed for the development of social inequality (Gardner, 1991). Others say it began with invasions by Indo-Europeans, also known as Aryans. Irregardless of causal factors, these agricultural and societal changes represented a shift from horizontally-based consciousness to a vertical one.

Earlier humanity had a horizontal perspective of life. For nomadic societies this meant that life itself was sacred. The shift to a vertical perspective required that one look upwards towards an ideal, a hero, hierarchical figure or a god. One relevant consequence was that we lost our foundation in the here and now. In his book, *Wandering God: A Study in Nomadic Spirituality*, Morris Berman points out that this new ideal of looking upward represented the onset of what he calls the *sacred authority complex* (Berman, 2000). The sacred could only be found outside of, and hierarchically above, life — thus a split between heaven and earth was proclaimed.

Patriarchy is a form of social organization, in which the male represents the supreme authority. It affirms that children belong to the male line, rather than the female lineage. It uses a hierarchical form of ranking. The hierarchical tendencies within patriarchy tend toward structures based upon superiority over others. The male dominates the female—a religion, race or nation claims superiority over another.

One cannot discount the fact that humanity has evidenced incredible architectural, scientific and philosophical development during the forward thrust of the patriarchal paradigm, including the manifestation and organization of the world's religious traditions. Religion has emphasized compassion and other noble qualities that bring one closer to the divine, but at the same time its patriarchal underpinnings have wrought much destruction. In short, humanity has both prospered and suffered under patriarchal reign. Author and philosopher Ken Wilber has pointed out that we cannot dismiss hierarchy itself as an inferior way, in that hierarchy is a natural process of evolution containing significant patterns of development. He suggests that rather than focusing on condemnation, we would better direct our energies by determining the pathological or dominating tendencies within this organizational paradigm and weed them out (Wilber, 1996). It is a fact that various people have gained greater proficiency and knowledge than others. There are teachers and there are students who seek to learn from them—not everyone has the capacity of an Einstein. Likewise there are those who are endowed with greater compassion, for example the late Mother Teresa of Calcutta.[1] Hierarchy of talent, knowledge and character exists.

A positive use of hierarchical principles is evidenced in Native American tribal organizations in that the majority of tribes choose their chief because of evidenced wisdom. Feminist psychologists have also promoted a very different power structure, one in which we empower one another to grow and develop. Understanding this principal, progressive thinkers propose that a new human organization—one that is based upon gender balance—will provide the impetus for an egalitarian world, thereby eliminating the superi-

---

[1] Sadly, Mother Teresa did not stand up against the patriarchal structure of the Catholic Church, even though she was aware of its dominating influence.

ority and artificial ranking that have fed and maintained the
hierarchical culture of prejudicial ways.

Prejudice, gender imbalance and rising fundamentalism
are core representations of the evil plagues threatening our
survival. The rise and dominance of patriarchy during the
last six thousand years has encouraged these human
plagues. When one examines the attitude of *prejudice*, it
becomes obvious that hostile feelings and opinions—
directed against racial, religious or national groups—
are widespread indeed. Also, pride is inherently related to
prejudice. This motivating force can be described as a "high
or inordinate opinion of one's own dignity, importance,
merit or superiority" (Webster, 1989, p. 1142). One aspect of
being prideful is to demean another, to portray them as inferior, in an attempt to elevate one's self. Prejudice is the
response to this pride. These two concepts are related to
patriarchy because of its insistence upon hierarchical organization. Someone has to be superior and the other inferior.
Therefore, prejudice and pride are intimately coupled with
one another. It is a fact that these powerful forces have conspired against the potential nobility of the human being
since the beginning of recorded history.

The more recent phenomena of *Fundamentalism* can be
described as the inability to comprehend and respect life
beyond one's limited view of the world. This attitude and
way of perceiving religion first manifested in the Western
world in the American Protestant movement that began
early in the 20th century. Its continued rise is considered to
be a reaction to Modernism. The dictionary tells us that fundamentalism began with Christians, in particular, and that
it stressed "the infallibility of the Bible not only in matters
of faith and morals but also as a literal historical record"
(Webster, 2000, p. 531). But this same phenomenon has evidenced itself with Muslims and their interpretation of
Qur'anic scripture. In fact, fundamentalism has been on a
steady rise within all of the world's religious traditions. As
patriarchy nears its end, it has tightened its grasp and fundamentalism is a manifestation of this fearful response to
Modernism.

One common attribute of all fundamentalists is their belief in the inerrancy of their belief system. They are unable to stand aside and look within for metaphorical or deeper understandings. In fact, one can find fundamentalist mind-sets not only in religion, but also in science, politics and other realms. Fundamentalism maintains a system of superiority and prejudice against *the other*, supporting acts of racial, national, class and gender injustice.

Gender-imbalance is the most powerful example of the repressive qualities exemplified in patriarchy for it demands that the female be subservient to the male. Men have held the monopoly and authority on administrative and religious matters since patriarchy's onset. In modern times, the Taliban regime portrayed gender imbalance for the entire world to see through the eyes of modern media. Only males were visible, as Afghan women were despised and hidden from view. The Taliban created its own interpretations of Islamic teachings. Its behaviors were predominantly aggressive and destructive as a result of the extreme gender imbalance. The Taliban men evidenced a lack of caring and respect for anything outside of their own rigid ideology (for example, not only their violent treatment of women, but also their destruction of art, including the precious Buddhist statues of antiquity and disallowance of music in any form).

But the Taliban men were not alone in these gender imbalanced attitudes. For example, Catholic and Protestant Christian denominations have followed the commandments of the apostle Paul, "Let your women keep silence in the churches: for it is not permitted unto them to speak; but *they are commanded*[2] to be under obedience, as also saith the [Jewish] law. And if they learn anything, let them ask their husbands at home: for it is a shame for women to speak in the church" (I Corinthians, 14:34–35). And, as noted, this was a Jewish law expecting females to adhere to male domi-

---

[2]   Italics are found in King James version, where they are not used for emphasis, but to indicate words not present in the original Greek text but added to convey its meaning into English.

nance so this thread wove itself through Judaism, Christianity and Islam alike.

From the onset of patriarchal dominance, every religion — from East to West — claimed male dominance over females. This stance must now change.

The Splitting of Heaven and Earth

Gender *balance* represents a significant element in restoring humanity from the brink of destruction. Women are inherently disposed to egalitarian principles because of their innate maternal and relational qualities.[3] Also, there is significant evidence to verify that gender-balanced, pre-patriarchal societies lived more harmoniously than those under patriarchal rule. The onset of patriarchy began approximately six thousand years ago. Anthropological explorations have revealed that Paleolithic (around 20,000+ to 8000 BCE) and Neolithic (approximately 8000 to 4000 BCE) cultures were primarily egalitarian (Eisler, 1987). Gravesites from that period also suggest egalitarian cultural values. For example, excavations of gravesites revealed that marital partners, children, animals and slaves were *not* buried along with the deceased. (That phenomenon, indicative of values associated with domination [Eisler, 1987], was evidenced in the later gravesites of patriarchal cultures.)

These prehistoric cultures revered the Great Mother. Numerous icons depicting feminine representations of God have been found as anthropologists and archeologists unearthed ancient temples and dwellings. Yet there were no indications that males were subservient to females. Dwelling places and gravesites were not suggestive of vast differences in wealth and status amongst the citizenry. These discoveries have also confirmed that earlier beliefs differed considerably from the later Judeo-Christian story of Adam, Eve, the rib and the fall from grace (blamed on Eve and

---

[3] Here we are talking about the nature of women, but do so with the understanding that oftentimes women are aggressive due to introjected patriarchal influences. Irregardless, there are innate hormonal differences between males and females.

damning the feminine) (Parrinder, 1971; Eliade, 1978). They provided evidence of a very different paradigm, one in which iconography suggests that females were revered because of their capacity to bring forth life (Stone, 1976) and also that earlier societies appeared to live more peacefully.

The shift to patriarchal dominance began to develop around 4000 BCE. Since patriarchy was based upon a strict male lineage, there was a distinct change in social organization and religious beliefs. Patriarchal ideology, by its very nature, required a masculine representation and definition of God. New creation stories were formed from the old ones. Jack Miles, author of the Pulitzer Prize winning book *God: A Biography,* notes how "Myth, legend, and history mix endlessly in the Bible," and "that Bible historians are endlessly sorting them out" (Miles, 1995, p. 13). But one thing that is consistent is that the Bible has been interpreted from a one-sided patriarchal perspective.

Religious historian Geoffrey Parrinder relates that during the time of transition to patriarchy "many cosmologies tell of the forcing apart of sky and earth, who [were] regarded as united in sexual union" (Parrinder, 1971, p. 155). These changing mythologies reflected the beginning of the split between mind and body, male and female — and the loss of any remnants of paradise (unity). Parrinder and other scholars believe that the rise of patriarchy was also associated with the dawn of rationalization, as Plato, Aristotle and other philosophers turned inward (away from physical and sensual life) and upward (a movement toward idealizing thought and the mental realm). As these early philosophers developed their theories around the inner meanings and representations of life, the representations became more important than life itself. For instance, in future times Christianity deemed the after-life more important than life in the here and now. (In our time we see this as corporate profit displaying itself with blatant disregard for all life.) These new developments opened doors of understanding and insight, but they also disconnected us from our bodies and the earth. As evidenced, by domestic violence, the destruction of other cultures, and the denigration of the earth, this split has not improved our humanity.

New religious beliefs emerged as Hebrews re-created the ancient Canaanite (Miles, 1995) and Sumerian myths (Kramer, 1963). Jack Miles explains that, "The God whom ancient Israel worshipped arose as the fusion of a number of Gods whom a nomadic nation had met in its wanderings" (Miles, 1995, p. 20). The qualities and personalities of male and female deities (El, Baal or Tiamat and Ashera) were incorporated into one deity, God.

But the gift of increased revelations came at a high price. On the one hand, Abraham's direct experience of God was a major development in human consciousness. His experience went beyond the symbolic archetypal[4] images that constituted pagan beliefs. He was able to see there was one Divine presence beyond all the archetypal representations. In short, his experience of enlightenment carried him beyond the collective unconscious into mystical unity. Abraham was having conversations with God. He had found a personal unity with the divine.[5] But this revelation lost its purity in that other paths were then deemed inferior. It soon became a religious movement based upon male dominance, and hierarchical structure.

For instance, biblical stories refer to the women of Babylon and other goddess-revering pagan cultures as "whores," and cheers their destruction. But, in reality, these stories and related events represented a process of social control, assuring that others would conform to this new patriarchal religion. The problem of *the other* was immedi-

---

[4] The psychiatrist Carl Gustav Jung (1875–1961) studied comparative religion, mythology and dreams, finding similar themes manifesting in all three. Jung recognized a universally shared collective unconscious and wrote that it was filled with instinctive primordial forces, symbols and mythological presences. He called these unconscious motivating forces archetypes, psychic structures containing psycho-biologically related patterns of behaviors consisting of certain qualities and expressions of being.

[5] It is believed that Abraham's realization initiated the monotheistic religions, although one can say that the core declaration within the Vedic teachings that "I am That" most certainly refers to a unitive experience of the divine.

ately evidenced – in that anyone outside of new-found
Hebraic understanding of God was automatically judged as
sinful.

Patriarchal interpretations established religious rules for
sexual behavior that had both positive and negative conno-
tations. The emphasis on marital commitment and family
represented a positive step in human relationship, but the
fact that the female was now under the control of masculine
authority denoted an ill-fated relational change. The policies established by patriarchal religious interpretations specifically controlled female sexuality and property
ownership. Those who disobeyed the rules were, and still
are, oftentimes sentenced to death (particularly if they are
women). Women have been, and continue to be victimized,
simply because they are women. The stories chosen for the
Bible proclaimed that the loss of paradise was a result of
Eve's eating the forbidden fruit, and women have been pay-
ing for this erroneous legend since its onset. As we shall see
in the following example, earlier legends were changed in a
manner to demean the female.

It is believed that history began with the Sumerian culture, over 6,000 years ago. Their mythologies were
inscribed in clay tablets, using reeds as pens. Examples of
well-known Sumerian myths include the heroic epic of
Gilgamesh, and stories of the Goddess Inanna, Queen of
Heaven, known as the evening and morning star, and her
consort Dumuzi. It appears that Sumerian stories were integrated into Hebrew allegories. For example, Sumerian
scholar Samuel Noah Kramer discovered that an earlier
Sumerian version of "the paradise legend" existed. The leg-
endary Dilmun was known as the land of the living –
described as pure, clean, and bright. When the Sumerian
water god, Enki , noticed that Dilmun was dry, he asked the
sun-god, Utu, to draw water up from the earth. The gods
thereby turned Dilmun into a garden laden with fruit and
green meadows. This image is again evoked in the following version found in Genesis 2:6, "But there went up a mist
from the earth, and watered the whole face of the ground."
Kramer also explained that the Sumerian paradise Dilmun

was considered to be east of Sumer. He noted the similarity to the Biblical paradise, which is "described as a garden planted eastward in Eden, from whose waters flow the four world rivers, including the Tigris and Euphrates, [and that] may have originally been identical with Dilmun, the Sumerian paradise-land" (Kramer, 1963, pp. 148–149).

Kramer also believed that this Sumerian paradise myth cast further light on the later Biblical version of Adam and Eve being cast from the Garden of Eden, after eating the forbidden fruit. In the Sumerian version, Ninhursag, the Great Mother-Goddess of the Sumerians, caused eight special plants to grow in the garden. Kramer says, "She succeeds in bringing these plants into being only after an intricate process involving three generations of goddesses, all conceived by the water-god and born ... without the slightest pain or travail" (ibid.). Ninhursag did not want these plants eaten, but Enki ate them one by one, and, as a result, Ninhursag condemned him to death. Soon Enki's health began to fail as disease entered into eight organs, and one of them was his rib. The Mother-Goddess was finally persuaded to heal Enki. She sat Enki by her vulva, whereupon she birthed eight deities (one for each ailing organ) and he was made well. The legend next tells its listeners that one of the organs, his rib, was healed by the goddess Nin-ti, "She who makes live," or the "Lady of the rib" (ibid.).

The pictogram "ti" means both "to live" and "rib." This double meaning, "lady of the rib" or the "lady who gives life" provides a great Sumerian pun. The Sumerian pun was then transferred into the Adam and Eve paradise story, when Eve, whose name means "she who makes live", is also connected to a rib (Dalglish, 1996). Kramer suggested the play on the words "rib" and "live" was lost in the Bible's new language (Mijares, 2003). Perhaps it was simply that the older version did not support the onset of the patriarch because of its positive representation of the female.

It is important to remember that earlier societies had a horizontal, embodied sense of unity with the natural world; it was deemed to be part of the sacred (a fact evidenced in modern indigenous cultures). As will be discussed later in this book, patriarchal religions placed a greater emphasis on heaven, and with the passage of time we see how this split has led to rampant destruction of our environment. The value of the earlier relationship *with* nature is that it automatically implies stewardship as opposed to *dominion over*. These earlier societies were governed by creation myths that gave meaning to their relationship with nature, and its oftentimes opposing and beneficent forces. Their allegories also provided ethical guidance in regards to the relationship with other forms of creation.

Creation Myths: Stories of Nature and Guidance

In order to better understand the development of the world's religious traditions, we also need to understand humanity's evolving consciousness as depicted in its ancient mythologies. Researchers and mythologists explain that creation myths represented early humanity's attempts to reconcile the various forces of nature. But at a deeper level the numerous gods and goddesses were also archetypal representations of the various qualities of divine manifestation. The Ultimate Oneness manifests its godly traits. This expression is acknowledged in the archetypal realm of consciousness, which constitutes the heart of early paganism and its abundant creation stories concerning the origin of life, good and evil, and heaven and hell realms. Although there are indisputable differences among various cultures, there are also similarities. They also represent the human soul's longing for harmony and balance, both intrapsychically and interrelationally. These forces take form in the world's mythological and religious stories illustrating the many powerful forces affecting human behavior. Carl Jung wrote, in his *Collected Works*, that

> All the most powerful ideas in history go back to archetypes. This is particularly true of religious ideas, but the central concepts of science, philosophy and ethics are no exception to this rule. In their present form they are variants of archetypal ideas, created by consciously applying and adapting these ideas to reality. For it is the function of consciousness not only to recognize and assimilate the

external world through the gateway of the senses, but to
translate into visible reality the world within us. (Storr,
1983, p. 16)

Our changing mythologies depict the evolution of consciousness. The world within us is so vivid, so powerful,
and so influential in our lives. The collective volumes of
mythological lore express this richness. The religious stories in holy books are not only meaningful to our conscious
minds, but to our unconscious minds as well. Most significantly, their unending guidance and creative power of
transformation are lost when bound by dogmatic translations. Each passage and each story can be interpreted from
many different levels, allowing for literal, personal, archetypal and spiritual understanding. This contemplation is
called *Midrash* in Judaism and *Ta'wil* in Islam.

One reads and interprets Middle Eastern scriptures in the
spirit of *Midrash*. The Hebrew word *Midrash* means "to seek
out" or "to investigate." The rabbinic literature provides
judicial principles and moral lessons, as well as a spiritual
wisdom. Midrash *Halacha* is a way of interpreting the legal
meanings to be found within Scripture, for example, religious ritual; familial and personal status; civil relations;
criminal law and relations with non-Jews. Midrash *Haggada*
concerns biblical lore. The Midrash Haggada elaborates on
and furthers scriptural meanings through the ongoing
study of legends, tales, parables, and allegories. Since the
entire Jewish theological and legal system depended on the
interpretation of the Scripture, there was a need to continuously update the meaning of the Bible, and to allow interpretations to evolve over time. The Midrash includes
numerous interpretations by many rabbis; therefore, it consists of repeating motifs that vary in points of view (including some that contradict one another). Midrash Haggada
thus became a vehicle for mythic expressions that evolved
and were absorbed into the culture. These mythological stories formed as Martin Buber explains, "a second Bible of legends, scattered in innumerable writings, around the
nucleus of Scripture" (Schwartz, 1998, p. 6).

Reading and understanding the underlying meaning of myths and sacred text is a continuous task to assure a deepening of our understanding of our inner lives. Neil Douglas-Klotz describes the fluid, intuitive consciousness required in order to truly integrate and be transformed by scriptural readings. He notes that

> in Midrash one attempts through contemplation to make a scriptural passage or a saying of a holy person into a living experience that can meet the challenges of the present moment. Most Sufi Muslims would understand [this] as *Ta'wil*, a style of translation-interpretation that again considers the possible multiple meanings of a sacred text in order to cultivate wisdom for one's everyday life. (Douglas-Klotz, 1999, p. 2)

Likewise the Yogic philosophers understand that Vedic/Hindu myths are multileveled allegories intended to guide one on the spiritual path of love, compassion and regard for all life.

Sadly, this is not a practice found at the fundamentalist level of any religion for their interpretations are based upon literal and unchanging interpretations of sacred allegories. Conservative and orthodox Jews (similarly to members of other religions) have also tended to get stuck in interpretations that were more appropriate for another time and place in history. The threat of fundamentalists' influence is that even the investigative processes of Midrash and Ta'wil can be halted. When selective interpretations are accepted as literal fact, followers no longer seek within for an ever deepening meaning. This creative process is necessary given the evolution of consciousness, the changes in environment, technologies and so forth. Myths are influenced by the natural environment. For example, guiding myths may differ for those in rugged environments compared to those emerging from peaceful, pastoral ones. Also the cultural era in which new renditions emerge has an influence on the interpretation and use of guiding myths. Problems occurred when mythologies were proclaimed as literal fact, and then used to promote patriarchal ideals and control the beliefs of others.

In a positive light, mythological allegories offer common themes. They guide our relationships in the physical world as they point us toward a yet higher level of existence. Cultural and collective myths provide ethical guidance for human development. Myths and archetypal themes depict the human journey, and guide us towards Self- (and Divine) Realization. The primary apparent function of myth is to provide answers for our questions regarding the origin, destination and meaning of life at a metaphoric level, and, secondly, "to justify an existing social system and account for traditional rites and customs" (Larousse, 1968, p. v). So they could be a source of guidance to solve the secrets of life, or they could be also a source of justifying dogmatism.

The above mixture of motivations influenced the development, and most certainly the interpretation, of sacred texts. One, albeit controversial, illustration of this is found in the Hindu Vedic scriptures, known as the *Rig Veda*. Another example is the Jewish scriptures compiled and contained in the Bible's Old Testament. The history and teachings in these texts represent the transition to patriarchy. Both documents also depict their heroes as warriors that conquered other tribes and other ways of life — testimonies of prejudice against the other.

Many creation stories simply provide ethical guidelines for living in harmony with nature and other human beings. These narratives are also filled with beautiful ideals and practices for living a spiritual life. For example, sacred texts and mythologies tell us that evil deeds cause destruction to the inner self; whereas good deeds generate spiritual growth and psychological contentment. This concept is expressed both literally and metaphorically. Unfortunately this guidance is often twisted into rigid and fanatical interpretations, leading people to follow the *forms* while overlooking the *meanings* of the rituals and rules. By emphasizing the underlying meanings of these myths, we can see how these symbolic systems guide spiritual evolution. Moreover, in these myths we read an explicitly implied message of tolerance and openness — that enhances psychological development and spiritual growth.

Numerous stories depict the consequences of behaviors related to good and evil, such as the following Native American creation story from the Hopi nation of Arizona. The responsibility for ongoing life and well being rests within the character, rather than gender, of its people.

The Hopis believe that the universe was created out of the mind of Taiowa, the Creator.

Taiowa created Sotuknang, who entered into the first world and created Spider Woman. She was given the responsibility of creating life. Spider Woman mixed earth with her saliva and created the first human in the form of twin beings. Life continued in this first world and its people were happy. They began to quarrel and divide. Then "there came among them a handsome one, Kato'ya, in the form of a snake with a big head. He led the people still farther away from one another and their pristine wisdom" (ibid., p. 12). This led to warlike behaviors. (Obviously Kato'ya represented pride and the quest for power leading people into opposition and destruction.).

Those who chose good behaviors were told the way to a new place being created for them, and they were saved from the destruction of the first world. The chosen people went to live with the ant people in the underworld while the second world was being created. They were then brought into this second world. Eventually the people began to create commerce, trading and bartering among one another. This led to fighting and wars along with destruction of the second world by ice. This time greed led them astray.

The people who still had the song alive in their hearts were taken to a safe place in the underworld with the ant people to emerge into the third world when it was ready. This time lust and gluttony led many people astray. Those who strove to keep the song and praise alive in their hearts were led by spider woman to leave and find their own way. In desperation after much journeying they "opened the doors at the top of their heads" (ibid., p. 20) and found the place of emergence into the next world. The old world was destroyed by water (the flood). They were told to follow the higher wisdom (available through this door at the top of their heads) and to not follow evil ways. Once they had found the fourth world, they traveled to all parts of the earth and then returned to carry on the plan.

It is the feminine creation, Spider Woman, who brings joy and balance into the world, represented as the twin beings. The Native American Hopi myth stresses that salvation is found when a person is freed from attraction to greed, lust, jealousy and so forth. A constant factor found throughout all native traditions is the belief that discord occurs when one is not living in harmony with nature. Mother Earth and Father Sky are equally revered. The indigenous traditions have cultivated a respectful balance between male and female, heaven and earth.

The Hindu Trinity: Stories of Wrath and Devotion

Hindu mythology contains great epics including numerous gods and goddesses. The stories from these ancient Indian texts, the Rig Veda, are estimated to be more than 3000 years old. Most likely a shift in story line occurred similar to the Hebrew re-versioning of the earlier Sumerian myths, supporting the rise of patriarchal religious and social structures. Colorful sagas depicted the manifestation of creation along with battles between forces of good and destruction. Gods often entered the world during a time of cosmic chaos to fight a particular evil or destructive demon. The battles resulted in victory of good over evil, and the cosmic balance was once again restored.

Goddesses and Gods ruled along side one another in India's early history, but the influence of the feminine diminished as patriarchal ideals were incorporated into Indian mythology. It appears that the Indo-European (Aryan) invasion of India had a primary influence on the development of religious thought and India's caste system. Creation myths defined and rationalized the Indian caste system, which designated its people into one of four social systems; namely the Brahmans (priests), Kshatriyas (warriors), Vaishyas (merchants and other common peoples) and the Shudras (those who serve the other three classes).

According to this religious mythology, it was one's karmic destiny to be a Brahman, Kshatriya, Vaishya or Shudra as one's lot in life was cast at birth. (A fifth class, the untouchables, was added later.)

Many believe that conquering nomadic Aryan tribes invaded India (as well as other lands), castes were established (oftentimes on the basis of color) and a leader known as the great Manu established rules for conduct among the castes. On the spiritual side there was a notion of spiritual "purity" at the highest (Brahmin) level; but this was tainted with the idea that only Brahmins represented purity. Following this hierarchical belief structure, the darker Dravidians (native Hindus) were delegated to be slaves of the lowest order.

It is said that the entire universe manifested from Ishvara, and that all gods and goddesses are a manifestation of Ishvara. The ultimate being of power manifests in the Hindu trinity of Brahma, Vishnu and Shiva (all males). One story tells us that, "when Ishvara creates the universe, he is called Brahma, when he protects, he is called Vishnu, and when he destroys, he is Shiva."[6] Each represents a state of mind, and this ultimate mind manifests powers of both creation and destruction. Purusha is another name for a manifestation of the ultimate being.

The Rig-Veda relates that Purusha pervaded the entire earth, and extended beyond it. He is seen as the lord of immortality and life manifested from his being.

> When they divided Purusha, in how many different portions did they arrange him? What became of his mouth, what of his two arms? What were his two thighs and his two feet called?
>
> His mouth became the Brahman; his two arms were made into the rajanya [kshatriyas], his two thighs, the vaishyas; from his two feet the shudra were born...
>
> With this sacrificial oblation did the gods offer the sacrifice. These were the first norms [dharma] of sacrifice. These greatnesses reached to the sky wherein live the ancient Sadhyas and gods. (de Bary, 1958, pp. 16–17)

[6]   http://www.exoticindia.com/articleprint/vishnu

The Creation myth has the act of creation itself placing people into caste systems according to where they emerged from Purusha's body. Another sacred Indian text describing the *Law of Manu* states that

> But for the sake of the prosperity of the worlds, he created the Brahman, the Kshaatriya, the Vaishya and the Shudra to proceed from his mouth, his arms, his thighs and his feet
> ...
>
> To Brahmans he assigned teaching and studying (the Veda), sacrificing for their own benefit and for others, giving and accepting of (alms).
> The Kshatriya he commanded to protect the people, to bestow gifts, to offer sacrifices, to study (the Veda), and to abstain from attaching himself to sensual pleasures ...
> The Vaishya to tend cattle, to bestow gifts, to offer sacrifices, to study (the Veda), to trade to lend money, and to cultivate land.
> One occupation only the lord prescribed to the Shudra, to serve meekly even these (other) three castes. (Muller, 1886, 12–14, 24)

The myths of the warrior and conqueror Indra are related in the Rig Veda, where prejudice against the darker race is clearly described: "Thou Indra, art the destroyer of all the cities, the slayer of the Dasyus [darker race], the prosperer of man, the lord of the sky" (Rig Veda. VIII.87.6); and another verse claims that "Indra protected in battle the Aryan worshipper, he subdued the lawless for Manu, he conquered the black skin" (Rig Veda. I.130.8).

The caste system also designates women to be subordinate to men. Uma Chakravarti notes how, "caste hierarchy and gender hierarchy are the organizing principles of the brahmanical social order and are closely interconnected" (Chakravati, 1993). As a result women's mobility and independence have been limited. In fact, women are vulnerable to domination regardless of their caste position. According to the Rig Veda, "Lord Indra himself has said that woman has very little intelligence. She cannot be taught" (Rig Veda 8.33.17). And to this day in many parts of India, a woman is denounced for bearing a female. She will bring pleasure to her husband if she births a son.

But like the Bible and other sacred books, beauty and wisdom stand alongside of evil traits such as prejudice and wrongful dominance over others corrupting the heart of humanity (and readers do consider that literal translations of sacred texts bind practitioners to these wrongful behaviors).

Patriarchal ideals of conquering others (and the ego) are also presented in the Hindu text known as the *Bhagavagita* for it depicts a famous battlefield scene in which the chaste and devoted warrior Arjuna is preparing for a great battle. He is grief-stricken when he realizes many friends and kin are among both armies. He laments to his god, Krishna, that if the men are killed, the women will become corrupt. The caste systems will then intermingle, resulting in destruction and hell.

Although this story conveys a rather questionable influence in suggesting that men must control women's corrupt nature and protect status and property, it also has a deeper spiritual intention. For example, Krishna tells him to "Cast off this weakness of heart ... the self is constantly born and constantly dies ...".[7] The reference to reincarnation along with the encouragement of detachment is emphasized in the Hindu-Vedic tradition. The story is really about the battlefield of the heart. Men have used warlike language to describe the purification process leading to unity with the divine. Therefore this story can also be understood as a metaphor with teachings on a multitude of levels.[8]

In summary, the above stories reveal the multileveled repercussions of the rise and reign of patriarchy in the East. The following reveals its continued influence as it spread to other lands.

Ancient Myths and Legends of China

The origin of the Chinese people is not known although there are speculations that the ancestors of the current Chi-

[7] http://www.wsu.edu:8080/~dee/ANCINDIA/GITA2.HTM
[8] The idea of the battlefield of the heart is similar to the frequently misunderstood reference to Islamic Jihad, which pertains to the Holy War of purification within one's self with the understanding that Arjuna's battle takes place within his own consciousness.

nese people may have come "from the west, from Akkadia or Elam, or from Khotan, or (more probably from Akkadia or Elam via Khotan, as one nomad or pastoral tribe or group of nomads or pastoral tribes)" (Werner, 1994, p. 17). Chinese history suggests invasions clearing forests, the pushing back of aboriginal peoples and the establishment of the Chinese culture around 2,500 or 3,000 BCE.

From its onset Chinese religion was primarily based upon ancestral worship — honoring and appeasing the spirits of the dead. Ancestral spirits entered into all forms of nature, including trees and rocks. The dead were buried with possessions (wives, food and other items) to assure well-being in the world of the ancestors. Oftentimes, the spirit was beseeched to enter a tablet, which would be taken home and placed in a prominent place for remembrance and worship. These departed spirits might have beneficent or malevolent influences so acts of appeasement were necessary. Basically this religion represents an "attitude towards the spirits or gods with the object of obtaining a benefit or averting a calamity" (ibid., p. 52).

In Chinese mythology everything on earth is a reflection of its heavenly counterpart. Therefore, the good and bad people in this world are counterparts of gods and demons in the heavenly world (ibid.p. 52). Its structure is patriarchal, which created somewhat of a caste system,[9] along with other problems. If everything is a reflection of its heavenly counterpart, then one can see how the emphasis given in regards to "saving face" when insulted is particularly important for the Asian.[10] If people are counterparts of the gods and demons in heaven, then the Asian idea of "saving face" denotes an even deeper cultural meaning. *Respect* takes on a multileveled meaning. If one is treated with dis-

---

[9]   Historians believe that India's caste system had an increasing influence upon Chinese social structure. A more rigid caste system began to develop after the late 1940s.

[10] "An individual in Chinese society always belongs to some groups which absorb and reflect that individual's glory or shame. Consequently, a person who does not want *lien* [face] may also be accused of 'losing lien' for someone or some group with whom he or she is closely connected" (Bond, 1986. p. 247).

respect, an insult has also been given to one's heavenly counterpart. Considering the power of mythological foundations in one's unconscious processes, it is easy to see how this background would by necessity initiate retaliation against a serious offence, or war against an enemy, in order to save face.

The Chinese belief system encouraged the following cultural hierarchical design,

> The general division of the nation was into the King and the People. The former was regarded as appointed by the will of Heaven and as the parent of the latter. Besides being king, he was also law-giver, commander-in-chief of the armies, high priest, and master of ceremonies. The people were divided into four classes: (1) Shih, Officers (later Scholars), consisting of Ch'en, Officials (a few of whom were ennobled, and Shen Shih, Gentry; (2) Nung, Agriculturalists; (3) Kung, Artisans; and (4) Shang, Merchants. (ibid., p. 28)

This hierarchal classification represented a male dominated paradigm.

Ancestral spirit worship may have had an adverse effect upon the development of Confucius' philosophy — for it became a sober tradition that discouraged an emphasis on supernatural forces. The great philosopher Confucius (551–479 BCE) believed in the spirit world, but was more interested in the development of moral character and social order. His was a humanistic doctrine and his teachings on work ethics and family loyalties still have a powerful influence on Chinese culture.

Taoism was founded by Lao Tsu (sixth century BCE). He taught the principles of the Tao to Confucius and had an influence upon his philosophy. A significant difference is that Confucius examined methods and behaviors for a good society whereas Lao Tsu believed that a moral and productive culture emerged as transformation occurred within ones character. The Tao is the way (a human should follow) and it is also the destination as it is believed that all things return into the Tao. References to creation are taught in the following manner. "The way that can be walked is not the Eternal Way; the name that can be named is not the Eternal

Name. The Unnamable is the originator of Heaven and earth; manifesting itself as the Nameable ..." (ibid., p. 88).

When the devotee finds peace within — knows and maintains a balance point between yin (receptive) and yang (active) — he or she has found the way. But, as pointed out in the Introduction chapter of this book, this ideal of a balance of yin and yang has not been encouraged in the outer world and fails as long as women remain relegated to a subservient position. Hence gender imbalance represents a manifestation of a wider chaos in the social and spiritual order of the world. (This becomes even more apparent as authors review the effects of patriarchal policies.)

Shintoism: A Native Religion of Japan

It is believed that China had a large influence on the development of early Asian culture and mythology. Japan's historical records (beginning around 552 AD) indicate that the Japanese people were organized into clans (uji). The one dominant clan, the Yamato uji, has continued and "by its extension, so has its Divine ancestors. The imperial family, which has continued in an unbroken line to the present, soon became the primary focus of Japanese myth" (Willis, 1993, p. 110). Its structure is patriarchal.

The native religion of Japan is Shintoism, a religion focused on worshipping gods, spirits (the kami found in all living things) and objects of reverence (which also have kami). Shintoism and Buddhism have co-existed since their appearances in Japanese culture, although Shintoism was the state religion in the Meiji government (1868–1912).

Takamagahara is the Japanese word for the highest heaven realm. Three invisible gods took form from this realm. Amanominakanushi-no-kami (Lord of the Center of Heaven) was the first god to emerge. Takaminmusubi and Kamimusubi followed. These powerful kami (spirits), along with two lesser deities, formed the "five primordial 'Separate Heavenly Deities. Then came seven more generations of 'heavenly' gods and goddesses, culminating with the Japanese primal couple: Izanagi and his sister and wife,

Isanami, in full Izanagi-no-Mikoto (the August Male) and Izanami-no-Mikoto (The August Female)" (ibid., p. 112).

It sounds as though a masculine and feminine balance is emerging, but as readers can see in the following narration, Izanami, like Eve, becomes the scapegoat for birthing a problem.

Izanagi and Izanami were commanded by the older and higher deities to complete the work of creating the world. They descended to a new island appearing below. Their first child was conceived. Izanami ends up being punished for birthing a deformed child called "Leech-Child," and lost her place of equality (an obvious support for male dominance) because of this ill omen. The Divine couple continued to give birth as many islands, gods and goddesses of many realms and the gods of nature sprung forth. Izanami died during the birth of the fire god in that her genitals were badly burned. According to the legend she was still bringing forth deities through her excrement, vomit, etc., as she died. In longing, Izanagi decided to go find her in the underworld, and finding her to be a rotting corpse, he fled in terror. In her outrage at this abandonment, Izanami sent the hags of the underworld after him. She transformed herself into a demon, pursued him and broke their marriage vow.

Following this discord between the sexes, Izanagi returned and purified himself by bathing. He then took on the role of a woman himself, as Gods and goddesses began to birth from his clothing as he bathed (ibid., p. 112).

Three significant deities in Japanese cosmology manifested at this time. Amaterusu-no-mikoto, Susano-no-mikoto and Tsuki-yomi-no-mikoto. Once again, a feminine power emerges. Amaterasu was known as the great Sun Goddess —the "August Person who Makes the Heavens Shine," (ibid., p. 114) —Tsuki-yomi, the moon god, and Susano as the storm god.

In Japanese mythology, Amaterasu (light and nurturance) and Susono (thunder and violent behaviors) birth out of the same divinity. Since their parents were birthed from the same source, everything is in relationship and emerges out of the formless and nameless sea. Thus Japanese mythology suggests a conflict in regards to the feminine, not only in its mythologies, but also in actual practice in that its patriarchal organization has suppressed and diminished the female. There is both a reverence of the feminine and a negation.

The Bodhisattva represents a positive manifestation of both male and female. The belief in Bodhisattvas was introduced to Japan through the Buddhist religion. A Bodhisattva is a divine being motivated by great compassion. This belief that a deity both heard and responded to the cries and needs of the world appealed to the Japanese. The Bodhisattva has given up Nirvana (state of eternal peace) until all sentient life knows the great enlightenment. These great ones act as lights to the rest of the world. Devoted believers turn to the Bodhisattva for protection, guidance and mercy to keep them from the evil evidenced in illusions, pride and other human vices. Male and Female Bodhisattvas are revered alike so this is a great image for gender balance in Buddhism.

Ancient Egyptians: The Dream of Paradise on Earth

Egyptian dynasties rose approximately 5,000 years ago, right in the middle of the ongoing shift into patriarchy. Although prejudice against women is not evidenced in its mythologies, and kings and queens existed alongside one another; some accounts suggest they kept slaves.

Ancient Egyptians had very sophisticated views, and their philosophy is worth contemplation (Wheeler, 2002). For a long period of time, it was believed that Egyptians were pagans who worshipped many gods and goddesses. It is more correct to say that they saw the universe as Divine entities, but that they were also aware of the one Divine origin, as the following passage shows.

> God is one and alone and none other existeth with Him. God is the one who hath made all things. God is a spirit, a hidden spirit, the spirit of spirits of Egyptians, the Divine spirit. God is from the beginning, and He has been from the beginning, he hath existed from old and was when nothing else had being. He existed when nothing else existed, and

what existeth He created after He has come into being, He is forever. His name remains hidden; his name is a mystery unto His children. His names are innumerable, they are manifold and none knoweth their number. God is truth and he liveth by truth and He feedeth thereon. He is the king of truth, and He hath established the earth thereupon- God is life and through Him only man liveth. He giveth life to man, He breatheth the breath of life into his nostrils — He begat himself and produced himself. He createth, but was never created. (Budge, 1967)

The Egyptians' world view was distinct; they saw everything in its relationship to other things. They felt a connection to nature, yet at the same time humanized nature. The famous picture of the sky depicted in a shape of a woman whose hands touched one end of earth as her legs stood firm at the other end, symbolized the close relationship between sky and the earth, and reflected the Egyptian view of the universe whereupon all living beings were connected, and female and male aspects of the universe were integrated.

Balance between masculine and feminine aspects in the universe overwhelms the Egyptian mythology. One of its most noted myths is that of Isis and Osiris. Nut and Geb were descendants of Shu the air force and Tefnut the water force. Nut the sky was married to Geb the earth. The couple begot Osiris, Set, Isis and Nephthys. Their offspring represented cosmic powers, depicted in forms of human beings. Evil has nothing to do with the feminine aspect in Egyptian mythology. The power of goodness was symbolized by the character of Osiris, and the power of evil was materialized in his brother Set. Isis was Osiris' sister and also his wife — his soul mate. Set deceived Osiris and killed him. Although Nephthys had married Set, she soon left him, to help her sister Isis. It was because of the dedication and struggle of Isis that Osiris was able to defeat death and be liberated from his body and live in the hereafter.

Osiris' message on earth was continued through his son Horus. Osiris' high rank in the after world is seen through these prayers which Ani, a deceased person offered him:

The stars in the celestial heights are obedient unto thee, and the great doors of the sky open themselves before thee.

> Thou art he to whom praises are ascribed in the southern heaven, and thanks are given for thee in the northern heaven. The imperishable stars are under thy supervision, and the stars which never set are thy thrones. (ibid.)

According to this myth, there will come a day when Horus will defeat Set forever, and Osiris will be resurrected, and return to earth, bringing with him all those who had been his own faithful followers.

The two powers of good and evil are always in opposition, thereby creating trouble. The dream of ending the power of evil has been embedded in the human psyche since the beginning of patriarchal history. Ending the patriarchal reign may not bring a complete end to wars and conflict, but gender balance will certainly soften and transform the dangers confronting humanity at this time. The patriarchal ideal of solving conflicts and imbalances inspires reformers and people of vision. It has both allowed for and created opposition, while longing to heal it. This shared, rather hypocritical, theme appears in many of its religions; for example, the coming of the Messiah for Christians, the Mahdi for Muslims, the Hidden Imam for Shi'is are a few examples. Regardless of whether this dream will come true or not, it continues to inspire human hearts towards compassionate acts or towards destructive ones—and humanity tends to mirror its beliefs.

On the other hand, the feminine aspect is rarely caught up in this masculine drama of being at war with the forces of the universe. Instead, the power of Isis manifests as a savior, and Virgin Mary becomes the giver of life to her son Jesus.

In contrast with the core message provided by these feminine deities, the monotheistic religions' followers believe that the return of their Prophet means victory for their religion over other religions. So the power of evil comes back disguised under the mask of goodness.

The Isis and Osiris myth demonstrated psychic activities on the individual level. The power of evil and goodness are embedded within our unconscious, and their conflicts are taking place deeply from within. With the help of the feminine power that represents compassion, mercy, motherhood, fertility, sacrifice and self denial, a human being is supported to choose goodness over evil, and witness a new birth. Isis was a symbol of that power. Therefore, drawings show her in a variety of forms and shapes, each of which captured one of her features.

Greek Influences

Plato, Aristotle and other Greek philosophers had a profound impact on patriarchal ideals. Through these great thinkers, humanity discovered its potential to contemplate nobler ideals and mental attributes. The shadow side of this evolutionary development is that mental concepts became more important than the body, any form of emotion or sensuality, and physical life itself. Plato's *philosopher kings* principle was used to justify authoritarianism. Aristotle believed women to be deformed males. He claimed that the "courage of the man lies in commanding, [whereas] a woman lies in obeying" (Freeland, 1994). These authoritative arguments swayed the course of history, and even the role of the feminine pantheon of Gods and Goddesses changed. The Goddess Athena had a primary position in earlier, pre-patriarchal Greek paganism. Some stories, based on symbols link her far back into African mythology. Athene was the daughter of Metis, whose threads lead back to African mythology. It was prophesied that Metis' unborn daughter would equal Zeus in wisdom, so Zeus ate Metis. The image of Athena was then recreated when Homer proclaimed her to be born from the head of Zeus rather than from a mother. Therefore the male was assured dominance.

The Greek and Roman pantheon of gods and goddesses represented many virtues ascribed as divine qualities. These same archetypal qualities are later recognized as holy attributes of God in both Eastern and Middle-Eastern traditions. For example, Buddhist and Yogic mantric practices, early Christians chanting various qualities of Jesus, and Muslims intoning the 99 Names of Allah (these may be fierce qualities as emphasized in Zeus, the wisdom and strength of Athena or gentle, homely qualities of the Goddess Hestia and so forth).

Hades was the god of the underworld. This was the place where human souls were judged. They were believed to be sent to a land that was blessed or to a dark, fiery one. The mythology was incongruent in that Grecian gods and goddesses[11] were capable of murder, lust, etc., without blame, whereas humans were to suffer punishment for such behaviors. This incongruence no doubt influenced Plato, Aristotle, Pythagoras, Socrates and other Greek philosophers' contemplation towards nobler ways. In fact, their beliefs were contrary to the sexual freedom enacted by their own Grecian warriors and its elitist society.

Ancient Middle-Eastern Roots

Some scholars have noticed that the mythologies of the Ancient Egyptian, the Sumerian and Akkadian cultures of Mesopotamia and the later Zoroastrian religion of ancient Iran had a powerful influence on the development of Middle Eastern (Jewish, Christian and Islamic) religious beliefs.

Mesopotamia was a fertile valley between the Tigris and Euphrates rivers. It extended "outside the borders of modern Iraq into Syria, and parts of Turkey and Iran" (Black & Green, 1992, p. 11). Mesopotamia's influence spread into Israel, Jordan, Egypt and other Middle Eastern countries. As mentioned earlier in this chapter, many scholars have noted the effects of its oral tradition upon the Bible stories in the Old Testament.

It was the Sumerians who invented writing around 3400 BCE. Their mythologies were left for future historians, anthropologists and mythologists to study. According to Sumerian scholar Stanley Kramer,

> One fundamental moral problem, a high favorite with Western philosophers, never troubled the Sumerian thinkers at all, namely the delicate and slippery problem of free will. Convinced beyond all need for argument that man was created by the gods solely for their benefit and leisure, the Sumerians accepted their dependent status just as they

---

[11] Roman gods and goddesses paralleled the Grecian pantheon.

accepted the Divine decision that death was man's lot and only the gods were immortal. All credit for the high moral qualities and ethical virtues that the Sumerians had evolved gradually and painfully over the centuries from their social and cultural experiences was attributed to the gods; it was the gods who planned it that way, and man was only following Divine orders. (Kramer, 1963, p. 123)

The Sumerian records reveal that Sumerian people "cherished goodness and truth, law and order, justice and freedom, righteousness and straightforwardness, mercy and compassion, and naturally abhorred their opposites, evil and falsehood, lawlessness and disorder, injustice and oppression ..." (ibid., p. 123). These values were evidenced by records of kings and rulers who reigned according to these principles. Female and male Gods ruled alongside of one another.[12]

As already alluded to, the emergence of patriarchal culture and domination included the development of religious ideals. Hebrew, Hindu, and Zoroastrian religions are primary examples of this early transition. The Zoroastrian religion began in ancient Persia (Iran), and was founded around the 6th or 7th century BCE. by its Prophet, Zarathustra (anglicized as Zoroaster). Its rituals and ceremonies were centered on the elements of nature. Although much reverence was given to the feminine aspect of Asha, divine truth, the principle deity was the sun god, Ahura Mazdah. The Zoroastrian cosmology was structured around the battle between good and evil, no doubt influenced by the harshness of the land in which they lived. Ahura Mazdah, and the evil god, Ahriman, (also known as Angra Mainyu) were the principle deities.

> To Zoroaster God is the Wise Lord, Ahura Mazdah, the one who creates heaven and earth, the first and the last, yet also a friend, the one who has called him from the beginning. God can have nothing to do with evil. His Holy Spirit establishes life, and creates men and women. He is opposed by

[12] There was no language depicting God and Goddesses, rather the defining element was the description of their genitals. Early historians were able to decipher who was male and who was female because of these gendered body parts and at the same time note gender equality.

the Evil Mind, the Lie, and Pride. Between these opposing
forces, these twin spirits, people must choose. If they follow the path of evil, their lives are full of evil thoughts,
words and deeds. But if they follow the path of truth, they
share in the Good Mind and attain integrity, immortality,
devotion and the kingdom, all of which are aspects of God.
(ibid., 178)

Much attention was given to fasting, purification, ritual,
and *Asha* — holy truth known through the pure heart. The
Middle-Eastern religions that followed (Judaism, Christianity and Islam) incorporated their ideas of heaven and
hell, good and evil. An end to this conflict between good
and evil was envisioned, with the devil being defeated following a trial by fire. One can see the threads that would
eventually be woven into the monotheistic religious beliefs,
although approximately six-hundred years later Jesus'
teachings and examples would place little importance on
fasting practices or practicing the Sabbath as evidencing
true spirituality. Instead his works emphasized the importance of healing, honoring women, challenging hypocrisy,
protecting others and creating good relationships. This is
the manifestation of *Asha* — the truth known through a pure
heart.

Another example of this thread is found in Islam where
the call directly addresses the freedom of the human soul by
explaining that there is nothing to fear or even to worship;
rather people need to discover their ultimate goal of life,
and establish the relationship between their earthly activities and the ultimate goal. Humans are thus directed to the
way this freedom can be achieved. This is the holy truth we
seek.

Both Jesus and Mohammad led their followers to look
within themselves in order to overcome evil. This inner
journey leads one away from projection onto and defenses
against other human beings into the cleansing and freeing
of the human heart. It is guided by what the alchemists of
mystical Judaism and Islam knew as the feminine archetype
— a receptive, reflective, inner nature of the heart. Ancient
Hebrews called her *Hokhmah*. In Islam the feminine aspect
manifests as divine Compassion. In Arabic the origin of the

word compassionate and merciful is derived from the root ra-ha-ma which is the same root for the word rahem, meaning the womb. By cultivating this feminine aspect in the psyche, human beings are likely to achieve balance and spiritual maturity. The Chinese Taoists recognized the feminine expression of divine manifestation as *Yin*. It is the pure feminine nature portrayed and honored in patriarchal religions, yet ignored in the outer world as living women were and still are defamed. The imbalanced psyche motivates separation between the ideal and the real, and encourages aggression and violence, the feminine aspect is a source of compassion that softens and balances masculine power and evil tendencies.

Satan's Fall from Heaven:
Evil in Judaism, Christianity and Islam

In particular, the creation stories found in Judaism, Christianity[13] and Islam specifically illustrate that superiority, prejudice and aggression against others is the root of all evil, hence Satan's fall. Many have attempted to name the sources of and behaviors related to evil, but have not given enough attention to the following stories from the monotheistic religions for patriarchy has well named its own evil. The following renditions tune right into the core issues that separate us from our natural unity (paradise).

The *Haggadah*, originally part of the Jewish Talmud, is one of a vast collection of Jewish stories. These stories were gathered around the fourth through sixth centuries CE. Previously they were part of the oral tradition of story-telling.

The following story, in particular, discusses the root of evil; it should be read in the spirit of Midrash. And, most importantly, readers will notice that this early myth, underlying the development of Middle Eastern religions, indicates that prejudice against the other (race, religion, gender) is the root of all evil.

---

[13] Until the Common Era, the majority of religious teachings were presented through the oral tradition. In fact, many Jewish and Christian scriptures were not written down until the first three hundred years of the Common Era.

The Creation story found in the Haggadah describes the fall of Satan.

> The extraordinary qualities, with which Adam was blessed, physical and spiritual as well, aroused the envy of the angels. They attempted to consume him with fire, and he would have perished, had not the protecting hand of God rested upon him, and established peace between him and the heavenly host. In particular, Satan was jealous of the first man, and his evil thoughts finally led to his fall. After Adam has been endowed with a soul, God invited all the angels to come and pay him reverence and homage. Satan, the greatest of the angels in Heaven, with twelve wings, instead of six like the others, refused to pay heed to the behest of God, saying, "You created us angels from the splendor of Shekinah, and now you command us to cast ourselves down before the creature which you fashioned from the dust of the ground!" God answered, "Yet this dust of the ground has more wisdom and understanding than you." (Barnstone, 1984, pp. 29–30)

According to this version of the fall, God asks Adam, the archetypal human being, to divine the proper names for the animals in his creation. The Haggadah narrates that Satan had failed this task that had now been given to Adam. Satan was forced to acknowledge the "superiority of the first step in creation." (ibid., p. 30). He then,

> ... broke out in wild outcries that reached the heavens, and he refused to do homage unto Adam as he had been bidden. The host of angels led by him did likewise, in spite of the urgent representations of Michael, who was the first to prostrate himself before Adam to show a good example to the other angels. Michael addressed Satan: "Give adoration to the image of God! But if you do not, then the Lord God will break out in wrath against you." Satan replied: "If he breaks out in wrath against me, I will exalt my throne above the stars of God, I will be like the Most High!" At once God flung Satan and his host out of Heaven, down to the earth and from that moment dates the enmity between Satan and man. (ibid., p. 30)

The passage states that human life manifested from the thought and creativity of the Divine, which then took form in matter. It also suggests that the ability to comprehend and name various forms of creation was a potential of human consciousness (perhaps this refers to the human capacity for reasoning and higher cerebral functions). The legend tells us that Satan was outraged that this earthly, human manifestation would receive more reverence than those created of pure spirit (angels). The idea that angels having been created from the splendor of Shekinah (feminine Hebrew word for holy light) and having "to cast ourselves down before the creature which you fashioned from the dust of the ground!" (ibid., pp. 29-30) was deemed unacceptable to Satan.

Elaine Pagels, , a Professor of Religion at Princeton University and author of *The Origin of Satan*, reports that

> In the Hebrew Bible, as in mainstream Judaism to this day, Satan never appears as Western Christendom has come to know him, as the leader of an "evil empire," an army of hostile spirits who make war on God and humankind alike. As he first appears in the Hebrew Bible, Satan is not necessarily evil, much less opposed to God. On the contrary he appears in the book of Numbers and in Job as one of God's obedient servants — a messenger, or angel ... (Pagels, 1995, p. 39)

The story tells us that Satan is an angel, which implies that he did not originate in evil (unlike the Zoroastrian god of darkness Ahriman/Angra Mainyu who is in constant struggle with Ahura Mazda, the god of light). It is the idea of superiority that prevented him from acknowledging Adam, and diminished his light.

In this story it is Satan's perception of himself as an alienated, separate being that evokes resentment of the other. The thought of separateness, creates jealousy, envy and hatred. Although Satan represents a symbolic, archetypal figure, he symbolizes our internal struggle between light and darkness, unity and division. For example, it serves Satan's purpose when one group of people considers itself to be chosen over others, or one nation or race proclaims itself to be superior to others, while these others are deemed as lesser, infidel, worthy of God's wrath, untouchable, and so on. This dark influence was accepted by the early Jews as the Old Testament clearly portrays prejudice when the Israelites are told to take slaves from among the heathens, rather than from their own relatives (Leviticus 25:44-45). In regards to prejudice against women, the scapegoating of Eve has created the greatest injustice. For example, I Timothy 2: 11–14 advises, "Let the woman learn in silence with all subjection. But I suffer not a woman to teach, nor to usurp authority over the man, but to be in silence. For Adam was first formed, then Eve. And Adam was not deceived, but the woman being deceived was in the transgression". The point of the legend of Satan's fall was obviously missed.

The Qur'an relates a similar story to the one in the Haggadah. In this version Satan is known as Iblis. The following is from the section Al-A'raf, Sura VII, (11–17):

It is We[14] Who created you and gave you shape; Then We bade the angels bow down to Adam, And they bowed down; not so Iblis; He refused to be of those who bow down.

(Allah) said: "What prevented thee from bowing down when I commanded thee?"
He said, "I am better than he: Thou didst create me from fire, and him from clay."

(Allah) said: "Get thee down from this: It is not for thee to be arrogant here. Get out, for thou art the meanest (of creatures)."
He said: "Give me respite till the day they are raised up."

(Allah) said: "Be thou amongst those who have respite."
He said, "Because Thou hast thrown me out of the way, lo! I will lie in wait for them on Thy Straight Way: Then will I assault them from before them and behind them, from their right and their left: Nor wilt Thou find, in most of them gratitude (for Thy mercies)."

The two primary themes of evil are again emphasized in this story. One is the theme of *prideful* prejudice against human creation (refusing to bow before Adam) and the other is that the inner, spiritual (created from fire) is superior to earthly matter (created from clay). Interestingly, matter and mater (mother) have the same roots so there is a relationship to the rejection of women, birthing, sexuality and so forth.

[14] The language of the Qur'an has the characteristic of changing the Divine pronoun from We to I to He. It all refers to God (Allah).

These Middle Eastern stories indicate that evil is clearly
defined and perceived as prideful superiority over others.
When we negate earthly life and deem it to be inferior to
heaven, we discount the all pervading influence of divine
creation. The Qur'an and other religious texts illustrate the
power of evil as it manifests rigid egoic thinking and negative feelings overtaking human hearts. Yet, despite these
illustrations, this evil is evidenced in the widespread mis-
use of religious myths that have led to the abuse of women.

We must find a way to eliminate the sharp lines that separate us from one another. Jesus recognized this and emphasized the value of a caring, loving spirit when he explained
that anger and hatred are the origin of all bad deeds,

> But I say unto you, That whosoever is angry with his
> brother without a cause shall be in danger of the judgment;
> and whosoever shall say to his brother, Raca, shall be in
> danger of the council; but whosoever shall say, Thou fool,
> shall be in danger of the hell fire. (Matthew 5:22)

In another discourse he added,

> Every kingdom divided against itself is brought to desola-
> tion, and every city or house divided against itself shall not
> stand. And if Satan cast out Satan, he is divided against
> himself, How shall then his kingdom stand? (Matthew
> 12:25–26)

So much misunderstanding has occurred over these metaphors. The image of Satan's "kingdom" (hell) should not
be taken as a literal existence of a political entity. This influence appears in the heart of human beings who choose
hatred, anger, and superiority as a way of life. It is a manifestation of the "small I", for the ego governed by these
qualities is manifesting the emanations of a hell world.
Light, wisdom, love and beauty are the emanations of
heaven. The projection of evil upon other groups has contributed to numerous wars, deaths and sorrow. The victory
over evil influence cannot be accomplished through hatred
and revenge, but rather by nourishing the spirit of love
within oneself and towards others. All revelations have
been guiding humankind to the way of love rather than

hatred, but it has been prevented due to the suppression of the female.

Evil is evidenced in the many conflicts existing throughout our planet. Ironically, the legends which explored these thematic principles metaphorically have been taken literally and used to nourish feelings of pride and superiority. The danger in taking our religious myths and legends literally (a danger particularly manifest in fundamentalist thought), is that we tend to ignore the message and, instead, demonize the other. For example, the stories in this chapter have described collective themes concerning dark or evil forces. They are evidenced in our violence towards others, especially if they differ in religion, color or gender. In particular, the Satan myth influencing Judaism, Christianity and Islam suggests that every time we demonize another human being, race, nation or religion, we have been taken over by this satanic archetype.

Conclusions

Although the many myths addressed in this chapter differ in form and content, there is a continuous stream advising human beings to respect other forms of life, and to find a way of living in peace and harmony. All mythologies and religious stories include a standard for ethical behavior and some form of teaching regarding cause and effect relationships, or consequences; in other words, that "one harvests what one sows." Examples of this are found in Judaism's Covenant; Buddhism's Eight-Fold path; Islam's Shari'a and Christianity's Golden Rule. Despite our guiding myths, deeply ingrained religious beliefs, and technological developments, a large amount of humanity continues to disregard the wellbeing of its brothers and sisters. Instead, people make the choice to kill one another and to endanger our environment. Oftentimes religious devotees support their destructive decisions by limited, fundamentalist interpretations from sacred texts. This choice reveals an apparent inability or refusal to integrate and act on the true ethical and religious teachings as revealed in our myths and spoken by our Prophets. Much of this refusal to abide by ethical caretaking of one another has a relationship to patriarchal dominance and as such represents an imbalance of gender. This is why many myths alluded to the splitting of earth and sky at the onset of patriarchal dominance (Parrinder, 1971, p. 155). Metaphorically they symbolized the irrational splits between heaven and earth, mind and body, male and female that have filtered through our religious institutions and created havoc in our human relationships.

We cannot change the past, but we can change our attitude toward it. Uproot guilt and plant forgiveness. Tear out arrogance and seed humility. Exchange love for hate — thereby, making the present comfortable and the future promising.

Maya Angelou

Chapter Two

Violence in the Name of One's God

Patriarchy's influence was clearly evidenced by 3,000 BCE. Its religious traditions began to emerge. The lineage of reigning Egyptian pharaohs (kings and queens) began around 3,500. India's Vedic teachings were founded during this time, containing the structure for the Yogic teachings that would later flow into Buddhism. Abraham proclaimed a revolutionary religious ideal embraced by the Hebrew people and strengthened by the patriarchs that followed. This was the belief that universally there was only one God. The old gods and goddesses were denigrated and left behind. It was the onset of a monotheistic lineage, which would eventually include Christianity and Islam. A new development in human evolution was sweeping through humanity, a mutation that would eventually bring us to our current predicament — for better or for worse.

Jewish feminist Louise Gerda describes how monotheism supported the patriarchal ideology. She explains that

> monotheism supports patriarchy by deviating from its own primary insight. When patriarchy takes the principle of unity and splits it in two. When God is removed from the world and set above it, when Divinity is no longer inherent in us but exists as an ideal outside ourselves — both god and world are exiled. The problem, in other words, is not the oneness of Divinity, but the otherness of Divinity. The problem is in our image of transcendence, through which we disempower ourselves as we portray God as power over us. (Dorff & Newman, 1998, p. 134)

This is how Morris Berman's *Sacred Authority Complex* was put in place.

Yet, despite its inherent faults, we cannot deny the fact that humanity has achieved much learning during this patriarchal era. This is evidenced in great works of architecture, poetry, art and music. It is found in noble philosophies, scientific progress and other endeavors. It is seen in the finer elements of religious life, wherein compassion, beauty and nobility are found.

The late Sufi teacher Hazrat Inayat Khan (1877–1927) had a beautiful way of describing the essence of the world's religious traditions. He equated true religion to music, saying that each individual religion

> strikes a note, a note which answers the demand of humanity in a certain epoch. But at the same time, the source of every note is the same music which manifests when the notes are arranged together. All the different religions are the different notes, and when they are arranged together they make music. (Khan, 1979, p. 19)

This harmony is evidenced in the beauty, power and wisdom of the great teachers and Prophets initiating each faith. The heart of each religion resonates from its onset with universal love, harmony and beauty. In other words, they are not repetitive, but rather originate from the same source in a new way, and in this manifestation each religion compliments one another. Irregardless, a destructive element grows within a new religion soon after the death of its Prophet as the followers attempt to concretize the teachings — often based upon their own interpretations. Dominating tendencies soon take over as the followers of a religious belief overlook the power and inspiration of the heart and depend solely on superfluous and patriarchal ways of thinking. Differences from other groups and belief systems are emphasized, and rules are established to assure one is a true adherent to the established hierarchy. Those outside of this new order are demonized, and the musical notes quickly turn to cacophony, no longer harmonizing in unity.

This chapter examines the development of major world religions, and notes the ways in which these religions have failed to live up to their own ideals. To begin with, the tendency to both claim superiority and to defend one's religion tends to be rooted in fear — and fear perpetuates violence (the topic of fear will be discussed in Chapter Three). Oftentimes our defenses are built upon that which we deem to be sacred; for example, religious teachings that affect our ideals, beliefs and feelings. But this honoring takes on a different quality once the ego has made its claim concerning any religious teachings. This problem emerges as a result of the ill-conceived belief of separateness, discussed in the analysis of Satan's fall. The tendency to claim *absolute truth* and enlist *blind obedience* fuels this evil (Kimball , 2002).

Most importantly, the violence perpetrated in the name of one's religion has little, if anything, to do with the religion itself — but rather with evil tendencies within the human ego. In the Semitic languages, the word evil basically means "unripe" (Douglas-Klotz, 1999, p. 1). This implies that one is using power before one has developed. True human development requires gender balance to bring hearts, minds and bodies into harmony. This gender balance leads to the felt experience of unity — the healing of separateness.

Each religion's core teaching asks that believers have love and compassion for one another — for these are the ultimate acts of spiritual humanity, and as the examples that follow indicate, many adherents of religion have failed to listen to its heart. Countless people of color have suffered due to religious prejudice and intolerance, and women of all races and religions have been ongoing victims of discrimination, murder and rape. This marks another primary difference between the sexes. For the most part, males experience heightened levels of testosterone in response to a perceived threat; whereas women tend to reach out and connect with others. This is why the role of women is so important at this stage of our human evolution. They will help shift the tide.

Sadly, due to the influence of the patriarchal warrior mentality, religious teachings have supported numerous and ongoing acts of violence. One example of this is found in the book of Judges (19:24–27), in the Judeo-Christian Bible. In this story, readers are told that the patriarch of the

home and his male guest are threatened by "sons of Belial."
The man responds "Behold, here is my daughter a maiden,
and his concubine; them I will bring out now, and humble
ye them, and do with them what seemeth good unto you:
but unto this man do not so vile a thing." For some reason,
the daughter is refused, but the concubine is "gang-raped"
(Eisler, 1987, pp. 101–102) and found dead on the doorstep in
the morning. This is but one of many Biblical examples of
prejudice against women. It is also important to acknowledge that women, as well as men, embody these patriarchal
influences and related behaviors.

A tragically meaningful example of this is given by
syndicated columnist and author Ann Coulter in her article
Why They Hate Us.

> Americans don't want to make Islamic fanatics love us. We
> want to make them to die. There's nothing like horrendous
> physical pain to quell angry fanatics. So sorry they're
> angry — wait until they see American anger. Japanese
> kamikaze pilots hated us once too. A couple of well-aimed
> nuclear weapons, and now they are gentle little lambs. That
> got their attention. (Coulter, 2002)

Obviously, females, as well as males, can embody a
destructive mentality. This ill-fated drive of superiority
appears throughout the world and throughout its patriarchal ideologies. If we are to survive the American driven
"war against terrorism," this paradigm will need to change.

Gender imbalance is a manifestation of the spiritual
imbalance initiated by a patriarchal ideology. Even our relationship with nature is patriarchal in that we use nature for
our own ends, without regard for its natural beauty and
future. God is over man, man over woman, human over
nature. One religion's God is superior to another's. These
views stand in stark contrast to a unitive understanding,
one that recognizes God is within all manifest life.

As noted at the beginning of this chapter, Patriarchy
encouraged a new perspective of life, which, for a period of
time, brought about significant religious and spiritual
growth. Philosophical and scientific pursuits, and rapid
material progress ensued, but we forfeited our sacred

relationship with nature. As Buddhism, Confucianism, Christianity, Hinduism, Islam, Judaism, Taoism and Zoroastrianism became the dominant religious teachings, the earlier Goddess-revering traditions disappeared into the shadows. Women were denounced, deemed inferior to the male.

Religious Founders and Gender Balance

Our Prophets revealed oneness with the divine; they manifested spiritual wholeness and taught us the way to unveil our human potential. They also demonstrated the love and compassion that is often associated with women, and the strength and knowledge that have traditionally been associated with men. In particular, both Jesus and Muhammad were egalitarian, and taught others to treat women with respect, reverence and equality. They represented *whole* and *complete* human beings.

The New Testament story of Jesus speaking to the Samaritan woman at the well (John 4:7–42) illustrated not only his egalitarian views but also his acceptance of *the other*. She questioned, "How is it that thou, being a Jew, askest drink of me, which am a woman of Samaria? For the Jews have no dealings with Samaritans" (John 4:9). In his response he accepted her as both a woman and a Samaritan, and also revealed how he knew the intimate details of her life. He than began a deeply spiritual discourse that led her to an inner understanding and spiritual discovery. The story tells us that she went on to share his message with other Samaritans and that they came to hear him. This is but one of the many examples of Jesus' gender balanced stance and inclusiveness.

The *Gospel of Mary*, part of the Nag Hammadi Library's collection of religious texts discovered in 1945, contains knowledge omitted in the New Testament version of Jesus' relationship to his disciples. In fact, Mary's Gospel reveals even more about Jesus' core teachings and his non-patriarchal relationship with women. The introduction to the Gospel explains that,

Peter and Andrew represent orthodox positions that deny
the validity of esoteric revelation and reject the authority of
women to teach. The *Gospel of Mary* attacks both of these
positions head-on through its portrayal of *Mary Magdalene*.
She is the Savior's beloved, possessed of knowledge and
teaching superior to that of the public apostolic tradition.
Her superiority is based on vision and private revelation
and is demonstrated in her capacity to strengthen the
wavering disciples and turn them toward the Good. (King
et al., 1990, p. 524)

Stories of Mary confronting Peter about his patriarchal
ways have been found in the *Gospel of Thomas*, *Pistis Sophia*,
and *The Gospel of the Egyptians* (ibid.).

The Prophet Muhammad's appreciation and respect for
the feminine was exemplified in his familial relationships.
His wife and soul mate, Khadija, for example, believed in
him and provided assurance when he doubted the validity
of his own experience. When Gabriel appeared before
Muhammad for the first time, it was Khadija who helped
him to trust his spiritual experience, assuring him of the
greatness of the revelation. From that moment, Muhammad's life changed.

In the early years of his Prophetic mission, he could not
have managed without her support and her spiritual counsel. Whenever Muhammad was attacked by his enemies or
shaken by the power of his mystical experience, he always
went straight to his wife for comfort and for the rest of her
life Khadija, the first person to recognize her husband's
exceptional ability, 'strengthened him , lightened his burden, proclaimed his truth. (Armstrong, 1992, p. 80)

Khadija shared the Prophet's message, not only as a
believer but also as an active partner who put her money
and efforts at his disposal. She bore his most difficult times,
and her passing caused the Prophet great grief. Nobody
could be dearer to him than Khadija, his first wife, for she
had provided love, faith and monetary support when the
rest of his world had rejected him.

Furthermore, his daughter, Fatima, was deeply loved by
Muhammad, and respected by all. She was admired for her
eloquence and for her ability to speak directly from the
heart. It is said that "when she spoke, people would often be

moved to tears" (Helminski, 2003, p. 11). Rather than considering women less valuable than men, Muhammad took their counsel seriously. Following the disappointments of the Hudaybiyya Covenant (a treaty with his enemies), he took the advice of his later wife, Umm Salamah, thus avoiding anger and rebellion.

Likewise, another wife, Aisha, holds a special place in Islamic history. Muhammad advised his followers to listen to her wisdom, and it is believed that Aisha established the "fundamental rules of Arab-Islamic ethics" (ibid., p. 15). In short, Muhammad was a compassionate and balanced man who was grateful for, rather than threatened by, the strength of his wives. He did not expect to hold dominion over them. Just as they contributed to the religious, political and ethical life of the community; so he contributed to the life of the home by repairing sandals, sewing garments, sweeping the house and caring for livestock.

The love, compassion and tenderness emanating through the founders of our religions are more illustrative of the feminine, maternal aspect of the ultimate Creator. This *gender balance* melded well with their undaunted courage, and strength — and divine wisdom and wholeness were manifest.

This chapter will describe the atrocities perpetrated in the name of religion as followers ignored the gender-balanced examples and teachings of their Prophets. It is difficult for adherents of a particular religion to face its dark side, but this is necessary in order to truly represent the heart of a religion. In order to transform old patterns we must be willing to examine our attitudes, beliefs and behaviors — and bring them into the light of consciousness.

Our faith and actions should be based in the heart of the religion and its founder's *exemplified* message, for it is this that bears truth rather than the controls and ideas of superiority over others established by later followers after the founder's death. Although a greater emphasis will be placed on the monotheistic religions of Middle Eastern origin; Judaism, Christianity and Islam, authors will also provide historical examples of religious violence enacted by followers of other religions. Our findings support the premise that this evil is deeply entrenched in humanity's collective shadow.

Failing to Hear and Heed: The Message of the Prophets

Fundamentalism is on the rise, and as recent world events indicate, fundamentalists are to be found in most, if not all, religious traditions. Religious historian Karen Armstrong suggested in a recent talk at the Council for a Parliament of the World Religions that this fundamentalism manifested as a "rebellion against modern secular society, because it is understood as a threat" and that it "takes root in the fear of being annihilated" (Armstrong, 2004). Rapidly changing technologies, greed-driven commercialism and fear of the unknown have contributed to this phenomenon.

The narrow-minded beliefs expressed in the *radical* fundamentalist mindset encourage destructive behaviors; they are the breeding ground for prejudice and pride. This has led to ongoing warring and genocide with little, if any, regard for the wellbeing of others. Religion-based fundamentalists often rely on sacred texts to validate their beliefs, and to affirm identity. But oftentimes we can find similar core beliefs and recurring narratives in many religions. For example, Jews, Muslims and Christians, all trace their heritage to Abraham. Although the versions vary somewhat, common themes can be traced back to the biblical generation of Isaac and Ishmael (in Arabic, Ismail) at 1800 BCE. Their story allows us a glimpse of the similarities as well as an explanation for the *otherness* influencing Jewish, Christian and Islamic religions.

The biblical story informs us about Hagar (Egyptian name meaning "migrant"), the maidservant of Sarah, the wife of Abraham. When Sarah found herself unable to have children, she gave Hagar to Abraham as a second wife (Genesis 16: 3), hoping that Hagar would bear a son. Hagar conceived Ishmael, but years later when Sarah had a child of her own, Isaac, Sarah became jealous. "Cast out this bondwoman and her son: for the son of this bondwoman shall not be heir with my son, even with Isaac," outburst

Sarah (21:10). When Sarah demanded the ousting of Ishmael, God reassured Abraham: "Let it not be grievous in thy sight because of the lad, and because of the bondwoman … I will make a nation of him, too, for he is your seed" (21:12-13). To avoid her mistress's wrath, Hagar escaped into the desert. Despairing over her weeping child, she received an oracle from an angel of God: "What aileth thee, Hagar? Fear not; for God hath heard the voice of the lad where he is. Arise, lift up the lad, and hold him in thine hand; for I will make him a great nation" (21:17-18). The Ramban, a famous thirteenth-century Torah scholar, blames the enmity between these two nations, the Jewish and the Arabs, on the harshness [and prejudice] of Sarah and the callousness of Abraham. Interestingly, Muslims share a different perspective on this story.

Muslims believe that Isaac and Ishmael were equally chosen as Prophets. According to Islam, Allah asked Abraham to travel with Hagar and her son Ishmael for a sacred purpose, which was revealed later when the father (Abraham) and son (Ishmael) rebuilt the Ka'aba, the house of God. When Abraham left Hagar and her son alone, he was sure that Allah's protection would save them from any danger, since he acted according to divine orders. Yet, much dispute has occurred between Jews and Muslims over this variation in story line in that, Muslims, unlike Jews, view Isaac and Ishmael as equals. In the Islamic perspective, both sons represented the religion of their father.

Despite the shared themes and common ancestors of Judaism, Christianity, and Islam, religion has been, and continues to be, used as a tool in generating disputes. It provides leaders with powerful narratives for uniting and motivating the masses. As will be further discussed, the patriarchal structuring of religion provides an effective tool to control and motivate people in a way that supports political conflicts, oftentimes with harmful consequences. The original sacred texts that aimed to deliver a spiritual message have been used to provoke hatred and negative feelings, thus creating a false assumption that conflicts between nations are unsolvable due to their religious origin.

Humanity's well being is threatened with the current conflicts amongst the monotheistic traditions: Judaism, Christianity and Islam. Hinduism, and, more recently, Buddhism
have evidenced an increase in violent behaviors. Therefore it
is important for us to better understand the light and the
darkness manifesting in each of these traditions.

The Jewish Story

Considering the fact that the Jewish population is small in
comparison to other world religions, it is phenomenal that
Jewish thinkers and the Jewish scriptures have had such a
profound impact on the world. Being the smallest of the
so-called monotheistic religions, Judaism has only about 12
million followers around the world (this accounts for only
0.3% of the world population, compared to approximately
33% Christians and 19% Muslims). Throughout the world,
Jews are a minority within the larger non-Jewish environment, and in the Middle East, Israel is a relatively small
country surrounded by a vast constellation of Arab states.

The ancient Hebrews both endured and perpetrated
many wars but throughout these hardships and contradictions they have held an image of peace as evidenced in the
following scripture: "And they shall beat their swords into
plowshares, and their spears into pruning hooks; nation
shall not lift up sword against nation, neither shall they
learn war any more" (Isaiah 2:4). It is an image of a world no
longer dominated by testosterone. The following relates the
chronological development of Judaism.

The Prophet Abraham was born into a pagan society,
worshipping many gods. He was one of the first to proclaim
that there was but One God (Melchizedek was another)
(Chacour, 1984). The monotheistic religions trace their
origins and faith to Abraham and his followers, a nomadic
group of Hebrews, dating back more than 5,000 years.
Abraham, his second-born son Isaac and his grandson Jacob,
are considered to be the patriarchs (or fathers) of Judaism.[1]

---

[1]   As noted earlier, Abraham is also considered to be patriarch of the monotheistic lineage that followed, which includes Christianity and Islam.

Their descendants were the people who would later be
known as the Israelites.

The scriptures relate that Jacob received God's blessing
and was given the name *Israel* after a night of spiritual struggle (Genesis 32). This story is worthy of much study, for it
plays a central role in current world problems concerning
the "outer" state of Israel. The first name, Jacob (Ya'acov in
Hebrew) means that he is seized by the heel of his brother.
The story tells us that he was in fear of being attacked by his
brother, Esau, and four-hundred men. He sent many gifts to
Esau, via his servants. He released all of his belongings in an
attempt to avoid violence. He was left alone. The scripture
explains that he wrestled with a man all night, without
success.

> And when he saw that he prevailed not against him, he
> touched the hollow of his thigh; and the hollow of Jacob's
> thigh was out of joint, as he wrested with him.
>
> And he said, Let me go, for the day breaketh. And he
> said, I will not let thee go, except thou bless me.
>
> And he said unto him, What is thy name? And he said,
> Jacob.
>
> And he said, Thy name shall be called no more, but
> Israel: for as a prince hast thou power with God and with
> men and has prevailed.
>
> And Jacob asked him, and said, Tell me, I pray thee, thy
> name. And he said, Wherefore is it that thou dost ask after
> my name? And he blessed him there.
>
> And Jacob called the name of the place Peniel: for I have
> seen God face to face, and my life is preserved. (Genesis 32:
> 25–30)

According to the sacred text, God then promises him: "A
nation and a company of nations shall be of thee ..." (Genesis 35:11). According to this story, Israel's new name was
given as a result of inner struggle and peaceful resolution
with his brother. Jacob-Israel's 12 sons were to become the
leaders of the 12 tribes of Israel. In short, this new name represented a *way of life* and the tribes (representatives) were
charged with the mission of carrying on Israel's example.

But these brothers were unable to follow this example,
and, being jealous of Jacob's favorite son, Joseph, they sold
him into slavery without their father's knowledge. A

strange turn of events brought Joseph into great favor in Egypt, whereas his brothers became destitute due to a famine. This led them to Egypt seeking refuge and goods from its royalty, and they found themselves in front of the brother they had betrayed. But the story reports that Joseph, the one off-spring who had been able to carry on the spiritual goodness and examples of his father, bestowed compassion and fulfilled their needs. This favorable time led many Israelites into Egypt.

Nearly 300 years after Joseph's death the rulers of Egypt turned against the Israelites, oppressing and enslaving them. The Scriptures tell us that God chose Moses to lead the Israelites out of Egypt. Another interpretation could be that he was an extraordinary leader who led an Israeli revolt to the point of leaving Egypt (a journey known as the Exodus) into the promised land of Canaan. Upon reaching Mount Sinai, Moses received from God the *Torah* that included the Ten Commandments and all the laws that would follow, forming the ethical foundation of Judaism. This detailed value system is built upon 613 commandments (Mitzvoth) regulating manners of worship and treatment of other people. The Prophet Micah summarized this system into three principles: Only to do justly, to love mercy, and to walk humbly before God. The Mosaic laws basically ask that there be justification and culpability for any injustice. Some scholars believe that this was the onset of the "eye for an eye" and "tooth for a tooth" belief system.

Whereas Abraham initiated the spirit of Judaism, Moses delivered its laws and principles. In discussing the patriarch of the monotheistic traditions, Abraham, in her book *The Origin of Satan*, Elaine Pagels quotes Genesis 12:3 "I will make you a great nation, and I will make your name great … and whoever blesses you I will bless; and whoever curses you I will curse," and adds, "So when God promises to make Abraham the father of a new, great, and blessed nation, he simultaneously defines and constitutes its enemies as inferior and potentially accursed" (Pagels, 1995, p. 36). Israel was thus defined as *us* against *them*.

Traditionally people tend to use holy texts to support their world view, but this same verse can be interpreted differently. It can be seen as an assurance that God would support the children of Israel because they were endowed with a great message as revealed first to Abraham, and continued through his descendants. This message was one of hope, that love and justice would one day rule all of humanity. The problem manifests in the literal interpretation that only a select lineage has God's blessing, rather than the blessings being inherent in a particular way of life. Elaine Pagels' interpretation defines this passage as the beginning of the separation between Jews and other peoples, and one that has contributed to much suffering. And, we see this same tendency repeated over and over again with world religions and various sects as it appears to be human nature for individuals and groups to take an egotistical view whereby an individual, a religious group or a nation considers their experience to be elite or superior (this will be addressed further in Chapter Three).

The Jewish law, for example, forbids marriage to a *goy*, and reveals a fundamental fear of religious mixing (e.g., a Jewish and Christian marriage). Yet, although Talmudic literature does not encourage religious integration, it clarifies a humanistic attitude towards non-Jews: "We support poor gentiles (*goyim*) with the poor people of Israel, and we visit sick gentiles as well as the sick of Israel, and we bury the dead of the gentiles as well as the dead of Israel, because of the way of peace" (Talmud, Gitin, 61a). However, also inherent within this proclamation is an insinuation that one is compassionate towards, yet elevated above, the other.[2] Patriarchy!

The idea of the Promised Land is a powerful aspect of Judaism. The concept has become a potent archetype for humanity, because it embodies the human longing to live in peace and freedom with love and justice for all. The Bible

---

[2]   Our commentaries are not intended to demean the Jewish people, or
      any other group, but rather to point out the divisive tendencies that
      separate us from God and one another. *All* religions need to
      re-evaluate similar premises.

alludes to a Promised Land, based upon the following scripture: "Now the Lord had said unto Abram, Get thee out of thy country, and from thy kindred. And from thy father's house, unto a land that I shew thee" (Genesis 12:1). Moses was the one, who after freeing his people from slavery in Egypt, led them through forty years of wandering in the desert, to the land that ultimately became their home. After finally settling in Canaan, they battled with the Philistines over the land and triumphed. Although they certainly warranted a safe place to live (free from abuse and slavery), this story also provides another example of the developing patriarchal model — one of conquering other peoples and claiming land.

Another monumental event — the building of the Temple — occurred during the reign of King David. In 1000 BCE, David, the second king of Israel, both a lyricist and a fierce combatant, captured Jerusalem after many gory battles. Jerusalem was proclaimed as the capital of his new kingdom and his son, Solomon, built the first Temple — a symbol of Jewish worship and power. From the mid-8th century BCE, this Promised Land was conquered by a number of different rulers, among them the Assyrians, the Babylonians, the Persians, and the Romans. In 586 BCE, the Babylonians exiled the Israelites and the Temple was destroyed, but King Cyrus the Great of Persia made the decision to allow the conquered Jews to follow their customs. They thereby rebuilt the Temple, housing many sacred symbols and riches within it. In 165 BCE there was a Jewish rebellion (called Hasmonean) against Greek rule. There followed a number of uprisings against Roman rule, prompting Rome to ruthlessly repress Judaism, forbidding the study of Torah, and renaming the land "Palestine". In 66 CE, when Jews were celebrating the festival of Passover, Roman soldiers marched into Jerusalem and stripped the Temple of its treasures. A year later, the Roman general Titus brutally destroyed this second Temple as he killed, enslaved and exiled the Jews — thus starting what is known in the Jewish history as the Diaspora (the dispersion of the

Jewish people). By this time many branches of Judaism had already emerged.

Historically, the Jewish people were scattered, living in tightly knit local communities. A unified Jewish belief system did not exist. According to Jewish scholar and professor, Daniel Boyarin (Boyarin, 2004), various dialects and ethnic differences contributed to differing interpretations and applications (and that the roots of Orthodox Judaism and church-like gatherings did not begin until around 300 CE). There were also numerous segments claiming to be the direct descendants of its early prophets. The decentralization that occurred after the destruction of the temple also adds to this story in that the various Jewish groups held differing beliefs regarding Jewish viewpoints and history. This led to intra-group as well as inter-group violence amongst the various Jewish groups (not unlike was what to happen among later Christian and Muslim sects).

The Jewish Scriptures portray numerous wars and cruel killings. The book of Judges describes a total of 13 wars with a repetitive theme. The first war described in this book is because the Israelites sinned by adoring the false gods. Jews believe that this led to their being punished by foreign invaders. The Jews were then freed again, adding to a total of 13 cycles of war and freedom. Apparently the Jewish Pharisees were the most adaptable during this time. With the destruction of the outward temple, the Pharisees recommended the practice of Shabbat. This practice enabled the Jewish people to acknowledge the temple within the home (and from a mystical perspective this practice also alludes to the temple within the heart). Jews then began to consolidate consensual beliefs and traditions during the first few centuries of the Common Era (ibid.).

The conversion of the Roman Empire to Christianity in the fourth century CE fueled persecution of the Jews. Church teachings instilled hatred of the Jews in the general populace. Restrictions against them by the church became the laws of the land. Jewish-Christian marriages were forbidden. Jews were restricted in property rights and barred from many public functions and offices. These restrictions stayed in place until the rise of Capitalism in the nineteenth century. In the Middle Ages Jews were blamed for the death of Jesus, giving rise to the Christian Crusades, the first massive killings of Jews by Christians. Countries like England, France, Spain, and Portugal, expelled Jews or singled them out, segregating them. During the 18th century in Poland, Jews were confined to living in an impoverished area called the Pale of Settlement. After being blamed for assassinating the Russian Czar, Alexander the III, organized anti-Jewish attacks broke out, often encouraged by the authorities. With very little to protect themselves from the pogroms (Russian word for "devastation"), the Jews had to flee. More then 2 million Jewish refugees fled Russia between the start of the pogroms in 1881 and the Russian Revolution of 1917. Out of the remaining Jewish population in Europe, six millions were murdered by the Nazis during World War II.

Although there have been numerous genocides (as described in our Introduction), the Jewish holocaust blatantly portrays the idea of one group (the Nazis) proclaiming itself to be a superior race and then deliberately targeting and destroying those deemed by its standards to be inferior (the Jews). Historically, the holocaust shockingly represents the most cold-blooded and calculated genocide of one group of people in human history. Alienation, persecutions and later on what was coined as anti-Semitism can account for the great momentum of the Jewish concept of a nation-state (now known as Israel). Many people view the modern state of Israel as part of the fulfillment of the Covenant. It is easy to see how it has violated a deeper meaning of that Covenant to justify the Israeli occupation of Palestinian land. For example, Ezekiel 36:24 is used by Jewish Zionists to justify the Israeli occupation and the reclaiming of Israel. The passage reads "I will take you from the heathen and gather you out of all countries, and will bring you to your land." A non-fundamentalist, and obviously more spiritually humane, interpretation could be referencing a freedom from all the lesser parts of oneself (and life styles that separate us from spiritual unity) with the promise of coming to true spiritual realization—a return to the true homeland to be found within the heart. Perhaps this helps to explain why the idea of "a promised land" has such archetypal power in human thought.

In modern times, many branches of Judaism, for example, Orthodox, Conservative and Reform sects, exist within Judaism. The Lubavitch Hasidism and Lurianic Kabbalah groups are associated with Orthodox Judaism. Orthodoxy is the division of Judaism that strictly follows the original teaching and traditions of the faith. Orthodox Jews regard the *Torah* as the actual words of God. This contrasts greatly with Reform Jews who believe that the words of these texts were not directly given by God, and are open to reinterpretation to meet the conditions of a particular time and place. However, some fundamentalist rabbinical scholars insist upon a literal interpretation of the Scriptures. When taken to extremes, this implies that each law within the tens of thousands of volumes of Jewish legal codes is to be regarded as sacred and infallible. These fundamentalists became so embedded in strict Jewish rituals that they forfeited the original humanistic spirit of the religion.

Although fundamentalism constitutes a relatively small portion of the Israeli population, its political influence has been growing. Fundamentalists have even demonstrated hatred for those Jews who opposed their views. An example of this is the murder of the Israeli Prime Minister Yitzhak Rabin in 1995 by an Israeli fundamentalist (Yigal Amir, the assassin, who claimed to be following the *Torah*'s laws).

The Torah, which brings a message of love and compassion, can be puzzling for an inexperienced reader. One of the first stories to portray the destructive, all-powerful, wrath of God, *the Flood*, is also suggesting an opportunity for a better world, filling the reader with hope. According to the scriptural narrative, Noah's generation was so sinful that its peoples deserved to die and therefore only Noah was warned of the great flood. However, this same story also brings a message of salvation and conveys archetypal symbols of peace, and a new beginning (similar to the Hopi Indian mythology).

The ancient Jewish literature conveys the moral, ethical, and cultural codes of a different era. Many of the concepts are unacceptable in modern thought. But this is yet another example of the problems with religious interpretations relying on literal translations — for these sacred texts are no longer read as a living, vibrant entity. The stories were meant to be continuously renewed, and the Midrash employed by the early Rabbis allowed for this ever renewing interpretation (Douglas-Klotz, 2003).

The Hebrew Scriptures are rich with stories of rivalries, revenge, and anger; yet, at the same time they contain eternal concepts of love and brother/sisterhood. King David, for example, was both a warrior and the author of one the most poetical books, the *Psalms* (known as the *Tehilim*). David's story portrays this dissonance by conveying a message of success achieved by war, and also of punishment for being a warrior leader. For instance, Jerusalem was won by war. King David had claimed the city after conquering the Jebusites (Armstrong, 1993). The Hebrew Scriptures describe his many fights, beginning with his use of the slingshot against Goliath, the Philistine giant, and continuing with strategically planned wars against other tribes such as the Amalekites. But David had to pay the price for being a wartime king, who had shed others' blood. David's son, Solomon, was chosen to build the holy temple, as he had never gone to war nor harmed another life. Solomon represented justice, good-will, discretion, wisdom and peace-seeking. The rabbis who wrote this Midrash used the example of David, and similar stories, to teach a moral lesson. The leaders of the community wanted to stress the merits of justice, equality, respect for all life, and social responsibility. These values represent the true heart of Judaism.

The Christian Story

A Jewish teacher called Yeshua of Nazareth (later known as *Jesus*) emphasized good (humane) works as the heart of Jewish spirituality. This principal was particularly evidenced in what are known as the *Beatitudes* presented in Jesus' Sermon on the Mount. The Beatitudes provided direction for living a spiritual life (at that time there was no religion called Christianity). Jesus simply presented the directions for living a spiritual life to his Jewish followers. The Beatitudes emphasized being merciful, humble, longing for God and, in particular, being peacemakers. "*Blessed are the peacemakers, for they shall be called the children of God*" (Matthew 5:9). Jesus never emphasized or advised his followers to be violent nor did he advocate the conquering of other nations, occupation of other lands or warlike behaviors in any form. He did not manifest patriarchal characteristics. Instead, he demonstrated love, compassion and inner and outer strength of character and will. Yet how many lives have been destroyed in the name of Christianity? The following history verifies the many times the Beatitudes and the golden rule have been ignored. Many Christians are ignorant of the history of their religion. Perhaps they are fearful of facing Christianity's shadow in that it could disturb their faith—but the choice of ignorance is really motivated by fear rather than true faith. The belief in and relationship with Jesus goes far beyond the written word.

The early Christians began promoting the doctrine of *rebirth in Christ* soon after Jesus' crucifixion. The Christian baptism required one to denounce all life before the conversion. Christianity had begun to establish itself as a religion separate from its Jewish roots. This *rebirth* tended to demonize previous religious and social affiliations. It was based upon a commitment to a particular church and its beliefs about Christianity rather than the actual rebirth from separateness into mystical experience—a ritual imitating Jesus' baptism whereupon he *realized* his unity with God. A doctrine of superiority was carefully established in the first few hundred years following Jesus' death, for soon thereafter Christians began to impose their religion upon others.

Karen Armstrong explains that "during the first century, Christians continued to think about God and pray to him like Jews; they argued like Rabbis, and their churches were similar to the synagogues" (Armstrong, 1993, p. 90). Many scriptures were written and passed around. Debates about the nature of Jesus ensued. The Council of Nicea occurred in 325 CE. The Roman Emperor, Constantine the Great, gathered early Christian leaders together to discuss the dispute regarding the nature of Jesus Christ. In particular, this was based on the historical disagreement between the bishop Alexander and Arius, a priest. Arius questioned that if the father (God) had begat the Son, (Jesus) then the latter must have had a beginning, there was a time when he didn't exist, and therefore the Son was created as the rest of creation. Numerous biblical teachings supported Arius' stance. Psalms 82:6 proclaims, "I have said, Ye are Gods; and all of you are children of the most High" and Jesus taught, "Blessed are the peacemakers: for they shall be called the children of God" (Matthew 5:9, King James version). The Bishops voted against this way of thinking initiating instead what was to be called the Nicene Creed, the doctrine of the Trinity (a doctrine that Jesus himself never taught):

> We believe in one God, the Father All-sovereign, maker of heaven and earth, and of all things visible and invisible;
> And in one Lord Jesus Christ, and the only-begotten Son of God, Begotten of the Father before all the ages, Light of Light, true God of true God, begotten not made, of one substance with the Father, through whom all things were made; who for us men and for our salvation came down from the heavens, and was made flesh of the Holy Spirit and the Virgin Mary, and became man, and was crucified for us under Pontius Pilate, and suffered and was buried, and rose again on the third day according to the Scriptures, and ascended into the heavens, and sits on the right hand of the Father, and comes again with glory to judge living and dead, of whose kingdom there shall be no end:
> And in the Holy Spirit, the Lord and the Life-giver, that proceeds from the Father, who with the Father and Son is worshipped together and glorified together, who spoke through the Prophets:
> In one holy catholic and apostolic church:
> We acknowledge one baptism unto remission of sins. We look for a resurrection of the dead, and the life of the age to come.

This statement proclaimed there was only one definition of Jesus, and of Christianity.

Constantine was a Roman who honored Roman gods. He presented an image of Jesus that was more that of a Roman God than a Jew with a profound realization of unity with God. To say this does not negate the divinity of Jesus Christ, but rather it takes into consideration the influences which diminished Jesus' teachings and his examples for living a spiritual life and, instead, empowered the Church. The Emperor Constantine set the precedence for future popes and positions of power. Just as Romans had bowed to the gods and goddesses, they now bowed to a pope — and the church became the only true authority. And this church was decidedly male!

Jesus had also referred to himself as a Prophet. The Bible tells us that he was rebuked by citizens of Nazareth and that "they were offended at him. But Jesus said unto them, A *Prophet* is not without honour, but in his own country, and among his own kin, and in his own house" (Mark 6:3-4). Matthew 21:11 tells readers "And the multitude said, This is Jesus the Prophet of Nazareth of Galilee." The Beatitudes speak for themselves in presenting the heart of Jesus' simple message. They represent *a way* of living, rather than proclaiming the superiority of a specific ruling authority (The Church).

During the Nicene council, decisions were also made regarding the numerous religious texts: What would be incorporated into the New Testament? And what would be discarded? Also, verses were added. But even earlier than that, prior to the Nicene gathering, Origen (185-254 CE), a theologian and scholar, had noted that "The differences among the manuscripts have become great, either through the negligence of some copyists or through the perverse audacity of others; they either neglect to check over what they have transcribed, or, in the process of checking, they lengthen or shorten as they please" (Metzger, 1992, p. 152).

The books retained, and the verses within them, have influenced Christian beliefs, in ways both good and bad. Some verses are not congruent with the teachings and

examples of Jesus. For example, one verse attributed to Paul
(1 Thessalonians 2:14–15) has greatly contributed to anti-
Semitism "For ye, brethren, became followers of the
churches of God which in Judaea are in Christ Jesus: for ye
also have suffered like things of your own countrymen,
even as they have of the Jews; who both killed the Lord Jesus
and their own Prophets, and have persecuted us; and they
please not God, and are contrary to all men ..." This added
passage obviously encouraged anti-Semitism.

Towards the end of the 4th century the Emperor
Theodosian gave orders to "suppress all rival religions,
order the closing of the [Jewish] temples, and impose fines,
confiscation, imprisonment or death upon any who cling to
the older [pagan] religions" (McBade, 1971). By the time of
the council of Toledo (697 CE), "Jews were taken into
slavery, their property confiscated and children forcibly
baptized" (Deschner, 1962, p. 454).

Another prominent influence on Christianity's development occurred via Augustine (354–430 CE). Augustine was
a medieval philosopher, who was particularly influenced
by Plato's philosophy. Accordingly, one did not seek "to
understand the mind or the world in its own terms, but only
as clues to the invisible reality of God in heaven" (Leahey,
1997, p. 79). Therefore, sensate life, the here and now,
became the lesser reality as the truer life was based on faith
in the unseen. What this tended to do was to reduce the
meaningfulness and sacredness of the material world (that
which had form) and ordinary life. Two dilemmas occurred
as a result of this interpretation.

Firstly, it separated heaven and earth in a way that was
contradictory to Jesus' understanding as an indigenous
Middle Easterner whereupon heaven (the divinity uniting
us all) and earth (form) interpenetrate one another
(Douglas-Klotz, 1999). A rich example of this understanding (one that the church rarely emphasizes) is Jesus' revelation that the "Kingdom of God [heaven] is within you"
(Luke 17:21). This vital heart of his message has been basically ignored in traditional Christianity.

The second dilemma was that the emphasis on spirituality as being unseen and otherworldly made us less responsible for the here and now — which included responsibility for our behaviors towards other ethnic and religious groups, and also our environment. The after-world (death) had become more important than the gift of life itself.

The psychological effect of this negation of human life was to encourage detachment from the sacredness of life in the here and now. Another result of this continued expansion of the church is that it also expanded the empire, and thereby its wealth and power. Acts of disregard for and violence against *the other* increased. Brutality committed in the name of Christ was evidenced during the Crusades. The so-called *Holy Wars*, originally launched in the 11th Century against Muslims in the Holy Lands, eventually expanded into several major attacks against Muslims, Jews, Pagans, and other "heretics" in the Arabian, Byzantine, Persian, and Turkish Empires as well as "minor" attacks on "heretics" in Europe as well. These wars in the name of Christianity continued into the 14th century.

In her book *A History of God* Karen Armstrong tells us that in 1492, Christians expelled Muslims from Spain while demanding that Jews either convert to Christianity or leave. Prior to the invasion of the Christian crusaders, Spanish Muslims, Jews and Christians had lived in peace. Next, the *witch craze* began. It influenced and dominated both Catholic and Protestant denominations. Thousands of people, primarily women, were tortured and killed. Armstrong notes that this collective fantasy was based upon a repressive religious ideology and that the "fantasy was linked with anti-Semitism and a deep sexual fear" (Armstrong, 1993, p. 175).

In 1521 the Emperor Charles V issued a decree known as the Edict of Worms (a German city) against the founder of the Protestant sect, Martin Luther. Luther was declared an outlaw and his murder would have been sanctioned. Protestants saw themselves as reformers of the Catholic Church. Catholics saw Protestants as enemies. For example, many Irish Catholics were massacred by Irish Protestants in 1641, and to this day ongoing violence between Protestants and Catholics in Ireland continues. Christians have acted destructively against other religions and even towards those who differ within their own tradition.

Violence in the name of Christianity was evidenced more recently in Kosovo as the Serbs massacred ethnic Albanians (Christian Orthodoxy is the dominant religion among the Serb population, whereas the majority of Albanians are Muslims). This violence in the name of Christianity continues to be the catalyst for devastating conditions in many "third world" countries. Its adopted conquering spirit fueled the colonization of Africa and the Americas, and continues to impact impoverished nations through fundamentalist-backed missions. As mentioned in the Introduction, in Sudan, Christian non-governmental organizations pressure the Sudanese to convert to Christianity in exchange for much needed humanitarian aid. Similar activities have led to a backlash, whereupon many countries either ban or control Christian activities, particularly in Southeast Asia.

Religion is also a distinguishing difference evidenced in the occupation of Iraq in that George W. Bush is a Christian who believed that the war and occupation were backed by God, therefore fulfilling a holy mission. Prior to his re-election campaign Bush often used a strict good-and-evil compass to influence national issues. Iraqis are primarily followers of Islam. The Iraq invasion was translated in the mind of many Muslims as a declared enmity to Islam. Arab television networks continue to broadcast bloody images of the aftermath, and the ongoing acts of terrorism and violence in many ways remind Muslims of the historical atrocity of crusaders in the Middle Ages. In fact, at the onset of the war Christian programs began training and preparing missionaries to convert Muslims to Christianity under the guise of giving humanitarian aid. According to syndicated columnist Ann Coulter of the New York Daily News:

> This is no time to be precious about locating the exact individuals directly involved in this particular terrorist attack. We should invade their countries, kill their leaders and convert them to Christianity. We weren't punctilious about

> locating and punishing only Hitler and his top officers. We
> carpet-bombed German cities; we killed civilians. That's
> war. And this is war. (Asaeed, 2001)

This comment appeared in newspapers around the world,
representing American Christianity.

One should ask: "Where is Jesus in Christianity?"
Certainly, there have been many reformers and movements
incompatible with the religious hypocrisy demonstrated
throughout Christianity's history. St. Francis of Assisi,
Hildegard von Bingen, St. Teresa of Avila, St. John of the
Cross, George Fox, Thomas Merton, Mother Teresa,
Matthew Fox and many others are examples of the undying
Christian spirit that persists despite the fallacies of its
churches.

The Islamic Story

The Prophet Muhammad identified his message of Islam
with that of Abraham; he called it the Primordial Religion.
According to the Qur'an the Primordial Religion *addin
al-hanif* is the religion of Abraham and all other Prophets
(HQ 3:67).

The Primordial Religion and Islam are synonyms; they
point to the hidden innate light within the human heart that
is revealed to all seekers for truth (regardless of religious
affiliation). For example, the Qur'an advises:

> So Thou set thy face in the right direction to receive the Pri-
> mordial Religion, the Law of Allah, that Religion which is
> inherited *innately* for people to follow. No change in what
> Allah has set forth. That is the Religion to be appreciated:
> but most among mankind understand not. (HQ 30:30)

Before the revelation recorded in the holy Qur'an,
Muhammad (an orphan) lived a modest life with his uncle
and then married his employer, Khadijah. He was known
and respected for his honesty, sincerity and wisdom. Oftentimes he spent hours in a quiet hillside cave in isolation and
contemplation. One day the archangel Gabriel appeared
before him and commanded Muhammad to "read". The
order came with such a spiritual power that it totally transformed his life. Muhammad came to realize that he was to

carry this message of Allah to the world. The Archangel Gabriel continued to communicate with Muhammad by reciting the verses and having Muhammad repeat them back. Later Muhammad recited them to his companions who memorized them by heart and then recorded the sacred text. The transcribed verses were collected eventually comprising the book to be known as the "Qur'an", the holy text for Muslims. The word qur'an is derived from the verb qara'a "to read," or "to recite".

A local Arabian pagan tribe, the Quraysh, sought to destroy Muhammad and his message. They inflicted persecution and tortured followers of the new religion, but Muhammad was unwilling to respond with aggression. During their 13 years in Mecca, his companions were asked to bear the unbearable, and never to hurt their persecutors. Escaping the determined decision of Quraysh's leaders to kill him, Muhammad fled to an oasis called Yathrib, 275 miles away from Mecca, later known as Medina (in Arabic "Madinah" means city). He then established the first Islamic society. His enemies continued their attempts to demolish this new religion, but were surprised by the resistance, courage and organization of the Muslims, who valiantly fought for their lives and their belief in Islam.

The Prophet decided to go to Mecca on a spiritual pilgrimage. He and his followers dressed in the ritual attire, and left their weapons behind. But members of the Quraysh attempted to prevent them from accomplishing their trip. To avoid any bloodshed, the Prophet made a treaty with the leaders of the Quraysh in Hudaybiyya (628 CE), which is near Mecca. Although these men had threatened the existence of the Muslims (believers of Islam), Muhammad wanted to demonstrate that his message was about peace and not war. An attack by Meccan allies upon Muhammad and his followers led to the latter's denunciation of the treaty of al-Hudaybiyya. Unforeseen, he marched into Mecca in January 630 CE with 10,000 men (*Encyclopedia Britannica*, 2003). Peace and victory were assured for they entered Mecca without resistance from their former enemies. The Prophet then decided to forgive all those who had sought to harm him, offering a way of peace to all.

His message was in the same spirit of Abraham, Moses and Jesus. As a matter of fact, he believed the message to be a continuation of previous Prophets. In the Qur'an, we read the following verses that link the revelation to Muhammad with previous revelations:

> Say ye: "We believe in Allah, and the revelation given to us, and to Abraham, Isma'il, Isaac, Jacob, and the Tribes, and that given to Moses and Jesus, and that given to (all) Prophets from their Lord: We make no difference between one and another of them: And to Allah we surrender" "We gave Moses the Book, and made it a Guide to the Children of Israel, (commanding): "Take not other than Me as Disposer of (your) affairs." (HQ 17:2)
> And in their footsteps We sent Jesus the son of Mary, confirming the Law that had come before him: We sent him the Gospel: therein was guidance and light, and confirmation of the Law that had come before him: a guidance and an admonition to those who are remindful of Allah. (HQ 5:46)

Ideally, people who adhere to these three religions should have lived happily in peace and respect for each other, for regardless of differences in rituals and habits they all were directed towards the same goal, that is, to be in peace from within and to spread peace to others. In Islam, the emphasis on the oneness of all religions was somehow distorted as believers mistakenly decided theirs was the superior revelation, and therefore superior to the others. This misunderstanding resulted in unnecessary fights, not only among adherents to different creeds, but also among Muslims who differentiated among themselves, each claiming to hold the absolute truth.

Muhammad's vision and teachings had challenged the tribal ethics and dogma. The core message of Muhammad was to spread the knowledge that all people are created from one originating source, and that this relationship existed irregardless of color, race, gender or any other worldly difference. Diversity thus should be respected. For example, the Qur'an states, "We created you from a single (pair) of a male and a female, and made you into nations and tribes, that ye may know each other (HQ 49:13).

The Prophet Muhammad sought to establish a positive relationship with Jews and Christians. He asked his companions to migrate to Abyssinia to escape persecution and terror because he assumed that the Christian Emperor Negus would be understanding and helpful. Negus was impressed with the respect that the Qur'an paid to both the Virgin Mary and Jesus. He decided to protect the Muslims and provide them hospitality for as long as needed (see Chapter Five).

When Muhammad migrated to Yathrib (Medina), the first thing he did was to establish friendship with the Jews who were scattered into three separate tribes. In her book *Muhammad*, Karen Armstrong draws her readers' attention to the fact that the Prophet had believed the Jews would understand his message, because it came from the same source. He demonstrated his respect in calling them the "People of the Book" (the Qur'an's term for other revelations, in particular, Christianity and Judaism) He made a treaty with them to join as one nation to defend one another against foreign attacks. Although Muhammad befriended the Jews, they did not accept the Muslims. Disappointed because of their infidelity, Muhammad expelled two tribes from Medina, one after the other. Unfortunately, they then formed allies with the Muslims' enemies, worsening the situation of the Muslims. One Jewish tribe, the Qaynuqah, attacked Muhammad and his followers, who, in turn, destroyed the entire tribe. Muhammad regretted this, but the stage had been set for enmity between Jews and Muslims despite Islam's inherent respect for Jewish Prophets.

The politicization of Islam started early in its development, when the key persons in Quraysh tribe who had fought Muhammad for more then twenty years surrendered to his military and political power. When they saw the twenty-thousand Muslims coming to conquer Mecca, they feared defeat, and declared their surrender to Muhammad, assuring their security. The Muslims then walked into Mecca, without any major resistance. Members of the

Quraysh, including some figures who had plotted to kill
Muhammad, were converted to Islam. In reality, they
wanted to use it as a vehicle to achieve their political ambitions as later events revealed. Political conflicts rose and
religious rhetoric was used in a way that resulted in great
confusion and sectarianism. This sectarianism in Islam is
very complicated and requires a multi-dimensional explanation. Yet, despite these oppositions, Muhammad
established a reign of peace over all of Arabia.

   Islam as a religion of love and peace has been misinterpreted and misrepresented, for the tribal spirit, which
should have diminished as a result of the Islamic message,
revived itself shortly after the passing away of the Prophet.
We can barely hint at how this once tolerant, loving religion
changed and became a source of violence and prejudice for
many of its groups.

   Disputes began after Muhammad passed away in 632 CE
in Medina. In fact, they began even as the funeral was taking
place. Companions, originally from the Quraysh tribe,
along with those known as "helpers of Medina" assembled
in the house of one of the helpers. After some dispute, they
decided to choose Muhammad's companion, Abu Bakr, as
his successor. Meanwhile Ali Ibn Abi Taleb, the cousin of
Muhammad (and also his son-in-law) was at the house of
the Prophet preparing for his funeral, and therefore unable
to attend the assembly. Taken by surprise about the decision that Abu Bakr was to be the Prophet's successor, Ali
declined from giving Abu Bakr the pledge of allegiance
saying,

> We know well thy pre-eminence and what God hath
> bestowed upon thee, and we are not jealous of any benefit
> that He hath caused to come unto thee. But thou didst con-
> front us with a thing accomplished, leaving us no choice,
> and we felt that we had some claim therein for our nearness
> of kinship unto the Messenger of God." Then Abû Bakr's
> eyes filled with tears and he said: "By Him in whose hand is
> my soul, I had rather that all should be well between me
> and the kindred of God's Messenger than between me and
> mine own kindred"; and at noon that day in the Mosque he
> publicly exonerated 'Alî for not yet having (recognized)

him as caliph, whereupon 'Alî affirmed the right of Abû
Bakr and pledged his allegiance to him. (Lings, 1983, note 3,
p. 344)

These events were reconstructed once again after the killing
of Othman, the third Caliph (successor of the Prophet) and
the emergence of disputes that turned into a war in regards
to who had the right to be a successor: would it be Ali Ibn
Abi Taleb this time or the Son of Abu Sufian? The dormant
political ambitions of Muhammad's old rivals were soon
evidenced as they plotted against Ali. Ironically, events led
to the victory of Mu'aweyya, the son of Abu Sufian over Ali
and his party. From that moment on, there was a great division between Muslims who called themselves Shi'is, which
literally means *the partisan of Ali*, and those known as Sunni.
After the assassination of Ali, both Shi'is and Sunni reconstructed Islamic history to support their beliefs. Their differences created a split that reverberated throughout Islam.

The Shi'is accused Abu-Bakr, and the other two Caliphs
who followed him, of conspiring against Ali. Although
Fatima, Mohammed's daughter (and Ali's wife) had held a
distinguished place for the Shi'is, for the most part, the
Sunni were not interested in focusing on her religious
authority within the Islamic community. Shi'is formed their
own theology seeing Ali, Fatima and their descendants as
spiritually blessed leaders intended to lead the Muslim
community.

Mu'aweyya initiated a new era that lacked the harmony
conveyed in Islam's original message. Not only did this
style of governance deviate from the original Islamic ethics,
but differing schools of thoughts began to emerge from it,
some of which were propagated from pre-Islamic values,
such as fatalism.[3] These were disguised under the Islamic
rhetoric and called *Qadariyya*. Montgomery Watt concludes
that:

With such ideas current it was easy to go further and say
that to deny that God had given the caliphate to the

---

[3]   Fatalism is the belief that *predetermination* has power over man. It is
      destiny that brings men their successes and above all their
      misfortunes. The pseudo Islamic version replaced Allah.

> Umayyads was unbelief and that to disobey them or their
> agents was sin. This was the intellectual context in which
> Qadarism appeared. (Watt, 1985, p. 27)

With that approach, people were manipulated to surrender
to their rulers, and to lead apathetic lives. As with its predecessors, Judaism and Christianity, the core message of Islam
was lost in the politicization of the religion.

A major intra-group example of "we" against the "others" had its root in the *Khârijite*. Their chosen title is interpreted as "those who changed their situation from being
supporters to rejecters". The Khârijite emerged as a separate
group during the great sectarianism after the killing of the
third Caliph, and the arbitration between Ali and
Mu'aweyya which ended with the defeat of Ali. They considered both Ali Ibn Abi Taleb and Mu'aweyya ibn Abi
Sufian as heretics, and deviants. Their basic principle,
which had been formulated in Qur'ânic words to justify
their disagreement with Ali, was "no decision but God's" (*lâ
hòukma illâ li-Ilâh)'*; by this was meant that judgment was to
be given in accordance with the Qur'ân. They overlooked
the fact that no text is clear in itself, as it is understood
through our multi-leveled interpretations. The Kharijites
initiated the trend that many extremists would follow. The
Brotherhood in Egypt, Wahhabis in Saudi Arabia, Taliban
in Afghanistan and other fundamentalist Islamic movements consider themselves as the ultimate possessors of
truth, and their sublime duty is to spread their views
around the world. Although they all repeat the same ideas,
they vary in their implementation. Women's oppression is a
common practice among them all, indicating the imbalance
in their psyches.

If we move to the present time, we find that one of the
most influential policies in modern history is the Wahhabi
doctrine. It emerged in Saudi Arabia in the 18th century.
and was named after its founder, Muhammad Ibn Abdel
Wahhab (1703–1791). This doctrine had great influence on
many movements in the Islamic world, from India to North
Africa, to the Taliban in Afghanistan. Abdel Wahhab
deemed that all intellectual contributions following the

third century after the migration were non-Islamic. The Saud tribe of the Arab Peninsula accepted this version of Islam, deciding to wage war against those with any differing points of view. They were convinced that they represented the way of God. They killed any Muslim who didn't accept the Wahhabi view, and soon expanded to establish their version of the Islamic kingdom. It took more than a century to organize the political territory now known as Saudi Arabia. By claiming its legal interpretations to be divine, the political system in Saudi Arabia refused to allow the establishment of any other political parties, or any opposing civic institutions. Moreover, it created a security system ruled by religious police called *Mutawwa'in*. In the Report on Human Rights in Saudi Arabia, among other critical points we read the following

> The Mutawwa'in, or religious police, constitutes the Committee to Prevent Vice and Promote Virtue, a semi-autonomous agency that enforces adherence to Islamic norms by monitoring public behavior. The Government maintained general control of the security forces. However, members of the security forces committed human rights abuses.[4]

This never happened during the lifetime of the Prophet for he never imposed rules on any one. Muhammad taught that God does not consider one's appearance to be as important as what is in one's heart. Ironically Islam, the way of peace intended to liberate the human mind and soul, is now oftentimes used to suppress free expression, and maintain gender imbalance.

The Hindu Story

Hinduism differs from the previous religions in that it does not have a specific founder, even though Krishna represents a central figure in its mythology. Also, the Rig Veda has many references to the mythological Indra and a political

---

[4]   US Department of State, Saudi Arabia Country Report on Human Rights Practices for 1997, released by the Bureau of Democracy, Human Rights, and Labor, January 30, 1998. http://www.state.gov/www/global/human_rights/1997_hrp_report/saudiara.html

figure known as the great Manu, who obviously had a large influence upon the forming of its patriarchal structure. Divine forces manifest from Brahma, who represents "both Creator and Divine Consciousness" (Mijares, 2003, p. 200). Stories of numerous mythological deities are intertwined with the rules for its social structure.

As noted in Chapter One, the Hindu-Vedic teachings are over 3,000 years old. Its sacred texts contain guidance for a spiritual life leading to states of realization. All is considered to be a manifestation of the divine, caught in the world of illusion. As in other religions, beauty and wisdom reside alongside of the destructive elements. There are numerous Yogis and many Yogic schools. There are various levels — from the most superstitious to a precise, scientific process intended to bring the devotee to realization of the divine. This process includes the use of the breath, intoning of mantras, purified diet, bodily exercises in specific postures, mental discipline, devotion and service. It represents the deeper side of Yoga — moving beyond the sacrifices of animals for temple gods and goddesses still occurring to this day. The Hindu pantheon includes many goddesses, oftentimes consorts to the gods, suggesting the importance of gender balance. But as portrayed in Chapter One the primary deities were still designated as males.

The Yoga paths within the Hindu religion emphasize the quality of Ahimsa, a way of non-harm to oneself or towards others. Mohandas Gandhi called it "a quality of the heart" (Merton, 1964). Hindus have a long-tradition of bowing to one another as a way of acknowledging the divine manifesting in each human being. They also affirm the practice of Karma Yoga — service to all life.

Although the caste system reveals a deeply rooted prejudice within its own religious and social system, until recent times it has been accepting of other religions. For example, a relationship developed between Muslims and Hindus early in Islamic history, as Muslims traveled to India carrying the message of Islam. In fact, India was led by Muslim rulers from 1200–1526 CE. Despite the current separation of

Pakistan, Muslims still compose about 12% of India's population.

Conflicts between Muslims and Hindus became increasingly apparent during the nineteenth and twentieth centuries. Increases in fundamentalist thinking emerged on both sides as each group asserted their religious identity, and began to see the other as an enemy. The problem of "separateness" began its evil influence. Questions have been raised as to why religion formed the basis of cultural identity rather than social or cultural differentiation. Syed Nassr Ahmad believes it to be related to changes in the world economy along with the emergence of the unique Indian identity (see Ahmad, 1991, p. 1). Ahmad excludes religion as the main factor in the alienation of Hindus and Muslims. He argues that the Muslim and Hindu population were closer than most scholars can imagine. No doubt the fear of modernism and the influences of Colonialism had a negative influence.

Violence between Hindus and Muslims increased with the creation of Pakistan as a separate nation from India (see Chapter Five). This move encouraged divisiveness between the people representing these two great religions. A recent example of violence occurred on February 27, 2002, when Muslims torched two carriages of a train carrying 58 Hindus activists in Gujarat, India. In response, Hindu fanatics began an ethnic cleansing campaign against Muslims throughout Gujarat.

> ... a three-day retaliatory killing spree by Hindus left hundreds dead and tens of thousands homeless and dispossessed. The looting and burning of Muslim homes, businesses and places of worship was also widespread. Muslim girls and women were brutally raped. Mass graves have been dug throughout the state. Gravediggers told Human Rights Watch that bodies kept arriving, burnt and mutilated beyond recognition ... in many instances, police officials led the charge of murderous mobs, aiming and firing at Muslims who got in the way.[5]

---

[5]   Human Rights Watch at
      http://www.hrw.org/press/2002/04/gujarat.htm

In his book, *In the Belly of the Beast: The Hindu Supremacist RSS and BJP of India An Insider's Story*, Partha Banerjee proclaims that the Rashtriya Swayamsevak Sangh (RSS), Shiv Sena, Hindutva and other radical Hindu groups do not differ from the Taliban or other radical Muslim groups (Banerjee, 1998). Dr. Banerjee, a one time member of the RSS, also sees a similarity in the attitudes of extreme Christian fundamentalists such as the Christian Coalition and the Promise Keepers[6]. Their ideologies are fueled by beliefs of superiority over others. Their hatred, targeting and murder of Muslims is oftentimes based upon an admiration of Hitler and the Nazi policies used on Jews (Savarkar, 1939). The RSS is particularly active in movements against peaceful negotiations between India and Pakistan.

Thus Karma Yoga, defined as *service to all life*, has failed to include the Muslim population. It is difficult to know of such atrocities being committed in the country that claims one of the greatest exemplars of non-violent activism in our human history, Mohandas Gandhi. In the final words of his autobiography Gandhi advised, "So long as a man does not of his own free will put himself last among his fellow creatures, there is no salvation for him"(Gandhi, 1957, p. 505).

The Story of Buddhism: The Path of Compassion

Buddhism began in India in the sixth century, B.C. with the teachings of Siddhartha Gotama. Siddhartha was raised in the foothills of the Himalayas, a protected son of a leader of the Sakya clan. Stories relate that the future Buddha "encountered successively a man tortured by disease, a man in the last stages of senility, and a corpse being carried out to the cremation ground, followed by sorrowing relatives and friends" (Parrinder, 1971, p. 263). As Siddhartha reflected on these tragedies of life, an ascetic (holy man) walked by. This revelation prompted Siddhartha to leave

---

[6]   In particular, the Promise Keepers is a male-only organization challenging female equality (hidden behind ideas of a healthier family and a healthier America), and promoting the patriarchal family model.

his family, belongings and heritage to find a way of resolving human problems that brought so much despair.

Eventually he found himself exhausted by the severe disciplines within the life of an ascetic — finding that these had not encouraged spiritual awakening. He decided to give himself totally to meditation until he experienced enlightenment. Stories relate that Siddhartha was meditating when,

> He was assailed by Mara, the Evil One, who, with his three daughters, sought by means of various stratagems to deflect the Buddha-to-be from his purpose. Mara's efforts were, however, all in vain, and after a night of spiritual struggle, all the evil factors which in the Buddhist view, tie men to this imperfect, mortal existence were overcome, and he became the Awakened, the Buddha, and entered a transcendental, eternal realm of being. (ibid., p. 264)

Mara, a Hindu god of pestilence, disease and lust, was unable to disturb or terrify Siddhartha and this led to his enlightenment. The Buddha (the "Awakened One") then had another realization. He had attained freedom. In so doing he felt a great compassion for humanity. Therefore he decided to teach others the way of enlightenment — that they, also, would know this nirvanic freedom. But, the struggle between good and evil had not ceased as the Mahaparinibbana Sutta tells us that Mara, the Evil One, continued to tempt the Buddha right up until his death. But Mara was unable to stop the development of Buddhism and the increasing numbers of nuns and monks who embarked upon its path (ibid., p. 264).

Tibetan Buddhism, in particular, has many demons, but the interpretation greatly differs from the Abrahamic religions. These demons are seen as awakeners. They may frighten us into spiritual realization, release us from the wheel of karma, and facilitate enlightenment — the goal of life.

The revelation of a way that led followers beyond human suffering appealed to many. Monks and laypersons alike still follow the eight-fold path, a way of moral conduct established by the Buddha. The eight items follow:

- Right Understanding
- Right Thought
- Right Speech
- Right Bodily Action
- Right Livelihood
- Right Moral Effort
- Right Mindfulness
- Right Concentration

The education and wisdom of a religious follower has a deep impact on how these teachings are translated. Understanding the nature of our world, the meaning of life, developing the mind, directing the body and living with honesty and morality are the guidelines leading to a compassionate life. The goal is to go beyond an ego-centered existence based upon the belief that ego states are impermanent. It is a path of compassion, and liberation from fear and desire.

But Buddhism has had its own share of warfare and strife although various religious groups are normally able to live tolerantly among one another in Asian countries. For example, Buddhists sects, Confucians, Shintoists and Taoists have practiced their religions respectively alongside of one another for long periods of time (Parinder, 1971), although history reveals that political structures and motivations created oppositional forces resulting in religious strife and repression. Brian Daisen Victoria's book, *Zen War Stories* (Victoria, 2003), depicts incidents of Japanese Buddhist monks' involvement with assassinations of political figures, and the Nanjing massacre (against civilians). There are familiar themes in regards to current battles with radical Islamic fundamentalists. For example, the Japanese ideology of late Imperial Japan (before and during World War II) lent itself to "holy war," "suicide attacks" and was supported by Zen Buddhist teachings (Victoria, 1997). Buddhist philosophies supporting an indifference to life and suffering were used in military training and thus supported the "suicide attacks" carried out by the Japanese pilots against the West. They were also involved with the colonization of Japan's neighbors (yet another story of occupation).

A recent example of prejudice and fundamentalism is evidenced in Sri Lanka. An ethnic conflict between the Sinhalese Buddhist and the Tamils has taken thousands of lives in the last couple of decades. In a conference, *Buddhism and Conflict in Sri Lanka*, Professor Asanga Tilakaratne noted that

> it is widely believed that the Buddhist monks in Sri Lanka hold an exclusivist world-view narrowly defined in the lines of the Sinhala language and ethnicity and Buddhism and that this world-view is largely responsible for non-accommodation and discrimination of the minority communities in general and the Tamils in particular ...[7]

This violence has been occurring for decades during which time Buddhist monks have both killed and committed violence against the Hindu Tamils, Christians, Muslims and other groups. In his book *Terror in the Mind of God*, Mark Juergensmeyer explains that

> The great military conquests of the Sinhalese kingdoms in Sri Lanka, for instance, have been conducted in the name of the Buddhist tradition and often with the blessings of Buddhist monks. In Thailand the tradition called for those who rule by the sword as kings to first experience the discipline of Buddhist monastic training ... Using violence non-defensively for the purpose of political expansion is prohibited under Buddhist rules. But armed defense — even warfare — has been justified on the grounds that such violence has been in the nature of response, not intent. Like Islam, the great expansion of Buddhism in various parts of the world has been credited in part to the support given it by victorious kings and military forces who have claimed to be fighting only to defend the faith against infidels and to establish a peaceful moral order. (Juergensmeyer, 2000/2003, p. 114)

In 1995 members of a new religious cult, Aum Shinrikyo, in Japan, terrorized over 5,500 people, killing twelve and injuring numerous others (ibid.). The leader of this move-

[7]   Buddhism and Conflict in Sri Lanka. An International Conference. June 28-30, 2002. http://www.bathspa.ac.uk/conferences/buddhism-and-conflict-in-sri-lanka/abstracts.htm

ment, Shoko Asahara, justified the violence based upon his own interpretation of Tibetan teachings, saying that

> ... the persons killed are scoundrels, or are enmeshed in social systems so evil that further existence in this life will result in even greater negative karmic debt, then those who kill them are doing them a favor by enabling them to die early. (ibid., p. 115)

There is also a more subtle type of prejudice that occurs in Buddhism as well as all other religions. That is the tendency to believe one's one form (lineage, denomination, etc.) to be superior to others (for example, whether one follows the Hinayana, Mahayana or Vajrayana schools). But for the most part, in comparison to Judaism, Christianity and Islam, differing Buddhist schools have existed alongside of one another without extreme acts of violence.

The form of prejudice and fundamentalist thinking changes from culture to culture, but the story remains the same — destroy or shun others who are unlike us or who are unwilling to give up their ethnic or religious identities.

Native American

Native Americans (First Nations Peoples) have sayings such as "never judge another until you've walked a mile in his moccasins" (anonymous). Dr. Terry Tafoya explains that this saying has a "more visceral meaning" in Native American traditions because "the soft deerskin actually molds to the foot ... when the sole gets wet, it molds exactly to the shape of the foot and then dries hard that way, making each moccasin really unique to the wearer" (personal communication). So to walk a mile in someone's moccasins is to have a direct, felt sensation of this person. Also, animals and nature are recognized as brothers and sisters, and there is a greater connectedness to nature.

The Navajos have a ritual to restore *hózhó* (peace and beauty) when disharmony has occurred. It is called the Beauty Way ceremony. They believe the world is filled with this *hózhó*.

An Apache myth relates that when Yusn, the Mountain Spirit, "brought the Apaches out upon the earth to live, he did so only after instructing them how to walk in the holy Life-way. They should be kind to each other, generous to the poor, and respectful in hunting and warfare" (Haley, 1997, p. 74).

But are Native nations free from discord with one another? Are they able to walk in peace with their brother and sister tribes? Both of the above Indian nations were inspired by ethical values similar to those found in other world religions—and both nations evidenced similar failures in following the guidance given. For example, historical records indicate that Apaches and Navajos were enemies (ibid.).

Territorial wars occurred in some tribes. The winners gained power in attaining larger territorial controls. According to the history narrated by Peter Wright in *American Indian Leaders: Studies in Diversity*, "the Shoshones needed the assistance of federal troops to defend their homeland from the more numerous Sioux, Cheyannes, and Arapahoes" (Edmunds, 1980, p. xiii).

There is another explanation for tribal warfare. Tafoya explains that the majority of historical conflicts among the Native plains area communities were directly related to the incursion of white settlers who displaced Native groups. One example is the Lakota tribe, who were originally woodlands culture. They were forced further West, which then disrupted the Native peoples living in those areas. Tafoya reminds us that Native people were forced onto reservations at gunpoint, and access to their traditional hunting and gathering territories was prevented. This heightened the conflicts amongst Native cultures, because of the damage it did to the Native people's relationship to the land.

Also, Tafoya explains that disputes amongst Native American tribes are territorial rather than ideological. For example, the Navajos and Hopis have had a long-time dispute over land rights. He noted that,

> One of the reasons the Navajo have had difficulty with many of the other Indian Nations over the years is that they are simply the largest population group, and as a result, have far more political clout and power than other Native

> Nations ... The Zuni have also had a history of problems
> with land and resource disputes with the Navajo and
> Apache, although the battles are now won in courtrooms.
> (Tafoya, personal communication)

However, battles over territory are inherently spiritual
because a Native American's spirituality is grounded in the
land. This differs from the theological factions between religious denominations as evidenced in the Christian (Protestants and Catholics) and Islamic (Shiite and Sunni) faiths. It
is not a matter of one tribe fighting with another over religious differences, but rather over the intrusion or violation
to one's land (affecting one's identity). Religious splitting
occurred when some Hopis converted to Christianity,
but they simply moved to respective camps within the
community—a different ideal or religious belief was not
threatening to the tribe.

Native Americans have suffered greatly because of early
Christian missionaries enslaving them and forcing them to
become Christians. In recent decades Native Americans
have felt freer to practice their own religious beliefs. Many
people are discovering that indigenous peoples throughout
the world have much to teach us about respect for our environment and reverence for divine nature.

Religious Beliefs and the Problem of Obedience

A major problem of organized religion is its emphasis on
obedience to its hierarchical principles. Religions emphasize moral principles and obedience to them (e.g., the Ten
Commandments). But *obedience* itself becomes a problem
when human beings fail to consider the morality and consequences of destructive behaviors. History evidences the
many times that dictatorial rulers (e.g., Hitler) and wrongly
guided religious leaders encouraged "blind obedience"
from their followers. A destructive mass influence then
takes over as one ethnic or religious group slaughters
another without considering the morality of the behavior.
One example is the earlier described incident in Gujarat,
India, whereupon Muslims incinerated fifty-eight Hindu
passengers on the Sabarmati Express in Godhara, as Hin-

dus killed hundreds of Muslims. In despair over the tragedy, the India-born writer, Roy Arundhati, asked of both
parties, "Precisely which Hindu scripture preaches this?...
Which particular verse in the Koran [or Qur'an] required
that they be roasted alive?" (Arundhati, 2003) Caught up in
religious gang violence and revenge, they forgot their
common humanity.

Religion is oftentimes used to mobilize people and support aggression. What is it that makes people act cruelly in
the name of any belief? If we are going to change this
destructive behavior, we need to further our understanding
of it.

Religions throughout history have acted upon a mistaken
sense of divine mission by attacking *the other*. Moreover,
religions have expanded their hegemony over and over
again by the use of the sword (and more recently through
guns, bombs and other weapons of destruction). The following is but another small example of the results of male
domination and the suppression of the more unifying feminine side of humanity.

Militant Christians attacked Islamic lands and led crusades in the 11th and 12th centuries, seeking to defend and
expand the Christian faith. Three centuries later, thousands
of Muslims and Jews were tortured in the name of the Holy
Inquisition in the Iberian Peninsula, followed by the burning of women and children accused of witchcraft. Meanwhile Shiite and Sunni Muslims battled, debating which
lineage represented the true Islam, killing one another over
minor differences — forgetting that the true Muslim is one
who submits to the love of Allah. Human rights groups
appealed to the United Nations for help in response to the
Janjaweed, radical Arab Muslims, committing genocide
against African tribes (darker skinned) Muslims in Darfur.
The list is endless as history has provided us with abundant
examples of patriarchally motivated violence.

Many of these fundamentalist religious soldiers
(ill-begotten militants for God) fail to question the true sanctity of their beliefs. For example, Al-Qaeda members believe
that they are acting in the name of God, and that their

actions are against God's enemies. This belief causes them to ignore that the Prophet Muhammad never taught nor exemplified ruthlessness and cruelty. Unquestioned faith often serves as the rationale for heartless behavior. An earlier historical illustration of this heartless violence was evidenced in Pope Innocent III's armed crusade against Albigenses Christians in southern France in 1209. When the besieged city of Beziers fell, soldiers reportedly asked their papal adviser how to distinguish the faithful from the infidel among the captives. He commanded: "Kill them all. God will know his own" (Haught, 1991). Nearly 20,000 were slaughtered following this order. Whereas obedience and compliance to authority can be a powerful means in keeping social order, it can also become a deadly tool and a dangerous mechanism used to drive common people into atrocious deeds.

Between 1939 and 1945 approximately 11 million people were killed as a result of the Nazi genocidal policy. Hitler convinced his followers (many of them Christians) that in order to have a pure "Aryan" race, all those deemed inferior by his regime were to be annihilated. Hitler attempted to exterminate Jews, Gypsies, Polish citizens and other Slavs, Jehovah's Witnesses, homosexuals, dissenting clergy, Communists, Socialists, political enemies and the mentally ill. In particular, he hated the Jews and believed they had to be destroyed. In his book, *A History of the Jews*, Paul Johnson explains that,

> Hitler accepted anti-Semitic conspiracy theory in its most extreme form, believing that the Jew was wicked by nature, was indeed the very incarnation and symbol of evil. Throughout his career he saw the 'Jewish problem' in apocalyptic terms and the Holocaust was the logical outcome of his views. (Johnson, 1987, p. 492)

This atrocity caused many Jews to be mistrustful of the civilized world.

> The overwhelming lesson the Jews learned from the Holocaust was the imperative need to secure for themselves a permanent, self-contained and above all sovereign refuge

> where if necessary the whole of world Jewry could find
> safety from its enemies. (ibid., p. 517)

But the Jewish nation, Israel, has blinded itself to its own violence committed against its Palestinian (Muslim and Christian) neighbors motivated by its fear and resultant defenses. The dividing wall is a symbol of the enclosure around its own heart.

"I obeyed orders," said the Nazi war criminal Adolph Eichman. "I acted according to the instruction," claimed American soldiers that participated in the massacre of civilian Vietnamese in My-Lai village during the Vietnam War. How far are people willing to go to obey orders? What makes some people deliberately slaughter millions solely because of their ethnic or religious group membership?

Blind obedience to an authority figure or an ideal has motivated numerous religious and ethnic groups to destroy one another. This is another example of the hierarchical principles in patriarchal mindsets — as those lower down on the scale of power are expected to act without question. This human evil is enhanced when we deem something to be *sacred*, and therefore to be protected. For example, we hold a belief, race, or nation as sacred; and, according to this mindset, it becomes superior to others. Once a group of people projects the archetypal sense of the sacred upon an ideal, belief or symbol, the group ego tends to take over (this is called ethnocentrism). A great deal of destruction has occurred from this tendency. To follow a leader or an ideal without a compassionate concern for the life and well being of the other is sacrilegious. Religious groups and nations need to recognize the true sense of the sacred that arises in the heart.

A New York Times article on September 25, 2003, informed that 27 Israeli pilots refused to bomb Palestinian citizens.[8] An Israeli newspaper also reported that these pilots were then discharged from service.[9] Imagine the

---

[8]   Greg Myre. (September 25, 2003). 27 Israeli Reserve Pilots Say They
      Refuse to Bomb Civilians. NY Times.
[9]   Amos Harel & Lily Galili. Air Force to oust refusenik pilots. Israel:
      Ha'Aretz September 25, 2003.

possibilities if all people began to examine their hearts and to honor the humanity of all people everywhere — refusing to cooperate with the destructive elements of patriarchy. What will it take for humanity to come to this realization? What would happen if women were in influential positions? Yes, throughout patriarchal history, women have also supported destructive behaviors — caught up in patriarchal ideas of revenge and destruction. But if women had equal leadership over a period of time, research suggests these destructive behaviors would change (Karam, 1998).

Conclusions

The sacred texts and spiritual founders of all religions emphasize community, tolerance, and love. Despite this emphasis, the same texts and recorded words of our religious prophets have been violated and misused by fundamentalists failing to understand the profoundly spiritual messages and compassionate teachings of each religion's founder. Historically, this failure has led to exclusion rather than community, prejudice rather than tolerance, and hate rather than love. Violence perpetuated by fundamentalists has been the result. Thereby, fundamentalism undermines the core teachings found in all religions. Also, radical fundamentalists are gender-biased. Males dominate; females are negated and suppressed. This bias is especially evidenced in Islamic Taliban and Wahhabi sects, the Christian Coalition and the Promise Keepers, India's Sangh Parivar and numerous other radical groups. We need to return to the egalitarian message taught by our prophets, and move beyond patriarchal interpretations of religious life.

Jesus sat with Samaritans, lepers and with all people alike. Jesus also included women as equals (King, 1990). The only recorded act of anger toward any group was in regards to the "money changers" in the temple who were taking advantage of others (Matthew 21:12). Instead, his teachings were based on equality and compassion.

The Buddha also taught a way of compassion for all beings. The Buddhist Bodhisattva vow[10] depicts a way of life that is totally devoted to humanity, animals and all of creation. Hinduism teaches that respect for the divine is to be found within all human beings. Likewise Native American spirituality honors the sacredness of all life.

The Qur'an opens with the acknowledgement that the first manifestation of Allah (the One God shared by all religions) is that of mercy and compassion. Muhammad equally respected and befriended Jews, Christians and women alike.

In the year 70 CE the Jewish Rabbi Yohannan ben Zakkai was approached for spiritual guidance by another Rabbi lamenting the loss of the temple. Rabbi Yohannan responded, " 'Be not grieved. We have another atonement as effective as this.' 'And what is it?' 'It is acts of loving kindness, as it is said: 'For I desire mercy and not sacrifice'" (Armstrong, 1993, p. 72). And, yet, the desire for superiority has been stronger than our love for our neighbors.

---

[10] A Bodhisattva is an enlightened being who at enlightenment makes a decision to not enter Nirvana (heaven world) and instead stay within earth's realm until all sentient life has known enlightenment.

Don't think of yourselves as being unfortunate because of having to live through these times. Think of it as fortunate, because you have an opportunity to work for justice and the welfare of other people. This sort of opportunity does not come to everybody all the time.

Aung San Suu Kyi
(Kyi & Clements, 1997)

Chapter Three
Who Among Us is Chosen?

Much of humanity is dominated by an earlier evolutionary stage of brain development, preventing us from realizing our spiritual potential. Evolutionary attributes of aggression and fear stifle the application of the learning gleaned from history, science and religion. It is therefore relevant to examine prejudicial behaviors from biological, psychological, and anthropological perspectives. Although there are some basic differences between males and females, fear and feelings of inferiority influence the development of prejudice and fundamentalism in both sexes.

In particular, the latter portion of this chapter focuses on the Israeli, Arab and Christian discord because it holds the attention of most, if not all, of the world. Much of this conflict centers around religious ideologies related to the "Holy Land," namely Jerusalem. It is not surprising that the late Sufi mystic Samuel L. Lewis declared that "There shall be peace in the world when there is peace in Zion [Jerusalem]" (Lewis, 1975, p. 17). Given its history of war and conflict, this statement makes sense. Once patriarchy had solidly established itself, Jerusalem (translation: "City of Peace") became an area of ongoing conflicts over political and religious rulership and land. Although it radiates with the reverence of three of the world's great religions, Judaism, Christianity and Islam, it has long been tainted with the blood of their martyrs.

Evolution and Aggression

In his book *On Aggression*, Konrad Lorenz shared years of research on the aggressive behaviors of fish, birds, mammals and human life. Lorenz' conclusions regarding these evolutionary behaviors provide insight into a disturbing human phenomenon, the tendency to band and cast race against race, religion against religion and nation against nation.

Lorenz found that aggression is a natural instinct. From an evolutionary perspective and under natural conditions, "it helps just as much as any other [instinct] to ensure the survival of the individual and the species." (Lorenz, 1967, p. x.) The use of aggression to preserve life is easy to understand when an individual, a family or a nation's security is threatened, but why are we determined to destroy *the other* when there is no threat? According to Lorenz, most species do not attack other groups, except as related to the food chain. Differing species of animals simply do not interfere with one another.

> Darwin's expression, "the struggle for existence," is sometimes erroneously interpreted as the struggle between different species. In reality, the struggle Darwin was thinking of and which drives evolution forward is the competition between near relations. What causes a species to disappear or become transformed into a different species is the profitable "invention" that falls by chance to one or a few of its members in the everlasting gamble of hereditary change. The descendants of these lucky ones gradually outstrip all others until the particular species consists only of individuals who process the new "invention". (ibid., pp. 20–21)

However, Darwin did address intra-specific aggression, or aggression within a species. He suggested that the purpose of intra-specific aggression was to assure a favorable future for the species by allowing "the stronger of the two rivals to take possession either of the territory or of the desired female" (ibid., p. 27). According to this analysis, the rivalry and aggression to preserve a given species is particularly played out by its males. The stronger, more dominant, male assured the survival of the strongest along with the opportunity for selective breeding. Lorenz explains that once the human species had mastered weaponry, clothing and social organization, "an evil intra-specific selection must have set in. The factor influencing selection was now the wars waged between hostile, neighboring tribes" (ibid., p. 39).

The development of agricultural societies, and the advent of surplus agriculture associated with the Neolithic period (beginning around 10,000 years ago), created an economic structure that led to increasingly complex societies. Morris Berman points out that this shift represented, "a long, drawn-out, and occasionally non-linear, process" (Berman, 2000, p. 53). Once patriarchy entered into the organizational structure, ranking orders were established.

The members of a patriarchal system know who has the power and who doesn't. The individuals in the group feel a sense of belonging and a bond is established. At the same time the awareness of the *other* is defined. While societal bonding and organizational strategy have served as evolutionary tools to reduce some forms of intra-societal fighting, aggression still abides. Hence the prevalence of familial and gender violence, political and religious opposition, racial and economic prejudice, which have all continued to grow. These acts of domination support Lorenz' idea of an "evil intra-specific selection" (ibid., p. 39).

Photographs and observational research of *inter-specific* behaviors of animals about to kill and eat their prey do not reveal the hostility that is present in *intra-specific* attacks.[1] *Inter-specific* aggressive behaviors include killing prey in order to eat, or warding off threats from another species. *Intra-specific* aggression is evidenced in behaviors ranging from "cocks fighting in the backyard to dogs biting each other, boys thrashing each other, young men throwing beer mugs at each other's heads, and so on to bar-room brawls about politics and finally to war and atom bombs" (ibid., p. 26). Given the overwhelming development of nuclear arms, the threat of intra-specific violence demands the wholehearted attentiveness of us all. It is the greatest threat to the ongoing preservation of life. Lorenz's description

[1]   Inter-specific refers to differing species whereas intra-specific pertains to within species.

strongly suggests that "intra-specific aggression" is a male driven behavior. In fact, social and evolutionary influences have conditioned men to be more competitive; they resort to fight-flight behaviors in response to stressful situations whereas women differ in that females tend to move toward friendships and children to process life's stressors (Geary & Flinn, 2002).

According to research by Drs. Taylor and Klein, women have a specific hormone, known as oxytocin, which supports the female propensity to tend and care for others under stressful situations (Taylor et al., 2000). This hormone is related to relational qualities—feelings of deep caring, nurturing and touch. Hence Lorenz's research portrays the patriarchical system (and testosterone-driven behaviors). His research also reveals that destructive behaviors are primarily evidenced in the *human* species.

Lorenz reports that when an animal attacks another as prey it does not evidence facial changes or other forms of expression related to aggression, but rather that these aggressive warning signals manifest when the animal is cornered or attacked (female animals respond aggressively when offspring are threatened). This is also apparent in humans. For example, a rancher typically does not have physiological signs of aggression when slaughtering animals for the market, but would certainly display aggression if put in fear-provoking danger. It appears that fear fuels aggressive and prejudicial behaviors. Research into the development of the human brain is particularly significant in addressing this issue.

Konrad Lorenz's research on aggression revealed that the male is the aggressor in most species. The female is more apt to turn toward aggression when her young are threatened. Here we have to point out significant differences between males and females. Anyone who has observed or worked with groups of young children knows that there are large differences between the play behaviors of boys and girls. Most of the boys are running around chasing one another with make-believe weapons or racing around in toy vehicles, whereas the girls are more interested in playing house, store or the like. When it comes time for free activities inside the classroom, boys are more interested in building towers from blocks (structures that rise up as high as possible) and knocking them over. Girls are playing dress up and relating it to some unifying event.

Early feminists claimed that this was the result of social modeling and cultural expectations. This is sometimes true — but more often it is not the case. Many parents choose to not provide toy weapons for their sons, but the boys create weapons from any available item. This difference is psycho-biologically related to hormones, namely increased testosterone in the male and oxytocin in the female. Although social conditioning plays its part, on an evolutionary level hormones fuel the protection and nurturance of life.

Beneath the Reasoning Mind

The oldest neural structure is the reptilian brain. Patterned, habitual behaviors are programmed into this system. Joseph Chilton Pearce explains that this reptilian brain is "skilled in deceptive procedures that were developed eons ago to elude predators" (Pearce, 2002, p. 24). It is pre-wired to respond when we feel threatened. Pearce adds that,

> This deceptive skill can be used on behalf of our high neo-cortex to develop strategies for succeeding in the worlds of commerce and politics, for instance, after which our high neo-cortex can skillfully rationalize and make morally respectable, at least to ourselves, our often quite immoral actions. Through the alliance of our neo-cortex with this deceptive low brain we learn to lie, gloating glee-fully when successfully deceiving, lamenting and self-pity-ing when deceived. (ibid.)

This system is important for the preservation of life. It relates with higher neural structures to ward off dangers.

The old mammalian brain is a later development. It includes the limbic system and plays a major role in emotional responses. Whereas the reptilian brain is limited to a primitive visual sense associated with defense mechanisms, the old mammalian brain includes the senses of smell and hearing — enhancing the development of emotion in all mammals (ibid.). Lorenz explains that from an evolutionary perspective intra-specific aggression (associated with the reptilian brain) is "millions of years older than [the development of] personal friendship and love" (Lorenz, 1967, p. 209) and notes that

> In an animal not even belonging to the favored class of mammals, we find a behavior mechanism that keeps certain individuals together for life, and this behavior pattern has become the strongest motive governing all action; it can overcome all "animal" drives, such as hunger, sexuality, aggression, and fear, and it determines social order in its species-characteristic form. In all these points this bond is analogous with those human functions that go hand in hand with the emotions of love and friendship in their purest and noblest form. (ibid., p. 211)[2]

In the above description we see the unfolding evolutionary development of the three-fold brain. For example, whereas the reptilian system focused on external conditions, the old mammalian brain was attentive to one's mate and the care of offspring. This encouraged a developing awareness of an internal, emotional world (Pearce, 2002).

The third level of brain development is that of the neo-cortex, the new mammalian brain. It is associated with verbal and intellectual skills, and allows us to stand aside from any given situation in order to examine and reflect upon it rather than simply respond through emotional and defensive behaviors (includes pre-frontal cortex/lobes). This higher brain "occupies five times more skull space than the reptilian brain and the old mammalian brain combined and consists of some hundred billion neurons" (ibid., p. 26). It allows for novelty, creative imagination and enables us to reflect internally. Pearce explains that,

> Our three brains develop in utero as a nested hierarchy in the order of their appearance in evolutionary history: The reptilian brain begins its function in the first trimester of gestation, the old mammalian in the second, and the neo-cortex, or human brain, in the third ... Whether we follow novelty's call to adventure or close ourselves in a defensive

---

[2]   The documentary film *March of the Penguins* (2005) is a good example of this. [Footnote added]

posture, refusing to engage, depends largely upon the experiences we have in the first three years of life. These years mark the time when our emotional system develops the foundation for our higher intellect yet to come. And that's why Jesus, our great model, said that if we "cause one of these little ones to stumble, it were better a milestone be tied around our neck and we be dumped in the sea." It is thus we are a drowning species. (ibid., p. 27)

In short, much of humanity has been influenced by childhood woes, and this backs many of its leanings toward revenge, sibling rivalry and so forth. It has impaired the ability to truly receive and give love—for hearts become armored in moments of fear or feelings of not being loved. This is part of our evolutionary patterning.

Social Ills and Sibling Rivalry

Alfred Adler was another great psychoanalytic contributor to early psychological theory. Adler believed human beings are naturally motivated to strive towards goals, and therefore can overcome the influences of the past. His theory of Individual Psychology focused on our social relationships with one another.

Adler was particularly interested in aggression and power, acknowledging their significance in human development and survival. According to Adler, our initial dependence, and hence inferiority, begins early in life when as helpless infants we are dependent upon others to take care of us. As toddlers we learn to walk, and begin the struggle toward independence. Adler called this a natural movement toward superiority. This drive can take either a negative or a positive direction. If we strive to become superior to others and increase personal power, then our goal is negatively based. If we are focused upon becoming increasingly superior to our prior conditions with the hope of making a greater contribution to our society, we have developed a deeper understanding of the use of power.

Adler coined the term *sibling rivalry* to refer to the tendency of children to vie for first place in their parent's attention. Although Adler named this phenomenon, it is certainly not a new one. Stories of sibling rivalry are found in the mythologies of various cultures. Examples include the Egyptian myth of Seth's murder and dismemberment of his brother the sun god Osiris and the Japanese tale (related in previous chapter) of Susano and Amaterasu. Although the latter myths are an attempt to explain the disappearance of the sun each evening as darkness emerges, what is it within humankind that relates jealousy and rivalry as its explanation?

A well-known story of significant sibling rivalry can be found in the Old Testament and the Holy Qur'an. These texts both relate that Eve bore Cain and later Abel, and that whereas Abel tended sheep, Cain toiled the ground. Both Cain and Abel bring the fruits of their labors to the Lord, but Cain's contribution is rejected. For some reason, Cain's labor is unacceptable in comparison to his brother's offerings. Cain, the first-born, was unable to tolerate his younger brother's success. Cain compares himself to Abel in rage, rather than striving to improve the quality of his own works.

According to Jewish, Christian and Islamic beliefs, Cain and Abel are the first human-born kin—and, sadly, it is a story of rivalry and destruction.

Then there is the biblical story of Joseph, the most beloved of 12 brothers. His father Jacob (Israel) made him a coat of many colors. The jealous brothers plotted to kill Joseph, but instead sold Joseph into slavery. A turn of fate led him into royalty. After a long famine in the land, his brothers unknowingly came to this highly respected leader (Joseph) requesting financial support. Joseph revealed his identity with an attitude of forgiveness and compassion. He pointed out that their act brought them all to this goodness. Joseph, Jacob-Israel's preferred son, did not act on revenge. This is an important story in Middle Eastern sacred texts—for Joseph did not follow the archetypal example set by the archangel Satan (who had lost his position in heaven due to his jealousy at the creation of man) (Barnstone, 1984). Instead, Joseph exemplified the heart of true spirituality, compassion (and, it is Joseph who is Israel's favorite son). This also represents the developed archetypal male, who manifests both feminine and masculine qualities. Joseph was not controlled by testosterone-motivated behaviors, but rather by his heart.

An Anthropological Perspective

The modern civilization is an outcome of an accumulation of struggles with our environment along with the attempt to understand the world and ourselves. The way human beings perceive themselves and their relationships with one another is historically diverse. It appears that when we feel secure we are more apt to feel at harmony with ourselves, others and the universe. Gravesites and other archeological findings reveal that early Paleolithic humanity was more at one with this harmony than the later tribal societies associated with the evolution of the Neolithic period, beginning around 10,000 years ago.

Anthropological studies illustrate that cultural identity forms through kinship relations, starting from small households, and widening to bands, lineages, and tribes. Our tendency to see ourselves as "we" against "the other" does not have its origins in ideological, religious perspectives — rather it began as a way to protect one group from an attack by another. Early humanity had to be strong in order to defend itself; otherwise it would have been annihilated.

Even though a tribe might maintain a period of peaceful living, the underlying fear remained. In order for a band, lineage, or a tribe to survive, members of the communities had to be ready to face an attack at any time. This fear of the "other" kept these evolving communities on their toes. Their standards for social control and implementation of laws differed. There was a process in place for judging crimes of murder and attempts were made to prevent feuds. Victims were often compensated for losses. The ultimate goal was to keep cohesiveness within the tribe. War was an inevitable outcome should a person from a differing tribe attack someone within one's own tribe. The Nuer in southern Sudan still exemplify this practice. Similar responses are found in the Jivaros of Eastern Ecuador, and were also evidenced in Arabia during the Prophet Muhammad's time.[3]

These anthropological findings indicate that fear of other people increases the motivation of violence. They also show that narrowing the circle of belonging to a limited social group is likely to create feeling of enmity towards other groups. It is not surprising that some Israelis have focused on their ethnic identity and felt superior to other people perceiving them as enemies. The same is true for some Christians who exclude other people from salvation because they do not belong to their circle. Likewise, some Muslims consider themselves as Ummah (community) and outsiders as unbelievers. Moreover, nationalities have replaced tribes in the way people identify themselves. So despite the social and political changes in our world, we still witness the tribal mentality; "we" against the "other".

Religion, Wars and Competition for First Place

The struggle for superiority is present in sibling rivalry, and it is also nurtured by a tribal mentality that manifests in the society at large: religion against religion, race against race and nation against nation. In his book *On Aggression*, Lorenz describes what an observer from another planet would see when examining the human population:

> If we suppose our extraneous observer to be a being of pure reason, devoid of instincts himself and unaware of the way in which all instincts in general and aggression in particular can miscarry, he would be at a complete loss to explain history at all. The ever-recurrent phenomena of history do not have reasonable causes. It is a mere commonplace to say that they are caused by what common parlance so aptly terms "human nature." Unreasoning and unreasonable human nature causes two nations to compete, though no economic necessity compels them to do so; it induces two political parties or religions with amazingly similar programs of salvation to fight each other bitterly, and it impels an Alexander or a Napoleon to sacrifice millions of lives in an attempt to unite the world under his scepter. We have

---

[3]   For full account of this point, see Peoples & Bailey (2000), pp. 194–195, and Armstrong (1992).

been taught to regard some of the persons who have committed these and similar absurdities with respect, even as
"great" men, we are wont to yield to the political wisdom
of those in charge, and we are all so accustomed to these
phenomena that most of us fail to realize how abjectly stu-
pid and undesirable the historical mass behavior of
humanity actually is. (Lorenz, 1967, pp. 228–229)

But the problem may not be humanity itself, but rather the
imbalance initiated in the patriarchal system. As discussed
in Chapter Two, a majority of wars are motivated by some
form of religious intolerance. For it is within the arena of
religion that instinctual aggression, based on fear of *the
other,* erringly influences ideals, feeding the childish drive
for superiority. This manifests across the religious spectrum. The following is an examination of a few of the many
groups who believe themselves to be "the chosen ones,"
and the dangers facing humanity unless we are willing to
scrutinize and change these destructive and self-centered
patterns initiated by a hierarchical ideology.

According to the biblical narrative, the Jewish people
were called to a special relation with God as well as to a
special social role. The Jewish religion is rooted in the Covenant, which is an agreement between God and the *Holy
Nation.* The first covenant referred to in the Jewish Scriptures is that with Noah on behalf of the whole human race
(Genesis 9:8–17). That covenant was a promise to never
again destroy the earth with a flood. The Abrahamic Covenant was the promise of a special blessing for Abraham's
descendants, the *chosen people.* This Covenant was reaf-
firmed and elaborated on at Mt. Sinai. It outlined obliga-
tions about living rightfully and justly in the form of the Ten
Commandments. Exodus 19 relates that speaking in God's
name, Moses told the Jewish people: "If you will obey my
voice and keep my Covenant, you shall be my own treasure
from among all the peoples."

This concept of the *chosen people* has caused the Jewish
people much grief throughout their history (Sears, 1998).
According to the Midrash (interpretation), being *chosen*
does not imply any superiority over others, nor that of
having exclusive wisdom. Rather, the Talmud, the authori-

tative body of Jewish tradition, stresses that, "Whoever speaks wisdom, although he is non-Jew, is a Sage" (Talmud: Megilla 16a). Therefore, it is not exclusive wisdom or superiority, but rather that of increased responsibility (for example, the responsibility and respect exemplified by Joseph and his father, Israel).

Greater responsibility is not necessarily desired by many people. This translation describes God as having revealed himself, not only to Israel but also to all nations. The story tells us that God went to the children of Esav and said to them, "Will you accept the Torah?" They answered, "What is in it?" Said He, "You shall not kill." Said they, "Lord of the Universe, the very essence of our father Esav is that he is a murderer. As it says, 'By the sword you shall live' (Genesis 27:40), we cannot accept the Torah." The children of Esav, Amon, Moav, and Ishmael, all rejected the Torah. The Children of Israel, however, said to God "We shall do and we shall hear!" (Lauterbach, 1976, pp. 233–236). This oftentimes quoted Midrash (Midrash Exodus Raba, a portion of the Mishpatim) suggests a subtle semantic transformation. Rather than Jews being the *chosen people*, they become the choosing people. The concept of free choice is an important factor when dealing with some rabbinic writings that suggest that God's covenant with Israel rests upon obedience rather than free choice. The Covenant and the Torah express God's demands, and these include individual and societal morality.

Throughout their history, the Jewish people usually found theories to decipher why God would bring suffering upon his *chosen people*. The Holocaust, which exhibited extraordinary evil, challenged these theories by demonstrating how human ideas and philosophies can justify such evil — for example, when the Nazis killed all those deemed inferior in their attempt to become the superior race. Although many Jews believe the creation of the modern state of Israel to be a *God-given answer to prayers,* in reality it was a *man-made solution.* Some Jewish thinkers, such as Martin Buber suggested a more pragmatic approach. According to Buber, the renewal of Judaism "can emanate only from a very specific soil, the soil of the homeland" (Buber & Schmidt, 1999, p. 206). Buber believed that in order to revive the Jewish spirit, the scattered Jews needed to return to their birth place. For many holocaust survivors who felt abandoned by God, the nation-state was the only answer. However, the positive effect of returning to the Promised Land has been undermined by the fact that it came as a result of human action, violence, and armed conflict, rather than reliance on the divine. God said to the Jewish People, "It is not because you are numerous that God chose you, indeed you are the smallest of people" (Deuteronomy 7:7)

From the beginning of the Diaspora, up until the nineteenth century, Jews, for the most part, were not allowed to own land. As much as this contributed to their yearning for a land of their own, it also undoubtedly had an impact on their characteristic of being a non-violent and passive people, bearing continual attacks by gentiles. It was not until the founding of the modern state of Israel, that they became aggressive in the manner of other nations. The instructive example here might be that without national borders, there could be less violence and war.

Had the Jewish people been a large nation with a powerful army, their successes in spreading the Torah spirit would have been attributed to their might and not to the truth of their ideas. The *chosen people* concept, therefore, should not be interpreted as implying that others are rejected or inferior. The only interpretation could be a greater responsibility for moral behavior among all children of God.

The message of Jesus was a message of love, not only for those later known as "Christians," but for all of creation. He gave a universal message, one that applies to humanity's relationship with the divine. Jesus never called himself a Christian. He was a Jew presenting a fresh understanding of Jewish scriptures, who simply disagreed with the interpretation of the spiritual life extolled by the temple leaders. He spoke of the universality of spiritual experience and taught that "The kingdom of God cometh not with observation: Neither shall they say, Lo here! Or, to there! For, behold, the kingdom of God is within you" (Luke 17:20–21). It is interesting to note that the word Catholicism literally means *universal*. However, the human ego distorted its connotation, and in so doing established power in the church as a political body rather than emphasizing that love, harmony and beauty are natural emanations of unity with the divine and available for all who choose to partake. Henceforth, the depth of Jesus' words were for the most part ignored. Whereas Jesus spoke from the heart, uniting us with our neighbors, creation and the creator; the later Christians interpreted universal in terms of dominance, believing their conceptual understanding of Jesus' words to be the only way to God's heaven.

Although Christianity began with a small group of people who chose as their teacher a man who emanated great love, who healed the sick and who advised his followers to refrain from judging others; it became, within a few hundred years a battle cry.

The history of apostolic succession is of particular significance here. Firstly it claims its beginnings in the apostle Peter according to Jesus' words "That thou are Peter, and upon this rock I will build my church; and the gates of hell shall not prevail against it" (Matthew 16:18). Jesus gave Peter the task of continuing his teachings with the claim that they are pure and therefore incorruptible. (The apostolic lineage is somewhat hazy regarding this leadership as Acts 15 notes that the first major Christian council meeting was led by James, and, likewise, the Nag Hammadi scriptures fail to support this belief.)

History records an emphasis on humility in the early Christians. The Beatitudes as presented by Jesus in the Sermon on the Mount described a way of life that included peacefulness, humility and goodwill. But within a few hundred years, Christianity experienced a drastic change upon the Roman Emperor Constantine's Christian conversion into the fold. His interpretation of Christianity was colored by his position as a Roman ruler. The church and politics became entwined. Pagan gods and goddesses were replaced with statues of the apostles; pagan holidays were changed to Christian celebrations. Proclaiming himself to be Christ's spokesperson, Constantine began to persecute others in the name of Christianity, even though he had previously mistreated Christians because of their refusal to bow to the pagan gods. Roman Catholicism claimed it was the only way to salvation and that faith and baptism in the Catholic Church were necessary requirements. *Extra ecclesiam nulla salus!* (There is no salvation outside the Catholic Church) (Rahner & Vorgrimler, 1965).

The reign of Constantine also saw the beginnings of papal power and authority. The pope was to be "obeyed in doctrinal matters regardless of his moral character."[4] However, the *Catholic Encyclopedia* and other writings contain historical accounts of adultery, murder and bribery within the papacy. Regarding Pope Boniface VIII (1294–1303) for example, "scarcely any possible crime was omitted; infidelity, heresy, simony, gross and unnatural immorality, idolatry, magic ... " (*Catholic Encyclopedia*, pp. 661– 662, quoted on website in fn. 4). Frederick II, in his Manifesto of 1230, referred to Gregory IX as "the great Dragon and Antichrist of the last days" (Adam, 1951, p. 8). There were various Catholic sects emphasizing a way of humility and mysticism in opposition to the Papal glamour and wealth, but they did so under the auspices of the Mother Church (for example, the founding of the Discalced Carmelite Order by St. Teresa of Avila and St. John of the Cross during the 1500s). It is not surprising that the problems associated with papal infallibility, along with outrage at the disintegration of true Christian teachings, led to the reformation.

It was the split into Protestantism that was to become a major influence in the development of fundamentalism and its focus on literal interpretations of the Bible. Martin Luther, the leader of the Christian reformation, denounced the pope and referred to him as the great harlot of the Apocalypse (Adam, 1951). Luther, instead, developed the principle of Protestantism as an act of faith alone. The only authority was to be the Bible and one's blind faith in its

---

[4]   http://www.acts1711.com/Jesus2a2.htm

infallibility. This was to be the gospel of salvation with Jesus as savior. The mystical communion with Christ, as practiced and experienced by the many great saints to be found in the Catholic Church was to be ignored. The split between Catholicism and Protestantism exists to this day. Although in reality both profess themselves as followers of Jesus Christ, each believes their position to be the one and only truth.

A significant problem with these narrow interpretations of scripture and authority are that the individual's ego identity is more impacted than his heart. Luther's righteous indignation at the papacy, and later towards Catholicism itself, made good sense; but he was often besieged with attacks of fear having been "early imbued with a strong, central experience of fear, an extraordinary terror of sin and judgment"[5] (most likely related to his father's firm hand). Luther's connection to his faith was primarily based in fear, rather than love. This suggests, on a biological and psychological level, that the hindbrain, associated with the old mammalian brain, was interfering with the pre-frontal lobe and heart relationship as it certainly doesn't bespeak of a loving, unifying relationship with Christ.

Much attention needs to be given to the knowledge gleaned from modern psychology. For example, it points to discrepancies between the idealized self and actual behaviors. Jesus, in particular, spoke against hypocrisy when he denounced the Pharisees of the temple. Recent decades have verified the failings of sexual misconduct by Catholic priests and bishops and in Protestant churches. The unconscious projections motivating the Irish Catholics and Protestants to hate and kill one another for the last several hundred years is obviously unrealistic. What dark force prompts and continues their behaviors?

These same behaviors are evidenced in Islam even though Islam is intended to be a religion of peace, freedom and love. Islam liberated Arabs from tribal prejudice and established human relationships based on individual merits. The suffering of the Muslims in Mecca during the

[5] http://www.ewtn.com/library/CHISTORY/RETREF.TXT

early period of Islam's call was due to the fact that Islam had an inherent value system that violated the tribal hierarchy. It defended the right of the poor and marginal segments of humanity. For example, Islam did not value the master over the slave. One of the most profound and salient principles in Islam was the equality between humans regardless of race, color, or sex. Mercy and compassion are among the highest attributes in Islamic ethics. "Bismillah Er-Rahman Er-Raheem" (In the Name of Allah, the Most Merciful and Compassionate) is repeated before reading any verse in the Qur'an as a continuous reminder to the reader and listener of these highly appreciated divine attributes.

Establishing a friendship relation with the Jews upon the migration to Medina, considering them part of the *ummah* (nation) demonstrated Islam's openness, tolerance, and respect to others. The Prophet did not try to impose Islam on the Jews or Christians or even the pagans. Quite the contrary, the Prophet paid great respect to both the Torah and the Bible. The Qur'an refers to "Muslims" (believers) several times as those who respect other revelations that preceded the revelation to Muhammad, for example,

> The Messenger believeth in what hath been revealed to him from his Lord, as do the men of faith. Each one (of them) believeth in Allah, His angels, His books, and His messengers. "We make no distinction (they say) between one and another of His messengers." (Holy Qur'an 2:285)

The Qur'an also reveals that Allah's relationship with humanity is not dependent upon their specific religious affiliation, but rather according to the nature of their beliefs.

> Surely those who believe, and those who are Jews, and the Christians, and the Sabians,[6] whoever believes in Allah and the Last day and does good, they shall have their reward from their Lord, and there is no fear for them, nor shall they grieve. (HQ:2:62).

---

[6] "The Qur'an briefly announces the Sabians as people of the book but provides no details as to who they were. It is only logical that considering there is no explanations on who they were is that either the Sabians were well known at the time of Muhammad or that the name Sabian describes who they were in one word," see the following site: http://www.geocities.com/mandaeans/Sabians8.html

Despite these Islamic principles, many modern Muslims believe that Islam distinguishes its followers and that God (Allah) prefers them to followers of other religions. This perspective then justifies acts of violence disguised as spreading the word of God. This erroneous thinking is due to the misreading of the Islamic teachings, as well as ignoring the various phases alluding to Islam's core principles and development. This misunderstanding has its roots in the early Islamic period.

After the passing away of the Prophet, the tribal spirit began to dominate among Muslim sects. This affected their interpretations of holy texts. The results were Islamizing the pre-Islamic attitudes. Muslims used particular verses in the Qur'an and the Prophet's traditions to justify their superiority over other religions and nations while overlooking other passages that failed to justify these limited interpretations. According to schema theory in cognitive anthropology, there are categorical rules in our mind, which regulate our perception, and hence our understanding of situations, events, or texts (D'Andrade, 1995). Muhammad's message introduced new concepts to the Arabs. It was difficult for them to conceptualize the true meaning at that time, thereby their interpretations were limited. For example when they took the following verses to justify their superiority, they ignored other important principles that formed the core of the Prophet's message.

> Ye are *the best of peoples, Ummah* evolved for mankind, enjoining what is right, forbidding what is wrong, and believing in Allah. (HQ:3:110)

> *The Religion before Allah is Islam* (submission to His Will): Nor did the People of the Book dissent therefrom except through envy of each other, after knowledge had come to them. But if any deny the Signs of Allah, Allah is swift in calling to account. (HQ:3:19)

> *If anyone desires a religion other than Islam, never will it be accepted of him*; and in the Hereafter He will be in the ranks of those who have lost. (HQ 3:85)

The idea of submitting to divine will is a core belief found at the heart of all religions. This is what is meant by "Islam."

But, reading these verses through limited schemas justified fanaticism. They narrowed their perception of Islam to include only Muslims who followed the ritual aspects of Muhammad's teachings, and ignored many of the verses addressing the wider scope within Islam that included all of the divine revelations that had preceded the revelation to Muhammad. Therefore they saw themselves as "chosen people" on the basis of affiliation to the religion of Islam, rather than an ethnic racial foundation as exemplified by the Children of Israel. However the result turned out to be the same. They felt superior over other people, similar to their Christian counterparts.

The tribal spirit became obvious in the fight between Mu'awiyah Ibn Abi Sufian from Omeyya branch in Quraysh tribe, and Ali Ibn Abi Taleb (the Prophet's son in law, his cousin, and fourth caliph) mentioned in Chapter Two. The victory of Mu'awiya over Ali was taken as a victory of Omeyya over Hashimite. The son of Ali ended the blood shed between Muslims after the killing of his father on the condition that Mu'awiyah would give the people the chance to choose their own governor. However, the canny Mu'awiyah made sure to take the pledge for his son's position before his death. The Umayyad dynasty continued for almost a century (661–750 CE), followed by the Abbasid dynasty (750–1258 CE). Mongols defeated the Abbasid and were later defeated by the Ottomans. It is significant that the Ottoman reign used military power to invade and impose Islam on the people of the conquered territory. There were also genocide crimes against Armenians, which still has its wounds and triggers hatred in the hearts of many Europeans. These behaviors were an obvious deviation from the Prophet's style of governance and words of wisdom.

Radical Fundamentalism:
A Serious Threat to Humanity's Survival

The wars between male-dominated religious and political ideals are becoming increasingly dangerous for us all. In fact, the development of radical fundamentalism represents a serious threat to the well-being of humanity, because of its narrow perspectives and related inflexibility. It is based upon an inflated ego-centric and ethno-centric perspective, as opposed to a heart-felt universality that includes all of creation. Pressure in the Middle East keeps building, fueled by erroneous religious beliefs on the part of Jews, Christians and Muslims. According to a PBS Frontline series,[7] June 1967 marked a significant event in the Judeo-Christian relationship. Jews were once again in control of Jerusalem for the first time in over 2,000 years. To Jews it was the answer to ancient prayers. Over thousands of years their passion for Jerusalem has not diminished. This city was conquered and re-conquered 38 times by Babylonians, Greeks, Romans, Crusaders and Ottomans. Though other nations have gained political sovereignty over the area, none but the Jews had ever made Jerusalem their capital city. The Jewish leader Ramban (Nachmanides, 1268 CE) declared, "The glory of the world is the land of Israel, the glory of the land of Israel is Jerusalem, and the glory of Jerusalem is the Holy Temple" (Ramban, 1978, p. 353).

But the Christian fundamentalist interpretation of the Bible presented an extended and different view of the Jewish victory for, as James Tabor writes:

> Not only did they laud and applaud the Jewish sovereignty, but they understood this as the beginning of the end, as a potential fulfillment of Bible prophecy, because in fact every scenario that you can read about in the prophets, from the Book of Revelation to the Book of Daniel, implies that in the last days Jerusalem would be ruled and controlled not by Turks, not by British, not by all the various cultures that have controlled Jerusalem for the centuries, but by, in fact, a sovereign Jewish population.[8]

To Zionists, the time is approaching for the rebuilding of the Temple. To Christians, this third Temple is the awaited sign announcing Armegeddon, the end of the world and the second coming of Christ.

---

[7] http://www.pbs.org/wgbh/pages/frontline/shows/apocalypse/
[8] http://www.pbs.org/wgbh/pages/frontline/shows/apocalypse/
     explanation/jerusalem.html

Frontline presented this special broadcast with the intention of educating the public and providing the biblical background explaining Zionist and Christian beliefs related to the millennium. The program highlighted literalist' interpretations of the Old and New Testaments encouraging superstitious beliefs and catastrophic prophesies. These Christian-Zionists (a name given because of the combined beliefs) were focused particularly on literal (a trademark of fundamentalism) translations of the Books of Daniel and Revelation. But, even though the new millennium came without any unusual occurrences, these beliefs continue to motivate this fundamentalist mindset.

According to the Book of Daniel catastrophes will eventually be released upon the Jews who have not listened to and obeyed the voice of the Lord. Daniel 9:11 reads that all of Israel "has transgressed your law and turned aside, refusing to obey your voice. So the curse and the oath written in the law of Moses, the servant of God, have been poured out upon us, because we have sinned against you." Daniel continues describing kings, power, greed and destruction from the north, the south, east, Persia, Greece, etc., and warns that a ruler will appear with even more vicious influence than the others and that "he shall go out with great fury to bring ruin and complete destruction to many" (Daniel, 11:44). The writer goes on with this dark prophesy and a word of hope for the righteous, "There shall be a time of anguish, such as has never occurred since nations first came into existence. But at that time your people shall be delivered, everyone who is found written in the book [kept in heaven]" (Daniel 12:1).

This is an archetypal theme of the righteous among the chosen people. It is a story of failure of a group of people to live a spiritually ethical life. For example, Chapter One related how the Hopi Indian nation tells of great periods of disaster and of chosen people who survived to be delivered into the next world. The Hopi myths are similar to the Judeo-Christian beliefs, but the Hopis do not specifically identify the chosen survivors as a particular nation or religion. Instead, they simply imply that chosen people are singled out as those living a humane, spiritually-conscientious life. Those who have not allowed greed and power to dominate have the consciousness to intuitively move into a higher plane of existence as the old one is destroyed.

Whereas the Book of Daniel was recorded by the Jews, the Book of Revelation was placed at the end of the New Testament in the Christian Bible. The Book of Revelation, which also has as its theme the Apocalypse, is filled with an array of symbols and metaphors. But, interpretations are highly suspect for the symbols allow for numerous projections from those who ask these questions. One such symbol, the mark of *the beast*, has troubled and continues to trouble many fundamentalists.

Who is the beast? Who is the antichrist? The book of Revelation mentions a sign or a mark that some will wear on their foreheads and their hands. Supposedly it is the mark of the beast, and it is recorded that the beast also has a number. James Tabor, a professor of religious studies, concludes that "the beast being some military ruler that controls the world at the end of time — as being 666" and suggests that,

> There are five or six main characters. One would be a false prophet. He's like a dragon, but he speaks like a lamb. He has horns. A beast that is non-descript, some sort of horrible creature that appears to stand for the Roman government to the early Christians, but today could be any power — some sort of evil empire of some type.[9]

The antichrist has been a topic of concern for many, particularly since the rise of fundamentalism early in the 20th century. Figures like Stalin, Lenin, and Hitler have been called the antichrist. Hitler, himself, characterized "the Jews as a powerful demonic enemy and [envisioned] a great final battle"[10] that would bring a new order in his Mein Kampf. The Book of Revelation seems to attract dangerous projections. Given that the entirety of Revelation is related in symbolism, totally lacking historical content, the anti-christ

[9] http://www.pbs.org/wgbh/pages/frontline/shows/apocalypse/explanation/brevelation.html

[10] http://www.pbs.org/wgbh/pages/frontline/shows/apocalypse/primary/mein.html

could simply refer to a way of acting rather than a specific individual. The mark upon our heads and hands could reflect the mental attitudes and behaviors that dominate our lives. For Christians, perhaps the more pertinent question is *"If in religious intolerance we destroy whole nations and commit genocide, are we truly living in Christ's love and light?"* The reality is that Jesus' words and works reflect a loving compassion towards all life. The true antichrist is anything that takes one away from one's heart and the message that the kingdom of God is within it (rather than in the external power of the church).

For Jews, the virtue of peace making is fundamental. It is written in Psalms: "Seek peace and pursue it" (34:15), and the Jerusalem Talmud explicates: "That is, seek peace in its place; pursue it when it is elsewhere (Pe'ah 1:1). Judaism provides scriptural proof that the Divine commandment of love and peace should be extended to all nations. The Torah clearly obligates the Jews in this matter: "And you shall love your neighbor as yourself" (Leviticus 19:18).[11] The intent of the term "your neighbor" indicates a person like oneself, who participates in civilization like oneself, and this denotes members of all nations (Sears, 1998). Hence, if the Torah is calling for mutual respect and acceptance, how can the Holy Temple be rebuilt upon bloodshed?

Nevertheless large numbers of fundamentalists place narrow interpretations and great importance upon the idea of rebuilding the third Temple and the descending of Jerusalem depicted in the Book of Revelation, hence the car bumper signs acknowledging "The Rapture." Whereas the Jews see a new life beginning for the chosen people as the third Temple is rebuilt, the Christians see it as Armageddon — the end of the world in fire and judgment, rising to a new life in Christ (sometimes called "the rapture"). Those who believe in Jesus as the savior of the world will be redeemed; those who don't accept "Jesus as their savior" will burn in an eternal hell. The new Jerusalem will descend from heaven. Also, Fundamentalists exert a political influence in

[11]　Jesus was not the first to proclaim what is considered Christianity's Golden Rule. As a Jew, he was simply re-stating this core principle.

regards to control of Jerusalem as both Jews and Christians have strong reasons for its domination. This whole tale is a blatant example of the dangerousness of this extremist ideology, and supportive of the need for a gender-balanced paradigm shift. But, tragically, stronger political backing exists for the radical fundamentalist stance, as suggested by the following examples.

Yehiel Eckstein, an Orthodox American rabbi, president of the International Fellowship of Christians and Jews, and Ralph Reed, ex-head of the Christian Coalition, and one of George W. Bush's advisors, have encouraged funding Jewish immigration to Israel and the building of illegal settlements in the West Bank to secure their image of Israel's future.[12] Israel continues to both invite and fund Jewish citizens of other lands to immigrate to Israel and increase its citizenry (primarily due to fear of increasing Palestinian population). More than 1,500 American Jewish immigrants were expected by Fall 2004 ,[13] and the relocations continue.

A problem is exacerbated in that Jerusalem also has a special value in the heart of Muslims. At the beginning of the Islamic message, Muslims literally turned towards Jerusalem when praying. Pilgrimage to Jerusalem is still highly desired. When the Prophet took the miraculous journey to the seven heavens, he passed by Jerusalem in what is known as *al-Isra' wa al-Mi'iraj*. It is said that the Archangel Gabriel took the Prophet in a mystical, inner journey to Jerusalem and from there, he ascended the seven heavens. Later, Muslims built the Mosque known as the Dome of the Rock at the place of Muhammad's mystical experience. It was also an honoring of Abraham and the temples beforehand.

Construction of the Dome of the Rock began in 685 CE and was completed in 691 CE. After completion of the

[12] Daniel Hass. (July 10, 2002) US Christians find Cause to Aid Israel, Evangelicals Financing Immigrants, Settlements. *San Francisco Chronicle.* http://www.haaretz.co.il/hasen/pages/ShArtVty.jhtml?sw=Israel +War+of+the+Jews+by+Daphne+Berman&itemNo=458105

[13] Israel's Plight Draws American Jews to Homeland. (July 18, 2004). *San Francisco Chronicle.* http://sfgate.com/cgi-bin/article.cgi?f=/ c/a/2004/07/18/MNG617NH0R1.DTL

Dome of the Rock, construction began to build a vast con-
gregational mosque accommodating more than five-thou-
sand worshippers. This was completed in 705 CE. Both the
Dome of the Rock and the Al Aqsa Mosque are included in a
sanctuary area called Al-Haram al-Sharif (Noble Sanctuary), which encloses over 35 acres of fountains, gardens,
buildings and domes. The entire area is regarded as a
mosque and comprises nearly one sixth of Jerusalem. The
area is the third holiest site in Islam after Mecca and Medina
(Daryle et al., 1996).

The 1967 defeat of the Arabs formed a turning point in
their history when one of their most sacred places fell into
the hands of Israel. Now, it is the dream of Muslims, not
only in the Arab world, but also in much of the Muslim
world, to claim Jerusalem and protect the Mosque, the
Dome of the Rock.[14]

Some Muslims see particular verses in the Qur'an as a
prophecy that Jerusalem will be theirs once again, and Israel
will be defeated:

> And We decreed for the Children of Israel in the Scripture:
> Ye verily will work corruption in the earth twice, and ye
> will become great tyrants! So when the time for the first of
> the two came, We roused against you slaves of Ours of
> great might who ravaged (your) country, and it was a
> threat performed. Then we gave you once again your turn
> against them, and We aided you with wealth and children
> and made you more in soldiery. If ye do good, ye do good
> for your own souls, and if ye do evil, it is for them (in like
> manner). So, when the time for the second (of the judg-
> ments) came (We roused against you others of Our slaves)
> to ravage you, and to enter the Temple even as they entered
> it the first time, and to lay waste all that they conquered
> with an utter wasting. It may be that your Lord will have

[14] The Mosque was set on fire on August 20, 1969 (waterlines were shut
off right before the extremist started the fire). In 1979 40 settlers
raided the Mosque. Explosive materials were found within it in 1980.
In 1984 100 kilograms of explosives were detected in time. In 1989
Israelis were protected by the military when they decided to pray
within it. Twenty Muslims were killed in 1990 in the Mosque square.
In 1996 an opening of the tunnel along the Mosque wall caused it to
fall as 85 Palestinians were killed and hundreds injured. Extremist
groups continue in their attempts to dig tunnels under its foundation
and there is a continuous threat of bombing.

mercy on you, but if ye repeat (the crime) We shall repeat
(the punishment), and We have appointed hell a dungeon
for the disbelievers. (HQ: 17:4-8)

Many fundamentalist Muslims believe that these verses
allude to two great events in the history of the "Children of
Israel." The first one occurred in 586 BCE when they were
taken into captivity in Babylon. The second event occurred
when Romans destroyed the Jewish temple in Jerusalem
and expelled them from the land of Israel, and they lived in
exile (called the "Diaspora"). Some interpretations suggest
that these two events occurred as a divine punishment for
deviating from Moses' guidance, and other harmful behaviors. They believe that if Israel doesn't stop its systematic
destruction of the Palestinians, it will reap the results of its
behaviors and Israel will end. Mustafa Mahmoud, an intellectual Muslim and prominent writer, believes the above
verses predict the end of the State of Israel.[15]

More importantly, the continued Israeli aggression
against the Palestinians can only lead to ongoing violence
and contra-violence, and the loss of precious lives on both
sides. Many Muslims believe that Israel is losing any opportunities for peace with its neighbors as a result of its continued aggression against the Palestinians. Also, those radical
fundamentalists who look forward to Israel's destruction
are aggravating the situation and providing the Israeli government justification for its continuous assault against the
Palestinians. In short, ill-willed fundamentalist mindsets
on the part of Muslims, Jews and Christians continue to
provoke violence in the Holy Land.

Conclusions

Extremist Zionist Jews have focused on the rebuilding of
the Temple,[16] forgetting that it is a metaphor for the true
Temple within the Heart; radical fundamentalist Christians
have focused to a greater extent on the destruction and end

[15] http://answering-islam.org.uk/Walid/12israel_quran.htm
[16] Jonathan Lis & Yair Ettinger. Police Ban Jews from Temple Mount for
      Tisha B'Av. (July 28, 2004) *Haaretz News.* http://www.haaretz.
      co.il/hasen/spages/456926.html

of the world, forgetting that Jesus told them the kingdom of heaven is within; whereas Islamic extremists have been dreaming ways for destroying those who differ from them, ignoring that the revelation to Muhammad emphasized the naturalness of human variations while emphasizing compassion and mercy to others. Each has failed to focus on the wisdom teachings of their prophets — who advised that love for one another was the core behavior of spiritual life.

This radical fundamentalism is contributing to increasing political discord and religious strife. The United States is rapidly losing its position as a world leader, the Israeli government is being reprimanded by much of the world, and most Arab nations are trapped in outdated lifestyles and misinterpreted laws. These behaviors along with political dominance, economic greed and a profound disregard for anyone outside one's identified group represent the true antichrist.

As it nears its demise, patriarchal religious and political stances are becoming increasingly more threatening. If humanity is to survive, we have no other choice than to examine the failures of our historical past while creating a vision and action plan for a healthy, respectfully balanced, relationship between *all* members of our human family. The future of humanity and shared organic life are at stake. Perhaps the course of this self- and other-destructive world view will change as women become more equally and actively engaged as co-leaders in humanitarian, religious and political domains.

At present our country needs women's idealism and determination perhaps more in politics than anywhere else.

Shirley Chisolm

Chapter Four

Tales of Democracy, Power and Corruption

A Collusion Between Politics and Religion in the US

A Systemic World View

A systemic world view offers a more collaborative perspective than a hierarchical one. Systems theory is egalitarian in that it recognizes that every element, person, interaction affects the whole. Considering the current threats to human safety, religious and political leaders (along with the general populace) have to take a larger world view in regard to these enormous clashes of power if there are to be any hopes of resolution and world peace. The knowledge gleaned from the scientific study of Cybernetics and General Systems Theory provides a greater framework for understanding that each nation, religion, racial and ethnic group is an organized element within the context of the organization of the larger world system. Each group has a function within that system even though it may perceive itself to be operating independently of it. Systems theory examines the principles common to mathematical systems, particles, cells, human beings, nations, etc. Cybernetics studies the communication and controls within these organizational systems.

General System Theory (GST) was the result of the biologist Ludwig von Bertalanffy's recognition that

> separate a living organism from its surroundings and it will die shortly because of lack of oxygen, water and food. Organisms are open systems: they cannot survive without continuously exchanging matter and energy with their environment. The peculiarity of open systems is that they interact with other systems outside of themselves...When we look more closely at the environment of a system; we see that it too consists of systems interacting with their environments. For example, the environment of a person is full of other persons. If we now consider the collection of such systems which interact with each other, that collection could again be seen as a system. For example, a group of interacting people may form a family, a firm, or a city. The mutual interactions of the component systems in a way "glue" these components together into a whole. If these parts did not interact, the whole would not be more than the sum of its components. But because they interact, something more is added. With respect to the whole the parts are seen as subsystems. With respect to the parts, the whole is seen as a supersystem.[1]

Further it is noted that a supersystem accommodates for

> all types of systems: societies consist of people which consist of organs, which consist of cells, which consist of organelles, which consist of macromolecules, which consist of molecules, which consist of atoms, which consist of nucleons, which consist of quarks. (ibid.)

Systems theory differs from the Cartesian reductionist mentality that has governed modern humanity for several hundred years. For example, family systems theorists do not take a reductionist view blaming one person in a particular family (typically referred to as the *identified patient*) for its problems. This same theory applies to groups within the larger world system. The reductionist considers one ethnic or religious group to be the designated problem, and fails to examine the complex interactions within the relationship itself. A systemic world view considers the relationship of all parts (nations and groups), seen and unseen, for each part is

---

[1]   Basic Concepts of the Systems Approach. Principia Cybernetica Web http://pespmc1.vub.ac.be/SYSAPPR.html

intimately related to the whole. GST recognizes that systems, both simple and complex, are evolving in some manner.

Systems (consider individual families, nations and religions as representing systems) have interrelated elements with specific characteristics that function in an independent manner. These create a structure—a membership within a given system or subsystem and a boundary between that system and its environment. There are patterns of interaction that develop within each system. The repetition of these patterns creates a certain equilibrium that tells its members how to relate within the system. Its boundaries determine whether the system has open or closed forms of communication. For example, there are rules within the religion or nation that either allow for or prohibit change. The boundaries containing the system can allow for new energies and experiences (these are called "open" feedback loops) or they can isolate its members from other systems (families, nations and/or religions) and therefore remain isolated and self-contained (these are considered "closed" feedback loops) from interactions with the larger system.

Each system has subsystems. A nation's differing political parties are subsystems within it. A fundamentalist religious group would differ from one based on deeper or experiential interpretations of scripture. These would represent two subsystems within a given religion. Various religious and political groups within a system would represent its subsystems. Each is representing a different voice (perhaps one not heard by members of other groups). This would include those who challenge and disrupt a system if it is the only means to bring attention to a missing perspective or imbalance. An individual may change from one subsystem to another at any given time as he or she takes a different position within the given system.

> *Closed Systems*: Closed system loops preclude questioning and deviation of any kind. The members of the system are locked into rigid boundaries and belief structures, a pervading sense of *absolutism* rules. Families cannot deal with emotions or talk about dad's alcoholism or mom's inability to express

her feelings. Members of closed political systems cannot question or go against its policies. Likewise, members of a closed religious system would be unable to think outside its basic teachings (typically literal translations of religious scripture). Members are kept in check with threats of loss of faith or being influenced by demonic forces. Even the protection of values and beliefs deemed to be sacred can encourage closure, and prevent further discussion and/or growth. No one is expected or even allowed to think or act outside of the system. Also, any evidence of hypocrisy is denied.

Open Systems: Open systems of communication allow for change. Family members are encouraged to express their feelings and share ideas. Males and females have an equal voice. They equally deal with problems and promote change. Open discourse, including conflict, would be allowed — even encouraged. A true democratic government would be an example of an open system in that all its members would have an equal voice (the leadership would not be dependent on buying votes and other questionable practices). Religious systems would appreciate individuals exploring their spirituality and discovering God. They would be respectful of religious diversity and the varieties of ways in which God manifests.

The increasing rise of fundamentalist mindsets adds to closed systems of communication. Also, gender imbalance has offset the homeostasis of the world. In the previous chapters we examined how the denigration of women was influenced by patriarchal religious ideals; let us now examine how this imbalance has affected our political systems. The next two chapters review the effect of patriarchal governmental systems, and the threatening influences of political power when combined with religion and economic/corporate greed. The motivation of power and greed fuels domination over others, while fostering political corruption, financial abuse and war. Closed religious systems have contributed to prejudice and hatred. The com-

bination of unilateral political systems and religious fundamentalism is a recipe for destruction. The following begins
with a description of Native American tribal life, for it represents an open system of governance, spirituality and gender balance. Its communal traditions also had a significant
influence upon the development of the United States Constitution. We discussed some of the early mythologies influencing religious development; and believe that it is equally
valuable to examine earlier influences on our political
development. This chapter reveals the sharp contrast
between the ethics and ideals of the First Nations peoples
who comprised the land now known as the United States, as
opposed to the later ideological development of what is
called "manifest destiny" leading to its current style of governance and maneuvers toward global dominance. Would
it have been different if women had been equally involved
in the development of this nation? A study of early Native
American traditions suggest it may well have been.

First Nations Peoples:
Democracy and Native American Spirituality

The dominant culture thinks little about the threats of
global warming and other environmental dangers in that all
of nature is seen as something to be used for profit. This
includes the way peoples of third world[2] nations are
exploited in the labor market, the destruction of natural
rainforests and other habitats, and the pollution of our trea-
sured elements — air, water and land. These attitudes and
behaviors differ greatly from the ways of indigenous peoples, who have a deep respect and reverence for "mother
earth".

The relationship of the United States and its indigenous
population of Native Americans is a significant one,
because its native inhabitants see all of nature as kin. This
provides a roadmap for saving the life on our planet from

[2]   A more recent term for Third World nations is "Undeveloped
Nations." This term denotes two things. One, that their cultures are
not respected unless they mimic our own; and secondly, that these
nations are ripe for economic exploitation.

destruction. Consciously or unconsciously, westernized Christianity disdains the natural environment (this is exemplified in the Bush regimes' undoing of environmental protection policies). As discussed in Chapter Two, the influence of St. Augustine's emphasis on building faith in heaven and the "hidden" God caused Christianity to become more concerned with the afterworld — a policy that ignored Jesus' proclamation that *the kingdom of God was to be found within.* (Luke 17:20–21) Why? It would appear that Jesus' emphasis on the kingdom of heaven being located *within* (the heart that knows unity with the Divine) would limit political power in the church and its religious influence upon government. It is this misinterpretation and misdirection that allows Christians of the Western world to turn a blind eye to greed and other destructive behaviors. Westernized Christianity has negated the sacredness of the earth — and erroneously excused its exploitation. This has contributed to a dangerous mix of politics and religion. Rather than it being a matter of stewardship of our environment and its inhabitants, this limiting paradigm suggested that the world is simply here for our use (and abuse).

Native American spirituality provides a missing ingredient for healthy spirituality because it includes respect and love for the many manifestations of God in life. Many tribes are matriarchal, in that the blood line is established through the mother rather than the father. The female has a prominent and equal place in Native American communities. Irregardless of matriarchal or patriarchal lineages, the majority of tribes do not have a hierarchal system that diminishes others by gender or any other natural state. Secondly, everyone has a significant place, and a voice, in the government of the community.

Political organization and spiritual beliefs are not separate domains in Native American life as their cosmological view is holistic. The cosmology includes heaven and earth in relationship (Father Sky and Mother Earth).[3] Humanity, animals, birds, reptiles, trees and elements such as air,

---

[3]   Father Sky is akin to the movement of the wind and the space in
      which we live, whereas Mother Earth is all of nature.

earth, fire and water are considered kin (a cosmological belief also held by St. Francis of Assisi). The word *spirituality* does not make sense to Native Americans in that it proclaims a duality that does not exist.

The following relates to some of the tribes in the early developmental years of the United States. Some tribes[4] had highly organized social and political structures, such as the Iroquois (Johansen, 1999). For example, they had civil chiefs, subchiefs and also stable and temporary wartime chiefs. At the other end of the spectrum smaller nomadic tribes existing with limited territorial rights required far simpler social organization and therefore less political governance. Many chiefs were chosen for their position because of their evidenced wisdom and exemplary behaviors (Hopi, Creek, and Iroquois among others). In other tribes a chieftainship might be claimed through accumulated wealth or simply an inherited right whereas the courage and ambitiousness of a warrior achieved chieftaincy in the Plains tribes. The chief guides the council comprised of tribal and clan representatives.

As noted, more clans (intra-tribal society often based upon a common ancestry) were matriarchal in that they traced their lineage through the female blood line (although Californian tribes as well as the Mohave and a few others traced their lineage through the father). This did not mean that a woman reigned over others, for hierarchal organization did not exist. Women and men had their respective roles. Women were honored — for they brought forth life. Each member of a clan was (and still is) woven into its fabric — a tapestry identifying the tribal identity.

Territories changed as Native Americans were forced into reservations. There are many historical examples of tribal governance both before and after these changes. In 1680, the Iroquois nation stretched across the North East, including portions of Pennsylvania, southern Ontario, Kentucky and New England. Kinship was determined by the women who also owned all Iroquois property. Historically,

[4]   This is based on historical research of early American tribal life prior to Native Americans being forced into reservations.

the Iroquois nation was known for its unity, sense of purpose, excellent principles and superior political organization. The League of the Five Tribes (Iroquois included Cayuga, Mohawk, Onondaga and Seneca) was founded on establishing and maintaining peace, security and the health of all, advocacy and defense of justice, equity and respect for the authority of law, and magic power.

Many Americans are unaware that our Constitution was, in part, influenced by the democratic organization of the Iroquois tribes (Grinde, 1994). Benjamin Franklin and other founding fathers sought to emulate the Iroquois in establishing our own ideals of democracy. Charles Brownell noted that "The nature of the [Iroquois] league was decidedly democratic; arbitrary power was lodged in the hands of no ruler ... A singular unanimity was generally observed in their councils" (Brownell, 1855, p. 287). They considered this way to be the *Great Commonwealth*, a term that would later be used by Benjamin Franklin, Thomas Jefferson, Samuel Adams, and other founding fathers of the US (Grinde, 1994; Champagne, 1994). Franklin and others were also impressed with the Iroquois' supreme law and highly structured system of checks and balances. They had complex and well-planned confederations, and its clans had representation in the tribal council. In fact, it was the Iroquois who suggested that the British colonies unite, and Franklin utilized their input in the development of the Albany Plan and Articles of Confederation (Champagne, 1994). The Iroquois represented an *open* system of governance, and this style melded well with the ideals of the founding fathers.

In a paper on *Religion, Politics and the Native American Land Ethic* presented at the Fourth North American Symposium on Society and Resource Management in 1992, Adolf Gundersen noted that,

> Village governance among Native American societies was expansive ... decision making processes paid special attention to individuals who felt most aggrieved ... Because the integrity of the community was seen to depend very directly on those who felt most oppressed by it, the community had good reason to woo disgruntled individuals. Meanwhile, disaffected individuals were asked to do more

> than simply object: they were asked to consider the vil-
> lage's welfare from an alternative standpoint. [This] was
> the true political genius of Native American societies: by a
> process of consultation and persuasion, the individual was
> at once respected as an individual and incorporated into
> the community. (Gundersen, 1998, pp. 181–203)

The majority of Native American tribes exercised democratic government. There was a natural unity of spiritual life
and political structure, and both of these were in relationship to the land in which they lived. Political governance
was intended to assure goodness and equality for all of its
members. Commodities were shared, as greed was not a
part of tribal life. Their lives and ways were severely disrupted when the white man arrived with the intention of
creating a nation representing its new ideals for freedom of
religion and democratic government, for although prominent figures, such as Benjamin Franklin, emulated the communal style of the First Nations people, the white man's
tendency towards dominance and greed eventually relegated the tribes to reservations.

The Separation of Church and State

The separation of Church and State, envisioned and
planned by the founding fathers of the United States, was a
unique attempt to prevent one group within the system
from having a potentially abusive power. A young, pre-
dominately Christian, nation created a vision that would
allow subsystems to exist and even evolve within it. It
created a Constitution and Declaration of Independence
grounded in democratic principles—a government that
existed to protect, rather than oppress, its citizens (Hart,
2004).

The founding fathers of the United States of America
intended a separation of church and state that would assure
the caretaking of these principles. In an address to the
General Assembly of the Commonwealth of Virginia, James
Madison began with the following:

> We the subscribers, citizens of the said Commonwealth,
> having taken into serious consideration, a Bill printed by

order of the last Session of the General Assembly, entitled
"A Bill establishing a provision for Teachers of the Christian Religion," and conceiving that the same if finally
armed with the sanctions of a law, will be a dangerous
abuse of power, are bound as faithful members of a free
State to remonstrate against it, and to declare the reasons
by which we are determined.

Madison's remonstration against the Bill is well thought out
and deserves much attention. He noted that,

Because we hold it for a fundamental and undeniable truth,
"that religion or the duty which we owe to our Creator and
the manner of discharging it, can be directed only by reason and conviction, not by force or violence." The Religion
then of every man must be left to the conviction and conscience of every man; and it is the right of every man to
exercise it as these may dictate ... We maintain therefore
that in matters of Religion, no man's right is abridged by
the institution of Civil Society and that Religion is wholly
exempt from its cognizance ... The Rulers who are guilty of
such an encroachment, exceed the commission from which
they derive their authority, and are Tyrants. The People
who submit to it are governed by laws made neither by
themselves nor by an authority derived from them, and are
slaves ...
... Who does not see that the same authority which can
establish Christianity, in exclusion of all other Religions,
may establish with the same ease any particular sect of
Christians, in exclusion of all other Sects?... If "all men are
by nature equally free and independent," all men are to be
considered as entering into Society on equal conditions; as
relinquishing no more, and therefore retaining no less, one
than another, of their natural rights ...
... During almost fifteen centuries has the legal establishment of Christianity been on trial. What have been its
fruits? More or less in all places, pride and indolence in the
Clergy, ignorance and servility in the laity, in both, super-
stition, bigotry and persecution. Enquire of the Teachers of
Christianity for the ages in which it appeared in its greatest
luster; those of every sect, point to the ages prior to its
incorporation with Civil policy ... Such a Government will
be best supported by protecting every Citizen in the enjoy-
ment of his Religion with the same equal hand which protects his person and his property; by neither invading the
equal rights of any Sect, nor suffering any Sect to invade
those of another ... Because it will destroy that moderation
and harmony which the forbearance of our laws to

intermeddle with Religion has produced among its several sects. Torrents of blood have been spilt in the old world, by vain attempts of the secular arm, to extinguish Religious discord, by proscribing all difference in Religious opinion. Time has at length revealed the true remedy. Every relaxation of narrow and rigorous policy, wherever it has been tried, has been found to assuage the disease ...

Thus began the argument and plan for separation of church and state. James Madison, and the other founding fathers, had examined the failures of the historical past. They wanted to create a country that allowed for true freedom — one that acknowledged individual expression, religious freedom and human rights. They proclaimed it was "the equal right of every citizen to the free exercise of his Religion according to the dictates of conscience" and that this was to be held with the same respect as every other right. Madison's document clearly spelled out an intention to separate religion from political government as history had evidenced the detrimental effects when these two power structures acted in cohort. This was an attempt to avoid religious fundamentalisms, recognizing that these would demolish the democratic ideal.

Diverse religious groups were associated with the founding of this country from its onset. There was a mingling of Christian groups and members of secret sects who held the vision of a new world order. Many of the founding fathers were Masons[5] (for example, Benjamin Franklin, Paul Revere, John Hancock) influenced by Sir Francis Bacon's vision of a new world, *the promised land of democracy and freedom* (Hall, 1944/1972). It appears that the symbolism (for example, the Great Seal) and each document influencing the

[5] The first known lodge of Masonry was founded in England in 1717, although there is evidence that Masons existed in the fourteenth century and some believe it can be traced back to Egyptian mystery schools. There are many levels to Masonry as depicted in the fact that the name refers to masons as "builders." There are 33 known initiatory steps in Masonry. Many Masons simply join for the membership in the fraternity, whereas others seek the power and influence it contains. The further one goes up the ladder, the more secretive and powerful the steps become. George Washington was a known Mason as well as the dark magician Alistair Crowley.

creation of the United States Constitution were carefully planned with the image of this new world order in mind. But some things were flawed from the start; *namely that these rights and this vision, in particular, applied primarily to the white, Anglo Saxon male.*

The Power of Symbols and the Problems of Capitalism

Symbols have great archetypal power and influence. One example of this is the power the swastika (originally a Vedic symbol) wielded over the German people during the Third Reich. Hitler had studied esoteric literature and knew that symbols emanated the power found in humanity's collective unconscious. He used symbolism to obtain power in order to create what he falsely deemed to be a pure humanity. Old films show Hitler speaking with the symbol of the Third Reich greatly enlarged — placed directly above and behind him. The power of the symbol affected the unconscious of those around him as much as did his words. He knew that symbols speak to the unconscious mind.

Symbols are chosen by leaders with meaningful intention. This is apparent in the design chosen for the Great Seal of the United States, presented by William Barton in 1782 (Hall, 1988). His original design had a bird rising from flames (indicative of the ancient Phoenix rising out of the transforming fire). This design was not accepted and the eagle was chosen instead. Numerous papers and books include descriptions of the vast amount of symbolism in the Great Seal, each detail carefully chosen with a specific intention. The number thirteen was repeatedly used in some of the detail. (Although there were thirteen colonies at the time being represented it also represented a mystical meaning given to the number.) Its formulation bespoke of the divine providence that fueled the creation of the nation. It was infused with religious, occult and Masonic symbolism. In particular, continued Masonic influence is more than suggested when one examines the backside of the "Great Seal" imprinted on a one-dollar bill (Hall, 1951). The image of a pyramid with the single all-seeing eye placed at the top point is symbolic of illumination, and is displayed in Masonic temples throughout the world. The all-seeing eye is also a world-wide symbol used by Freemasons, as are the masonry "blocks" within the pyramid.[6] This later symbol was designed by Charles Wallace and approved by Franklin D. Roosevelt, both 32nd degree Masons,[7] in 1935.

The two sides of the Great Seal are very significant. In fact, a quick Internet search reveals the vast amount of research, discussion and controversial conclusions regarding each aspect of the formation and the intent. On one side we read *E Pluribus Unum* (One out of many), whereas the reverse side, *Novus Ordo Seclorum* (a new order of the ages), affirms the vision of a society determined to influence the future of the world. At the top of this affirmation of a new order (above the all-seeing eye) we read *Annuit coeptis*, an affirmation "He [God] favors our undertakings." This symbolism is in the background of America's energetic drive towards commercialism, wealth, oil rights and its current plan for "global leadership."[8] It represents an affirmation and belief that God favors all US undertakings and supports its unilateral position. These symbols and declarations clearly depict the belief in a supreme nation — one of manifest destiny. In short, each attribute of the design was selected to represent the power of an ideology — one destined to represent a superior power in the world. The theme of the *chosen* people shows up once again.

On a practical level, slogans also serve as powerful symbols. For example, President Reagan referred to the Soviet Union as the "evil empire." and President George W. Bush often used the term "evil" when he spoke of Saddam Hussein's regime. David Frum, a speech writer for Bush, had originally coined the term "axis of evil" as "axis of hatred," and attributed it to any regime that sponsored terror such as Iraq, Iran, and North Korea. The term was changed to "axis of evil" to coincide with the theological

[6]   Solomon's Temple (discussed in Chapter Three) is also replicated in Masonic Lodges.
[7]   www.greatseal.com/levels/fdr1935.html
[8]   www.newamericancentury.org

language used by Bush following September 11, 2001. Extensive use of such phrases thus define "good or bad," "justice or evil," "us and them." In a subtle yet powerful way, these verbal symbols also affect the subconscious and shape attitude. They also affirm the American way as righteous and other ways as misguided, wrongful or just plain evil.

Manifest Destiny: The White Man's Burden

John L. O'Sullivan first coined the term *manifest destiny* in 1845 to explain the vision and power of America as it spread from the Atlantic to the Pacific coast. Within less than 250 years after the Declaration of Independence had been signed, the original thirteen colonies has expanded to an entire nation. Many believed the growth to be ordained by divine providence (as envisioned in the Great Seal) to rule and Christianize the land, whereas for others it was the expansion of the nation that increasing numbers of people might explore and partake of its riches. O'Sullivan proclaimed it to be "... the right of our manifest destiny to over spread and possess the whole of the continent which Providence has given us for the development of the great experiment of liberty and federative development of self government entrusted to us" (Brinkley, 1995).

The motivation and the term *manifest destiny* became a "rallying cry" throughout the nation.[9] Numerous peoples' lives and souls were trampled upon to serve the white man and his cause. Africans were kidnapped from their native homes and sold into colonial slavery; Native Americans were slaughtered and forced into reservations like animals; Mexicans were killed and forced from what once had been their territories; and when slavery became illegal, the

---

[9]   Michael T. Lubragge. Manifest Destiny. The Philosophy that Created A Nation. http://odur.let.rug.nl/~usa/E/manifest/manif1.htm

In November 1994 a group of students from the Arts Faculty of the University of Groningen in the Netherlands under the supervision of George M. Welling created a World Wide Web-site dedicated to the pre-World War I history of the United States of America. http://odur.let.rug.nl/~usa/ This website is a well-documented history of the US and Manifest Destiny.

Chinese "coolies"[10] were promised riches and tricked into coming to America so they could be used for menial labor (primarily to build the railways).

This manifesto was also referred to as the "white man's burden", a burden backed by the belief in the supremacy of the white man and his Christian religion. It was his task to lead and save the inferior people of the world from ignorance and darkness. This term and philosophy were based upon the poem, *The White Man's Burden* by Rudyard Kipling.[11] It justified the violence and maltreatment of the *other* (for the end result would supposedly be in the victims' best interests).

Manifest destiny also provided the rational for America's foreign policy, known as expansionism and imperialism. Some Americans who supported the policy of expansionism also justified their view with the theory of Social Darwinism. In 1893 Herbert Spencer, a British philosopher and sociologist, described the manner in which nations struggled for survival. Spencer believed that advanced societies flourished whereas undeveloped cultures became extinct. In his words, "Therefore, natural order obligates powerful, civilized nations to appropriate the limited resources of the weak" (McGrarth, 2003, p. 5). Spencer's argument, thus, served as an ideological base for expansion.

By the late nineteenth century, the growing industrial economy of the United States was producing more goods than the nation itself could consume. The United States looked for ways to secure its own economic future through a policy of expansionism. It needed new markets for its abundant industrial growth. European nations, such as England, Spain, France, Russia, Portugal, Germany and Belgium had been faced with the same issue and had

---

[10] The term "Coolie" was used for Chinese immigrants brought in to perform hard labor (during the gold rush and the building of the railways). They were typically disrespected, often beaten, ridiculed and paid the most minimal wage possible. Racist Americans became concerned over the number of Chinese and other Asian workers. They protested to the US government who then ended Chinese immigration in 1882.

[11] http://odur.let.rug.nl/~usa/E/manifest/manif5.htm

resolved it by claiming and colonizing land in both Asia and Africa. The United States began to follow this same path.

The vision of power and expansion was not a new concept, for approximately 2000 years ago, the Roman Empire had spread onto three continents and held more than one-fifth of the Earth's population. The United States differed in that it believed that it was led by "divine providence" and that God had given them this right to plunder other lands and victimize their inhabitants. This is where the Darwinian idea of "the survival of the fittest," combined with religious enthusiasm and the idea of the chosen few. It believed its position to be a right — endowed by its Christian foundation. The underlying belief was that the world would be in its rightful place if its inhabitants were converted to westernized Christianity. This is the point where religion and politics have remained in cohort since the beginning of the foundation of the United States — despite the claim on paper of the separation of church and state. It is out there for all to see in our current government as the beliefs and movements of the religious right have infiltrated our government. For example, at a recent conference for members of the religious right, the prior House Majority Leader Tom DeLay (removed due to his indictment for conspiring to funnel corporation funds to State political campaigns) called Bush's faith-based initiatives "a great opportunity to bring God back into the public institutions of our country." The political conference opened with a revised version of the pledge of allegiance: "I pledge allegiance to the Christian flag, and to the Savior for whose kingdom it stands. One Savior, crucified, risen and coming again, with life and liberty for all who believe."

The movement also has agendas that could very well undermine women's rights. We also have to consider the influence that religion and politics played in the abuse and denigration of the female — for these practices were also brought into the new land.

Women's Struggles for Equal Rights

The colonies followed British law concerning women's property rights. In short, property ownership was under control of their husbands. There were enforced requirements during prenuptial and marriage agreements, assuring any separation of property was to be controlled by a man. In fact,

> During the early history of the United States, a man virtually owned his wife and children as he did his material possessions. If a poor man chose to send his children to the poorhouse, the mother was legally defenseless to object. Some communities, however, modified the common law to allow women to act as lawyers in the courts, to sue for property, and to own property in their own names if their husbands agreed. Gradually, the states granted women limited property rights. By 1900 every state had granted married women considerable control over their property.[12]

In fact, women were not allowed to execute a will until 1809. It wasn't until 1839, when Mississippi passed a law granting women limited property rights, the beginning of a series of successes — part of a long arduous struggle.

Lucy Stone, Lucretia Mott, Sojourner Truth, Harriet Tubman, Elizabeth Cady Stanton, Susan B. Anthony, and other feminists saw a relationship between the rights of both women and blacks. The emancipation of slaves allowed the feminist movement to develop regardless of the fact that patriarchal translations of the will of God continued to undermine equality. These women worked equally for the rights of both women and blacks. They represented the true ideals of a democratic government, allowing freedom for all. For example, in July 1848, a declaration was created based upon the Declaration of Independence. Its author, Elizabeth Cady Stanton, wrote that "all men and women are created equal," noting how "the history of mankind is a history of repeated injuries and usurpations on the part of man toward woman" (ibid.) This resulted in the creation of a long list of resolutions addressing such issues as

---

[12] Excerpted from *Compton's Interactive Encyclopedia* (1994, 1995), posted on http://www.wic.org/misc/history.htm

equitable laws, equal educational and job opportunities, and the right to vote. Many of these women were imprisoned and severely abused, but nothing stopped them. Eventually both women and blacks were granted the right to vote.

One of the major controversies in the US government has been women's right to choose. Although the decision to abort should not be taken lightly, at the same time women's rights would be undermined by the rules of the men in charge. Within less than a month after Samuel Alito's appointment to the Supreme Court, South Dakota pushed forth a measure attempting to make abortions illegal and overturn the 1973 ruling known as Roe vs. Wade. The fundamentalist religious right is moving forward in its agenda; hence it is imperative that women not let these challenges stop them from having control over their bodies — a needed step in the struggle for gender equality.

As women continue to enter into governmental, religious, and corporate leadership positions, they could very well provide a needed balance and a healthier world view than the current movement toward globalization. This development may stem the tide of destruction as the patriarchal ideal makes its dying grasp for supreme power — evidenced by the US policies supporting a new world order.[13]

A New World Order:
Globalization, Commercialization and Greed

The project for the New American Century (PNAC) was formally established in 1997 by a think tank motivated with the intention of global leadership. There was considerable focus and concern in regard to sustaining "American influence around the world" and shaping "a new century favorable to American principles and interests."[14] It promoted the use of military might in order to secure American

[13] And it is only fair to say, that many progressive men are not in favor of this dominant stance, and that on the other hand women, some blacks and other minorities sadly agree with the dominant patriarchal stance.
[14] http://www.newamericancentury.org/statementofprinciples.htm

supremacy and safeguard it from any threats or challenges. The PNAC supported a "military that is strong and ready to meet both present and future challenges; a foreign policy that boldly and purposefully promotes American principles abroad; and national leadership that accepts the United States' global responsibilities" (ibid.). Agendas were clearly defined: "to increase defense spending significantly ... modernize our armed forces ... strengthen our ties to democratic allies ... challenge regimes hostile to our interests and values ... promote the case of political and economic freedom abroad ... accept responsibility for America's unique role in preserving and extending an international order friendly to our security, our prosperity, and our principles" (ibid.).

The escalation of war in the Middle East was part of a strategic plan created by the Project for a New American Century. The PNAC was founded by neo-conservatives Robert Kagan and William Kristol, and includes well-known members Dick Cheney, Donald Rumsfeld, Paul Wolfowitz (now heading the World Bank Organization), John Bolton (appointed as US Ambassador to the United Nations) and Dov Zakheim (who was later sworn in as the Under Secretary of Defense, Comptroller, and Chief Financial Officer for the Department of Defense in May 2001). Their goals were formulated in writing as early as 1997 and since that time the entire world has changed. Yet the populace has been led to believe that it is the events of 9/11 that solely initiated these massive changes.

The ideal of democracy had been distorted. Whereas *Democracy* was intended to be a form of government whereupon "the supreme power is vested in the people and exercised directly by them or by their elected agents under a free electoral system," (Webster, 1989, p. 384) the PNAC's global strategies were instead *forcing* their concept of American democracy upon other nations (for example, Iraq). This has been a highly questionable policy given the nature and definition of democracy. Apparently, the PNAC had taken the attitude that Iraq and other Arab nations would be hostile to America's *unique role* in global politics; therefore, plans had

been made to assure dominance and control over the Middle East. The fact that our oil reserves are running out plays a primary role in global politics. In his book, *American Dynasty: Aristocracy, Fortune and the Politics of Deceit in the House of Bush*, former White House strategist, Kevin Phillips, described governmental reports on oil needs in comparison to US consumption and related how Dick Cheney's energy task force,

> predicted that domestic oil production would decline 12 percent by 2020, compelling the United States to import fully two-thirds of its oil. Leverage would continue to swing to the Middle East, with Gulf producers alone expected to provide 54 to 67 of world oil exports in 2020. Next to Saudi Arabia's 262 billion barrels of proven reserves, Iraq was second with 120 billion…Indeed, Cheney and his chief of staff, Lewis Libby, had already participated in drafting a 2000 report for the Project for a New American Century that called for taking over Iraq—this was well before 9/11—as part of a larger, oil-minded Pax Americana. (Phillips, 2004, p. 255)

In the PNAC vision and plans, the United States is deemed to be above all reproach. The principle of checks and balances has been ignored, disagreement not allowed and those who dare to disagree have oftentimes been referred to as *traitors*. Certainly, this is an example of a *closed* system.

The underlying belief of manifest destiny has developed into the building of an empire—a vision of global dominance—with the idea that this will be accomplished "for the good of all." Plans have been formed behind closed doors (a rather strange contradiction to democratic ideals).

On September 11, 2001, Al-Qaeda attacked and destroyed the World Trade Center, and opened the door for the PNAC to obtain their goal of a vastly increased defense spending and military enlargement "in order to secure our safety." The rest is history. The United States moved into Afghanistan. It formed an allegiance with its allies (primarily Britain and Spain) and took over Iraq, while threatening Iran and Syria. The relationship with France, Germany and Russia was impaired due to their disagreement with the unilateral decision to attack Iraq. (No doubt leaders of other nations are also knowledgeable in regards to the PNAC agenda.) Yet rarely, if at all, is the PNAC agenda discussed at any length in media news programs.

In response to policies of secrecy and deception in the Bush regime, the "former US Treasury Secretary Paul O'Neill, for two years the administration's top economic official, a principal of the National Security Council, and a tutor to the new President" (Suskind, 2004, jacket) quit his position. After leaving his office, O'Neill insisted upon having copies of each and every document (adding up to nineteen thousand) associated with him and his position. Because of his inherent respect for openness, honesty and disclosure, he then handed these documents over to the former Wall Street Journal's senior national affairs reporter, Ron Suskind, with the intention of informing the populace of the Bush regimes' policies. This led to the book, *The Price of Loyalty: George W. Bush, the White House, and the Education of Paul O'Neill*, news articles and guest appearances on TV talk shows. But it seems that few influential Americans paid serious attention to secrecy and deceit. The news reporters quickly went onto new items, and serious issues became fleeting memories. Too many citizens have become compliant — unwilling to confront the truths staring them in the face. Many simply ignore the deceit — and cast our democratic ideals and freedom into the shadows of doom.

Robert Kagan, of the founders of the PNAC, proclaimed that Europe had gotten soft (weak and lacking in aggression). He supported the premise "that Americans [were] powerful enough that they need not fear Europeans...that Europe [was] not really capable of constraining the United States" and that since we did share common beliefs it was in our best interests to create European support (Kagan, 2003, p. 102). The move toward the new world order was already in full operation. When CNN and other news stations aired George W. Bush assuring the multitudes the United States would protect itself and rid the world of terrorism, they supported its agenda. Therefore, given this intention, all of its acts would be justified. The idea of democratizing Arab nations led by *evil* regimes and thereby freeing Arab peoples was planted. This implied that dropping cluster bombs and using other weapons of destruction on Arab people during the *Shock and Awe* campaign were to be considered compassionate acts. This premise supported the underlying belief that this was yet another task in the "white man's burden."

This belief in US Anglo-Saxon-style superiority has wrought much injustice throughout the world. More recently, the violent winds of Hurricane Katrina revealed major failures in the US paradigm as the government failed to follow through on its fantasized "burden" in that whites were quickly rescued from the floods and damage while blacks were largely left to fend for themselves. Does democracy truly exist?

The question of democracy is a significant one when one considers its definition: *a form of government in which the power is invested in its people*. Given this interpretation, the goal to replicate and *force* the current style of American democracy upon Arab nations, whether they want it or not, is rather questionable. The type of democracy espoused in the United States may not fit other cultural paradigms, and it is clear that diversity and cultural identity are irrelevant to the PNAC agenda. Also, Middle Easterners correctly ascertained that these newly formed "democratic" nations would in reality be controlled by American superpowers and their economic interests. Our hypocrisies have been clearly revealed.

A Clash of Civilizations

Political scientist, Samuel P. Huntington, foresaw and proclaimed that the "clashes of civilizations are the greatest threat to world peace, and an international order based on civilizations is the surest safeguard against world war" (Huntington, 1997, p. 13). He also noted that the West (primarily the United States and Britain) were the only civilizations to have monetary interests, economics and power affecting all other civilizations. Most other nations are dependent upon assistance from Western monetary systems in order to survive in the world market for they "own and operate the international banking system … provide the majority of the world's finished goods … dominate international capital markets … exert considerable moral leadership within many societies … are capable of massive military intervention … control the sea lanes … access to space … aerospace industry … international communications … and the high-tech weapons industry" (Huntington, 1997, pp. 81–82). Huntington noted that the West sustained its preemptive power by defining its interests as the welfare and security of the *global* community.

In the meantime, CNN and other news media reported how the spoils of war were to be divvied up as large corporations were granted a piece of the Iraqi pie and *the opportunity* to rebuild war-torn Iraq. We now *occupy* Iraq (*occupation* is defined as "the seizure and control of an area by military forces") (Webster, 1989, p. 996). The created Iraqi regime has not really lessened the American presence. It is not surprising that many Iraqis have lost their faith in the American government. They were initially told the US was coming to free them from Saddam Hussein's evil regime; whereas the Iraqi people soon learned that the US, having taken control of its resources, was occupying their country. (The continued disruption has also inflamed long held enmities between Shi'ites and Sunnis, resulting in numerous civilian deaths on a daily basis.)

Other non-Westerners (also members of this global community) have been observing this blatant hypocrisy as cultural norms and religious beliefs are disrespected, Iraqi resources plundered and lands controlled by the dominating Western power. The back cover of the book *Jihad vs. McWorld* clearly describes the result of a runaway form of capitalism and its clash with other civilizations.

> Political scientist Benjamin R. Barber offers a penetrating analysis of the central conflict of our times: consumer capitalism versus religious and tribal fundamentalism. These diametrically opposed but intertwined forces are tearing apart — and bringing together — the world as we know it, undermining democracy and the nation-state on which it depends. On the one hand, capitalism on the global level is

rapidly dissolving the social and economic barriers between nations, transforming the world's diverse popula- tions into a blandly uniform market. On the other hand, ethnic, religious, and racial hatreds are fragmenting the political landscape into smaller and smaller tribal units. (Barber, 1995/2001, back cover)

Barber makes it clear that

neither the politics of commodity nor the politics of resent- ment promise real liberty; the mixture of the two that emerges from the dialectical interplay of Jihad versus McWorld — call it the commodification of resentment — promises only a new if subtle slavery. (ibid., p. 219)

Barber, wrote a new introduction to a more recent edition of this book in 2001 noting that Al-Qaeda had struck the

temple of free enterprise in New York City and the cathe- dral of American military might in Washington, D.C. In bringing down the twin towers of the World Trade Center and destroying a section of the Pentagon with diabolically contrived human bombs. (ibid., p. xi)

In Barber's eyes, these two axial options are terrifying and destructive. The first trend leads to a world of numerous national-states (or tribes) engaged in a gory battle. The sec- ond trend emphasizes globalized economic power, thereby creating uniformity and undermining individual gains.

Renowned economist Joseph E. Stiglitz, a Nobel Laureate and chief economist of the World Bank, believes that global- ization can be a force for world good and that it has the potential to help economically deprived cultures and change the lives of poor peoples (if handled intelligently and ethically). He noted that the International Monetary Fund's (IMF) plan to help the Ethiopians and other poor nations had failed, and that the IMF's plans did not benefit others as envisioned because "the net effect of the policies set by the Washington Consensus has all too often been to benefit the few at the expense of many, the well-off at the expense of the poor" and that "in many cases commercial interests and values have superceded concern for the envi- ronment, democracy, human rights, and social justice" (Stiglitz, 2002, p. 20). In the meantime, one of the PNAC primary members, Paul Wolfowitz, was placed at the head

of the World Bank. We can only wonder what will befall the
American ideal with John Roberts and Samuel Alito heading the Supreme Court, as every one of Bush's appointees
appears to be a major player in this movement (either
because of Christian fundamentalist, large corporate or far
right think tank affiliations).

For many years world renowned political activist Noam
Chomsky has denounced US foreign policy, pointing out
that it undermines democracy, quashes human rights and
promotes the interest of the wealthy few. Functioning
democracy presumes relatively equal access to resources
and that decisions that affect the public are to be made in the
public arena. Chomsky suggests that "The most effective
way to restrict democracy is to transfer decision making
from the public arena to unaccountable institutions: kings
and princes, priestly castes, military juntas, party dictator-
ships, or modern corporations" (Chomsky, 1999, p. 132).

The project "Rebuilding America's Defenses: Strategy,
Forces and Resources for a New Century" plan[15] was created by the PNAC in 2000. It named four strategies, which
were "to defend the American homeland; *fight and decisively
win multiple, simultaneous major theater wars* [authors italics];
perform the 'constabulary' duties associated with shaping
the security environment in critical regions;" and "transform US forces to exploit the revolution in military affairs."
Some research on the readers' part will reveal the immensity of their vision. The group acknowledged that their plan
for "full spectrum dominance" would take a long time,
unless some catastrophic event similar to Pearl Harbor took
place. Therefore, 9/11 provided the opportunity to quickly
execute their plans, and take control of Iraq.

There is little, if any, hope for peace in the Middle East as
long as these ideologies influence the United States (and
Israeli policies). The PNAC plans for ongoing wars and the
redesigning of the Middle East coupled with the far right
Christian thirst for Armageddon is not very hopeful. Any
nation that is not in harmony with their agenda is targeted

[15] http://www.newamericancentury.org/RebuildingAmericasDefen
      ses.pdf

for attack. These neo-conservatives are unconcerned about "collateral damage" (the loss of American, Jewish or Arab lives), for the ideal and cause are more important to patriarchy than the lives of the average human being. *For the authentic woman, the person is the cause*.

Dreams and Realities

The noble idea of democracy manifest in the Declaration of Independence, the US Constitution, and even in Martin Luther King Junior's "I have a dream" speech, are thoughtfully examined by modern thinkers. We witness growing gaps between the rich and poor, huge corporate power structures, and low voting rates. The dream and reality seem to be parting ways — and the American society appears to be in a state of apathy. Robert Kaplan notes that,

> The rise of corporate power occurs more readily as the masses become more indifferent and the elite less accountable. Material possessions not only focus people toward private and away from communal life but also encourage docility. The more possessions one has, the more compromises one will make to protect them. (Goodland, 2001, p. 66)

The assumed democracy thus becomes non relevant to the masses — therefore losing its power as a tool for positive social change. Many social activists, for example Noam Chomsky, Howard Zinn, and Arundhati Roy, among others, poignantly criticize corporate power and political corruption as each undermines democracy and human rights. Roy observes that,

> Every "democratic" institution in this country has shown itself to be unaccountable, inaccessible to the ordinary citizen, and either unwilling or incapable of acting in the interests of genuine social justice…and now corporate globalization is being relentlessly and arbitrarily imposed on an essentially feudal society, tearing through complex, tiered social fabric, ripping it apart culturally and economically. (Roy, 2003, p. 41)

America has represented democracy to the world, and, despite its failures, many nations still strive to follow its examples. As a result of corruption, power and greed, it has led the entire world into chaos. Will Americans continue to support this destructive direction based upon an ill-fated ideology of cultural supremacy and the claim of God-given rights? Or is there still time to reevaluate the positive values established in true democracy? How did we get from A to Z? What has happened to the ideals established in our Constitution in regards to our current predicament? This nation began with the ideals of an *open* system and has now closed its doors to the policies that allow for dialogue, negotiation and ethics. We need to return to the root ideal and practice of democracy. Hopefully, the choice of Nancy Pelosi as the first female speaker of the newly elected Democratic majority House of Representatives represents a change in a positive direction.

Conclusions

The United States was born in rebellion against an imperial power, yet now, under the regime of globalization, it behaves as if there are no limits to its sovereignty. As Michael Hardt and Antonio Negri claim in their book *Empire* (Hardt & Negri, 2002), the US has transformed itself into a nation that dictates to others while claiming a position above international law. In its unilateral decision to bomb and occupy Iraq, the Bush regime ignored the intelligence and concerns of the United Nations, the NATO alliance, the Pope and many other religious leaders, Nobel laureates, and many of its own citizens and activist groups around the world. The Bush regime seriously damaged US relations with other countries, relying, in the end, upon financial threats and promises regarding who would be included in the spoils of the war during *the rebuilding of Iraq*. Its building threats against Iran may well further isolate us from the global community.

The idea of forcing democracy upon Arab nations is ludicrous. This chapter has proposed that the Bush regime and its project for a new American century of global "full-spectrum" dominance were entirely against the ideals upon which this country was founded. Many members of the Bush regime are fundamentalist Christians backing the radical Christian-Zionist ideas for control of the Middle East, and, in particular, Jerusalem (as discussed in Chapter Three). They are driven towards a planetary Armageddon that has nothing whatsoever to do with God, true religion or Jesus, and everything to do with the irrationality of radical, blindly-followed fundamentalist beliefs.

In a speech before the nation on April 13, 2004, George W. Bush noted that "we're changing the world and the world will be better off because of it." He repeated this and similar statements throughout his address. His claims precisely demonstrate the inherent, albeit misguided, belief in manifest destiny and taking up the tasks of "the white man's burden." This coupled with the military stratagem for *full spectrum dominance* (world control),[16] represents a threatening posture towards the global community.

Humanity is racing towards globalization. Sadly, this movement appears to be propelled by political power and corporate greed. And yet, an opportunity to truly know the many other peoples, religions and nations comprising the larger global system offers the promise of a healthier and more unified world—one in which we are more than dissimilar and combative parts. We believe this systemic change is dependent upon the equality and leadership of women for, as we will discuss in Chapter Six, research has shown that women are less apt to be influenced by corrupt political forces and, instead, are more concerned with education, health and social welfare (Dollar et al., 1999).

Global communication offers an opportunity to truly respect one another's differences and engage in an open system of inclusion and respect. In order to achieve that end, it is important to understand the historical events and underlying beliefs that have allowed the perversions of religion and government to dishonor other people, their lands and their religious practices. Throughout recorded history empires have justified their greed when dominating and controlling others. Author and political critic Edward Said (1935–2003) noted that,

[16] http://www.newamericancentury.org, and
http://www.dtic.mil/jointvision/

> Every empire, including America's, regularly tells itself
> and the world that it is unlike all other empires, and that it
> has a mission certainly not to plunder and control but to
> educate and liberate the peoples and places it rules directly
> or indirectly. Yet these ideas are not shared by the people
> who live there, whose views are in many cases directly
> opposite.[17]

During the last century the classical concept of imperialism
evolved into a blend of technology, economics, globalization, and modern politics. The previous era of imperialism
— a mixture of European dominance and capitalist expansion — has not diminished; it has merely changed its appearance. Moreover, we are still experiencing its devastating
effect as evidenced by the anti-colonialist reaction among
the peoples of Asia and Africa. This process of *Colonialism*
"the policy of a nation seeking to extend or retain its authority over other peoples or territories" (Webster, 1989, p. 291)
continues to spread, like a plague, even though it takes
other names and forms.

---

[17]   Al-Ahram weekly online: Issue 648. July 24-30, 2003. Cairo, Egypt.
       http://weekly.ahram.org.eg/2003/648/op2.htm

Freedom cannot be achieved unless the women have been emancipated from all forms of oppression. All of us take this on board that the objectives of [South Africa's] Reconstruction and Development Programme will not have been realized unless we see in visible practical terms that the condition of women in our country has radically changed for the better, and that they have been empowered to intervene in all aspects of life as equals with any other member of society.

Nelson Mandela
May 24, 1994

Chapter Five

Partitions and Global Conflict

Further Tales of Religion and Politics

The tale continues as we examine the results of patriarchal power on other peoples and other lands. Colonialism and Occupation, whereupon the indigenous inhabitants of a land are overruled by the dominating culture, offers a blatant example of the devastating effects of power and greed. Sadly, these atrocities are acceptable to those who commit them in that they deem themselves to be superior to those they rule.

Unfortunately, this ethnocentric thought has become a built-in attitude of Western civilizations towards the rest of the world. The relationship of the West to the East provides one such example. Upon "discovery" of the Orient, Western countries perceived Oriental culture as inferior to their own. In discussing this bias, Edward Said used the term "Orientalism" to show how ethnocentricity had shaped the intellectual structure of Western thinking toward Oriental nations. Said believed that Orientalism shaped the way in which Westerners have dealt with our Asian kin, "by making statements about it, authorizing views of it, describing it, settling it, ruling over it: in short, Orientalism as a Western style for dominating, restructuring, and having authority over the Orient" (Said, 1995, p. 3).

Stereotypical thinking can also be seen within the history of anthropology, itself, which began by studying cultures that were supposedly "primitive," "savage," and or "uncivilized." Early researchers were unable to see this hidden cultural bias. In other words, at its onset anthropology emphasized a unilinear perspective of evolution based upon ideas of the superiority of the Western civilization, and therefore considering other civilizations at lesser stages of development. Some anthropologists, such as Franz Boas, proposed a wider perspective. These new anthropologists pointed to the relativity of cultures. One culture was not deemed to be superior to another in that each culture was to be judged according to its own value system. Anthropologists have now found that the presumption of an absolute cultural standard has fostered arrogance and consequentially brought pain and suffering to those cultures who differed from the dominant culture.

Despite academic anthropology's emphasis on cultural respect, powerful regimes have continued to impose their cultural standards upon those with less power. This phenomenon has been behind both older and more recent conflicts around the globe. As demonstrated below, political conflicts in Asia, Africa and the Middle East are rooted in these ethnocentric approaches. They resulted in an explosion of economic and/or social problems. As the more powerful governments imposed their own model of the modern world and ignored the cultural ways of those they colonized, they created multi-hetero cultures. The resulting confusion has led to continued violence.

As mentioned in Chapter Four, the American political regime led by the current President, George W. Bush, is repeating similar mistakes to those evidenced during nineteenth century Colonialism in forcing the American standard of democracy on the Arab world. The underlying presumption that the West should enforce its reforms upon the Middle East implies an extremely ethnocentric, and dangerous, perspective.

We find ethnocentrism to be a modified form of racism. Although racism represents an ethically unacceptable stance, and a scientifically invalid notion, it continues to dominate in one form or another. It disguises itself as it shapes international relations and preserves social stratifications. Anthropologist Thomas C. Holt claims that "the meaning of race and the nature of racism articulate with (perhaps even are defined by) the given social formation of a particular historical moment" (Holt, 2002, p. 22). Racism is a modern word for the older tribal mentality (stories demonstrating this tribal mentality are found throughout the Old Testament and the Rig Veda). In other words, the tribalism evidenced in old societies, took on a new shape as cultures donned national and cultural identities, fueling prejudice and false pride. Tribal ethics were based on loyalty to the tribe, and fear of other tribes. That fear initiated violent and rough attitudes towards outsiders. This becomes more understandable when examined within the context of the social setting at that time.

Tribalism as such was based on "I" and the "others"; "I" as a group, a nation, one sex (male versus female), a religion, or a community is essentially founded on the idea of superiority. Modern tribalism is not based on that old loyalty to one's kinship relation; rather the grouping has become more complicated. For example, the nation state or a religious group represents the modern form of tribalism. Another primary grouping is that of gender in that the male has been deemed superior to the female across the globe. Racism, ethnocentrism and tribalism are all of facets of patriarchy. Unfortunately this patriarchal, racist spirit is nourished by pseudo religions which inflame hatred and justify oppressions. Neither race nor patriarchy represents a constant that is defined by some divine law outside social and cultural contexts. This is why it is important to review the following sections to examine the many ways this imbalance of power has contributed to oppression around the world, and how each case, as unique as it may appear, repeats the same pattern of "I" am superior, and "I" have the right to dominate and control *the other*.

Colonialism and European Expansion

The 19th century was seen as the great age of European expansion. Slave trade, and what could be considered to be an obscene profit, were common during this colonial era. Britain plundered India's rich resources and relied heavily on its raw materials; for example, the East India Company was used to rule and profit from a vast supply of tea and cotton.[1] The objective was to gain as much foreign territory as possible in order to provide a source of raw materials and preferential markets for British manufactures. In 1871, apart from the possessions of Great Britain in India and South Africa, of Russia in Siberia and central Asia, and of France in Algeria and Indo-China, the European stake in Asia and Africa was confined to trading stations and strategic posts. In South America, for example, Guiana alone was divided into British, Dutch, and French Colonies — and exploited by all.

Religion aligned with these aggressive political moves. During the colonization of America into the United States (occupied territory previously stewarded by its Native American population), Catholic and Protestant missionaries quickly organized to assure they would convert the heathens (a term often used to refer to Native Americans and other non-Christians).[2] Likewise, European missionaries were sent to East Indian and African Colonies to add the natives to their ranks of the saved. A world missionary conference was conveyed in 1910. Although its members were concerned with rampant imperialism and colonization, they were more than aware of the opportunity to win converts. They sided with the latter. Unfortunately, these missionaries wrought disease and death — and their disrespect for the sacred rites of the indigenous peoples often caused a

---

[1] English East India Company was originally a monopolistic trading body that became involved in politics and acted as an agent of British imperialism in India from the early 18th century to the mid-19th century.

[2] (a) Letting the World Know about Jesus: One Person at a Time
       http://www.crwm.org/wmab/wmab_hmt_1800.htm
     (b) http://www.lewisandclark200.gov/people_land_water/blue
       cloud.html

loss of soul resulting in alcoholism and silent despair —
sowing seeds of future wars. But this did not affect the move
to glean riches from the conquered lands and their native
inhabitants. During this era a large majority of women also
sided with the status quo.

In the mid-19th century colonial mercantile justification
had been demolished by Adam Smith and the *Manchester
school* of economists. The *Manchester School* was the term
British politician Benjamin Disraeli used to refer to the free
trade movement in Great Britain. The thriving trades of
Britain with the United States and South America indicated
that political control was not essential for commercial success. In 1852, Disraeli noted that the Colonies had become
the "millstones round our neck" (Barraclough, 2003, p. 244).
Although Disraeli believed in the expansion of the British
Empire, he also recognized the difficulties involved in ruling the Colonies. It took almost a century for all of these
empires to acknowledge their burden. Colonization was
not trouble-free, for the indigenous peoples demanded
their freedom (something the United States is currently
experiencing in its current occupation of Iraq). By 1881
nationalism was on the rise, and anti-colonial reaction
flared through Asia and Africa.

Hence, the Indian National Congress was founded in
1885, symbolizing a great revolt against the British Empire.
The First World War in 1914 also contributed to the incipi-
ent nationalist stirring. As early as 1904, flames of resistance
had been fanned by Japanese victory in the Russian-Japa-
nese war. This victory proved that European powers were
not invincible. During the First World War the European
empires shifted their focus from the Colonies. While
empires were busy in the war front, the Colonies began to
organize, thereby creating an opportunity for opposition
and revolt.

None of the powers, which had partitioned Asia and
Africa into numerous Colonies, were secure in its possessions. Throughout the globe, abused Colonies sought identity and independence and resisted the foreign occupiers.

Although the achievements of nationalists were relatively minor at this stage, they kept the flame of resistance alive.

But the patriarchal movement, fueled by prejudice and fundamentalist mindsets, continued to expand its power. In 1939 Great Britain, France, the Netherlands, Italy, Belgium, Spain and Portugal claimed colonial possessions. However, they shared a new conception of imperial rule, a temporary and limited one. This new perception, combined with a growing opposition in the Colonies, eventually led the empires to govern their Colonies with a greater degree of independence. But the transition from occupation to sovereignty was not an easy one. History tells us that the 20th century wrought increasing inter-racial tension in many of the former Colonies. Since the powers that be had intended to endow their colonial territories with political institutions having few indigenous roots, it is not surprising that colonial withdrawal was frequently followed by acts of revolutionary violence (contributing to the development of repressive regimes). The empires divided Europe, Asia and Africa according to their avaricious needs, disregarding any ethnical/cultural/historical logic, and then left their Colonies in the midst of a crisis. A good example of this is what happened in both Palestine and India. They were promised partition and the resulting crisis perpetuated war in both cases. The British Empire withdrew from Palestine and India (among other Colonies) when inter-racial and inter-religious tensions increased (a similar outcome is already occurring in Iraq even though American troops continue to occupy the country).

In short, the combination of greed, political power and religious prejudice is a deadly one. Its influence has spread throughout the world. The following portrays how these former Colonies paid and continue to pay a horrendous price for their re-definition as national entities. It also demonstrates the problems which continue to manifest as human beings attempt to find a relationship between religion and political organization. In our examination of the roles of patriarchal governments and religious organizations, we have come to the conclusion that humanity is actually exploring the use of these two motivating and organizing forces. And, interestingly enough, each nation seems to find its own unique blend.

It is beyond the scope of this chapter to cover the many incidents and results of Colonialism and occupation, but the following well documents its strategies and results. It is noticeable that Colonialism not only ignored ethnic and religious diversities of the Colonies, but also generated enmity between local peoples according to the principle of *divide and rule*. For example, the British Empire encouraged the Jews' migration to Palestine under the occupation, while overlooking the local inhabitants' interests and aspirations. As such it created a situation where conflicts between the migrant Jews and the indigenous Arab Palestinians would be inevitable. In India, after the Independence, this same power encouraged the spirit of separation between Muslims and Indians in its creation of Pakistan as a distinct Muslim nation, separate from India, while leaving the problem of Kashmir unsolved. This area continues to inflame hatred and wars between the once-friendly Hindus and Pakistani Muslims. The same story with minor differences has been repeated in Ethiopia, Eritrea and Sudan.

The Jewish-ruled state of Israel,[3] the Muslim State of Pakistan, Christian-ruled Ethiopia, and Islamic-ruled Sudan all share common features. They have closed systems where "others" barely survive as subsystems, or overlapping systems. Ruling powers adopt ethnocentric approaches mingled with racism. Religions become a banner under which racism and ethnocentrism hide (as evidenced in the stories below). We have given considerable attention to the Israeli-Palestinian relationship, because it threatens the balance of the entire world.

---

[3]   Actually both Jews and Arabs belong to the land once known as Judea (in that both Isaac and Ismael were sons of Abraham), but the interference of political powers fueling religious oppositions thereby prevented Jews, Palestinian Christians and Muslims from living in harmony (see Chacour, 1984).

Two People, One Land: Israel and Palestine

The Israeli-Palestinian conflict exemplifies the complexity of the themes discussed in Chapter Four — such as state and religious affiliation, the role of economy, and influence of external and internal political powers. In order to fairly address the issue we must take into account the unique history of the Jewish people who have been exiles without a land for almost two thousand years. Their experience of persecution throughout the many lands in which they have lived, culminating in the twentieth century's mass extermination of European Jewry, has deeply impacted the Jewish psyche. For the Jewish people, the creation of the Israeli state represented a return to the Promised Land. It enabled the Jewish people to feel a vital sense of place in the world, after the holocaust and centuries of abuse in foreign lands. At the same time we must acknowledge the fact that the indigenous inhabitants (the Palestinians) had occupied Palestine consistently over a long period of time, and Palestinians were already living on shared land with Jewish people when a limited number of Jewish migrations began during the 19th century.

The Jewish identity is deeply embedded in this area of the world, for it hosts the sacred location of the first and second Temple. Likewise, for Muslims, Jerusalem was the site of the Prophet Muhammad's inner journey from Mecca to the "Furthest Mosque" and his spiritual ascension led by the angel Gabriel. The "Furthest Mosque" became the Al-Aqsa Mosque in Jerusalem (see Chapter Three), the site of the first and second Temples. Muslims once bowed toward Jerusalem, just as they now bow in the direction of Mecca.[4] Given this history, clearly both groups have a deep religious affiliation with the land now known as Palestine and Israel.

More attention is given to this section in Chapter Five because it holds so much power for Jews, Christians and Muslims alike, and, as noted, the tension and fighting is

[4] "Local legend had it that Abraham had visited Ismael in the wilderness and that together they had built the Kaaba in Mecca, the first temple to the one God in Arabia." From foreword by Karen Armstrong to Chittister et al. (2007) p. xi.

affecting the balance of the entire world. The Israeli-Palestinian conflict is too wide for this section to fully explore, and it is not likely to be resolved in the near future. (In fact, the escalation of Israeli attacks on Lebanon as of July 12, 2006, indicates that the situation worsened as a result of a sequence of incidents.[5]) However, our glimpse into past events reveals the roots of the conflict and the role of foreign nations upon Israel's inhabitants. The story did not begin as merely an internal land dispute between Israelis and Palestinians, but rather it represents a clash of far greater forces. Israel was (and continues to be) backed by the all-powerful US, while the Arab world supports the Palestinians. External forces and their need for power and control have deeply impacted this conflict. It is representative of patriarchal patterns, with little concern for the well being of *the other*.

The Creation of a Jewish State

Daniel Boyarin, a scholar of Near Eastern Studies and Rhetoric, explains in his book, *Border Lines: The Partition of Judaeo-Christianity*, that "Jewish" people did not inhabit the area called Palestine at the time of the Roman quashing of the futile Bar Kochba uprising from 132–135 CE, as only Aramaic-speaking people, descendants of the biblical Hebrews, lived in the land. Historically, some of these Semitic people would later become Christians whereas others became Jews after the advent of Rabbinical Judaism. Also, Arabic peoples were from Arabia, and only a handful

---

[5]   According to a report from Noam Chomsky on July 14, both Israel and the US were increasing tension on the Palestinian governance and citizenry in retaliation for voting in Hamas. Also, there was some annexing of the Palestinian territory, and a plan had been announced that Israel was taking over the Jordan Valley. Next, the "Israelis abducted two Gaza citizens, a doctor and his brother. They were taken to Israel, and no one knows their fate. The next day militants in Gaza, probably Islamic Jihad, abducted the Israeli soldier..." Nine Palestinians were killed, and a quarter pound bomb was dropped on the home of a militant leader killing his entire family. Hezbollah then abducted two Israeli soldiers at the border for two reasons, one a ploy for prisoner swap and the other to divert Israeli attention away from the Palestinians. The latter has been proposed by various analysts and was included in an article in London's Financial Times.

would have been that far north. According to Boyarin, origi-
nally there were no boundary lines for either "Israel" or
"Palestine" as the Romans had divided the territory into
Judea, Galilee and what is now Western Galilee (which
included part of Lebanon). In short, boundary lines for
Israelis or Palestinians in the land now called Israel (by the
Jews), and Palestine (by the Palestinians) did not exist in
ancient times (Boyarin, 2004).

The Arab population itself began to increase with the
advent of Islam. When the Muslims ended the Byzantine
rule in 638, the Arabs converted to Islam, although a number of these Palestinians were, and remained, Christians. A
small Jewish minority also resided in the area throughout
these changes.

The Crusaders conquered and established the Latin
kingdom of Jerusalem (1099–1187). This ended when
Salaheddin liberated Jerusalem, and established a regime
whereby Palestine was ruled by Egypt. It was then incorporated into the Ottoman Empire until that empire disinte-
grated, and British forces took over the land. Arabs
represented a much larger majority by that time.

However, the proportion of inhabitants began to change
during the late 19th century as Jews from Eastern Europe,
persecuted by the Russian regime, immigrated into the
area. In 1917, during World War I, the British government
stated in the *Balfour Declaration* that it looked with favor on
the establishment of a Jewish National Home in Palestine.
Forming a Jewish national home under British protection
would circumvent both the promise to the French to inter-
nationalize Palestine and the inclusion of Palestine in the
Arab zone. By offering to help the Zionists establish this
home, Britain could place its own troops in Palestine and
thereby control that strategic prize near the Suez Canal as
well as preside over the holy places in Jerusalem (Lesch &
Tschirgi, 1998, p. 8). Ideals and strategies were formed, with
little consideration for the rights and needs of the indigenous Arab and Palestinian people.

Jewish immigration from Europe increased sharply in
response to Hitler's policies. In 1922, Jews formed 11 per-

cent of the population. This increased to 29 percent by 1936, partially because of illegal immigration (Barraclough, 2003). During the mandate years (1921–1948), Britain restricted immigration in order to defend their control of its Arab population, needs and interests. This resulted in human tragedies as holocaust survivors and refugees, trapped on vessels in the Mediterranean Sea, found themselves unwelcome on any shore. For example, in 1941, the '*Struma*' ship was the last to leave Europe during wartime. The '*Struma*' carrying 769 Jewish refugees was forbidden from entering Palestine or embarking in Turkey, and eventually went down in the Black Sea.

Following the holocaust of European Jewry, the Jewish people demanded that the survivors be allowed to immigrate to Palestine. The Anglo-American Committee of Inquiry in 1946 supported the holocaust survivors' settlement and proposed that Palestine become a joint Jewish-Arab state (Lesch & Tschirgi, 1998). There was considerable Jewish American pressure to support this move. The Arabs, however, feared that such immigration would change the demographic balance, in which they were the majority. The increasing intensity in the region caused the British government to declare its intention to withdraw from the territory.

In 1947, the United Nations General Assembly adopted a plan to partition Palestine into Jewish and Arab states, whereupon Jerusalem would be under international control, despite a fierce opposition from Arab governments. At this point the dual-entities existence became the central issue in Middle East politics. The Soviet Union and the United States were the primary "super-powers" shaping the region during the Cold War. Although both these nations supported the partition idea, they each had their own agenda.

Soviet support was probably based on Moscow's desire to see British rule in Palestine ended as soon as possible as this would open possibilities for the extension of Soviet influence. American support was based more on popular sympathy for the statehood project, which had been carefully cultivated by the Zionists during World War II, and on

President Truman's interest in alleviating the Jewish refugee problem (Taylor, 1991, p. 26).

Noam Chomsky explains in his book, *The Fateful Triangle* that the United States had hoped to create a strong relationship with Gamal Abdel Nasser, Egypt's past President, in order to gain a more stable footing in the Middle East. Nasser had been supported by the CIA, whereas the US-Israeli relationship was weak at the time. Chomsky writes that, "From the late 1950s, however, the US Government increasingly came to accept the Israeli thesis that a powerful Israel is a 'strategic asset' for the United States, serving as a barrier against indigenous radical nationalist threats to American interests, which might gain support from the USSR" (Chomsky, 1983, p. 3.).

More recently, Chomsky called Israel a military arm intended to support US interests in the Middle East. In fact, Israel is the biggest recipient of US military funding. For example, the Jewish Voice for Peace reports that the United States "pays for the guns and ammunition, F-16 bombers, and Apache helicopters that are used to carry out Israel's occupation of Palestinian land and people." A lot of money, power and religious ideals have been used to support the state of Israel, but this Jewish group points out that the occupation "serves neither Israelis, Palestinians, nor Americans".[6]

Top advisors in these powerful nations shaped policies that added to the conflict. During Nixon's presidency (1969–1974), Henry Kissinger heavily emphasized the Israeli-United States relationship. Kissinger believed that the United States should rely on Israel and have a greater role in the region in order to contain the Soviets. Washington considered "Israel's surrogate role more important to American interests than the conclusion of peace between Israel and Arabs, including the Palestinians" (Taylor, 1991, p. 131). In other words, the power interests stand supreme in comparison to the lives and well-being of the people (a primary difference between masculine and feminine values). This led to an increasing repression of the Arab and

---

[6]   http://www.jewishvoiceforpeace.org/publish/article_17.shtml

Palestinian occupants of the land — who lacked a voice in any of the decisions being made.

During the last decade we have witnessed yet another aggravation of the situation with growing despair on both sides. Benny Morris wrote extensively on the Zionist-Arab conflict in his book, the *Righteous Victims,* and quoted the poet W. Auden in his assessment of the ongoing violence: "I and the public know what all schoolchildren learn: Those to whom evil is done do evil in return" (Morris, 1999).

Jews, who were an uprooted minority for centuries, now control Palestinians in a military occupation. They regularly attack and kill militants, innocent civilians and their children. In response, Palestinian refugees shoot into Israeli settlements, and send suicide bombers to kill innocent Jewish civilians, and their children. Both are motivated by the tribal law of an eye for an eye and a tooth for a tooth, although it is obvious that the Israelis have the military power and exercise a disproportionate amount of violence. The threat of suicide bombers has initiated much fear in the Israeli people, just as military attacks keep Palestinians in a heightened state of fear. The Israelis fail to acknowledge that oppression fosters this violent response, just as their own history of oppression has fostered their current stance. Israelis and Palestinians may have more in common than they believe. Civilians on both sides have been traumatized. In short, it is the tragic story of two peoples, tangled in a gory struggle — both fighting for the land, religion, security, dignity, and sovereignty. Tragically, these ideals have been the ploy for military aggressions and erroneous, and irrational, religious fundamentalist agendas.

The High Price of Sovereignty

On the day of British withdrawal, 14 May 1948, David Ben Gurion proclaimed the state of Israel, as the war between the Jews and Palestinian Arabs began. Literally, on the day the State of Israel was declared, the Arab countries initiated a massive attack in opposition. "Egypt sent troops into the Gaza strip and Negev, Trans-Jordan dispatched its Arab legion to the West Bank, the Syrian army approached the Sea of Galilee, and Lebanon sent token forces into northern Galilee" (Lesch & Tschirgi, 1998, p. 11). These colossal forces were defeated and the greater part of Palestine became Israel.

For the Jewish people it was a 2,000-year-old dream coming true; some saw it as metaphorically alluding to the David and Goliath story in which the young and the determined had overcome the dreaded giant. Many believed that God had ordained Israel's victory. The war had a huge effect on Arab countries as well. Their defeat led to a string of events. It perpetuated a *coup d'etat* (putsch, takeover) in Syria in 1949, the assassination of King Abdullah of Jordan in 1951, and a *coup d'etat* in Egypt in 1952, led by Colonel Gamel Abdel Nasser. Following the war, two thirds of the Palestinian Arabs became refugees in Jordan, Gaza, Syria, and Lebanon. The neighboring Arab countries allowed for the immigration of many Palestinians, but numerous other Palestinians were turned away. Also, many Palestinians did not want to leave and relinquish the land they had always known, but their property rights were often taken away, and they were relegated to confined areas. From the Israeli perspective, its political stance was based on its love of the land it cherished as a religious ideal, as well as its mistrust of the surrounding Arab countries that had refused to recognize its existence as a nation. (The latter contributed to its fear of persecution and the belief that aggression would lead to and assure success.)

An intervention by external forces led to further wars. After a swift victory in the Six-Day war in 1967 (which began when Egypt closed the Straits of Tiran to Israeli shipping), Israel began its governance of the Golan Heights, the West Bank, the Gaza Strip and the entire city of Jerusalem. The Israelis reacted to this ownership with amazement, jubilation, and relief as they flooded into East Jerusalem to visit holy places. Jews could pray again at the Wailing Wall in the old city of Jerusalem, the remaining section of the Second Temple. This had been the only section the Romans had left standing in the demolitions of 70 CE. Whereas the Israelis rejoiced, the Palestinians were left in increasing despair—a breeding ground for growing resistance movements.

David Ben Gurion was the guest of honor at the Labor Party conference shortly after the war. But Ben Gurion was not festive. He believed that "Israel was overextended, that it had bitten more than it could chew and that it should return nearly all the conquered territory immediately" (Lazare, 2003, p. 25.). The Israeli government found itself unable to formulate a coherent policy. Some viewed the lands as a bargaining chip in the return to peace, some wanted to deepen the buffer zone against the vast Arab front and others saw the land as part of the promised Jewish kingdom. Since 1967, Israel has contended with a desperate, and increasingly hostile, Palestinian population, which it placed under military rule, as the Arab-Israeli tension steadily mounted.

The situation might have gone in a healthier direction if the Jewish people had blended with the people already inhabiting the land; but there were powerful political and religious forces in the British and US governments supporting the development of what was to be a solely Israeli government. No one provided the psychological and spiritual support to enable the changes to work effectively for both the Jewish and the Arab peoples. The following section provides a history of the development of the Israeli state.

The Blending of Religious and Political Influences

The Israeli-Palestinian conflict is essentially a territorial one, propelled by external powers with strategic interests in the region. There is an obvious religious demarcation (Jews versus Palestinian Arabs who are primarily Muslim), but it appears that politics may have more to do with the problem than religion. Arabs and Jews shared the land for many years before these nationalistic aspirations took hold. The nature of affiliation to the land was altered by the role of *realpolitik when* practical and material factors rather than theoretical or ethical values began to shape politics. We should bear in mind that in ancient times the current Middle

Eastern nations simply did not exist as separate territories; rather, they were all part of the "Fertile Crescent."

Historically, the Greeks and Romans called this land *Palestina* because of the many Philistines who lived in the area, and it was generally known by its Arabic name, Filastin, during the Ottoman period when the land was part of Syria (*Columbia Encyclopedia*, 2000). It could be that some Palestinians are descendants of the ancient Philistines of Canaan whereas others are immigrants of Arabian descent. Ancient peoples were nomadic,[7] including the early Israelite[8] and Arab peoples. But, despite oppositional views regarding which group has more rights to the land, history indicates that both groups have a long history in the region, and, as noted earlier, there are no ancient claims to any specific piece of land for either group as the boundaries have continually changed over a long period of time. It is also a fact that the Palestinians have consistently lived on the land for several hundred years. Both have equal ownwership. Genesis 15:18 clearly states that Abraham was told by the Lord that the land was being gifted to his "seed," and this includes both Ishmael and Isaac.

Historically, Muslims have identified themselves as a single entity — the *Ummah*, (the Nation). However in its beginnings, the Ummah was not exclusive to Muslims, for Jews and Christians were included as believers in one God (monotheistic tradition). In the twentieth century, British and French governments created a separate Syria, Lebanon, Jordan, Saudi Arabia, and Iraq, thus carving the Ummah, into distinct entities. The current Israeli-Palestinian conflict reflects this severance and the problems caused by the policies of patriarchal religious ideals and political regimes on both sides. The following presents some of the background of Zionist ideology, and its influence on the Israeli nation.

---

[7]   We also have to keep in mind that scientific discoveries are confirming that all of humanity began in Africa and eventually spread into other lands. We are all immigrants.

[8]   The early Israelites were descendants of Jacob, i.e. nomadic tribes. Genesis 32:28 clearly denotes that the Lord changed Jacob's name to Israel to honor *his transformative state of consciousness* after a night of wrestling with an angel (as discussed in Chapter Two).

Historically, Israel was conceived within the concept of a *Jewish State* as Theodor Herzl envisioned it in his 1896 manifesto (Lazare, 2003, p. 23). The Zionist Revisionist ideology was initiated by Ze'ev Jabrotinsky and Menachem Begin in the 1920s. The movement rested on three pillars, namely, "the Jewish people, the Jewish language and the Jewish land: and all three had to be reclaimed in their entirety in order to insure the integrity of the Zionist project" (Kaplan, 2005). This movement, coupled with the dilemma of the many Jews who needed refuge following the Holocaust, set the stage for the current plight of the Israeli Jewish people, the Arabs and Palestinians.

Since Herzl called that First Zionist Congress in 1897, Zionism "has been under ideological and political assault" as many people have not agreed with its tenets (Lazare, 2003, p. 24). The political Jewish movement, known as Zionism, gained momentum in the late 19th century in response to growing anti-Semitism. It sought to reestablish a Jewish homeland in Palestine. Zionism (or Jewish Nationalism) derives from the Zion hill of Jerusalem on which the City of David was built. The 2,000 years of yearning for Zion encompassed all aspects of the Jewish spiritual life. For example, a daily prayer includes Psalm 137: "If I forget you thee, O Jerusalem, let my right hand forget her cunning." The longing for a land of religious heritage has been a major theme in Judaism. This is why Herzl used the slogan: "A land without a people for a people without a land" to promote his ideology. The statement, however, undermined the history and aspirations that the Arab population had for the same land — for each has a valid claim. Also, this patriarchal ideal of conquering and claiming lands, while abusing the natural inhabitants, is an ill-begotten one. It can only lead to continued violence for its foundation is corrupt. Yet history keeps repeating itself, and apparently will continue to do so until we heed its message.

The Israeli-Palestinian dispute has been intensified by religious differences. Therefore, a solution of secular democracy in a bi-national state for both Arabs and Jews would not easily be obtained. The ideological debate over such ideas in Israel is bitter, serious, and a continuous one. Although religion is not the entire cause of the problem, it has provided a powerful unifier. Both males and females are united in the patriarchal notion of a holy mission. This is evident in the attitudes of the settlers residing on Palestinian lands. The majority of the settlers in the occupied territories in Israel use biblical texts to justify their right over the land (as discussed in Chapter Three). For example, Ezekiel 36:24 is used by Zionist fundamentalists to justify the Israeli occupation and the reclaiming of Israel. The passage reads "I will take you from the heathen and gather you out of all countries, and will bring you to your land."

As evidenced, there were many influences leading to the building of the Israeli State. The Revisionist, Yehoshua Heschel Yevin had believed it was important for the Jews to develop strength, whereas A.D. Gordon, the initiator of what is called Labor Zionism, believed it was important to first establish a strong society by laboring the land. During the pre-Israeli State, the Labor Zionists focused on

> creating social institutions that would allow for the development of a viable and productive society [for example, the kibbutzim settlements]. They created a network of companies, unions, and social services that would be the backbone of the emerging Jewish community in Palestine ... The Revisionists, on the other hand, had no interest in social projects; they did not establish settlements, agricultural or otherwise. For them, Zionism had to pursue a single goal: namely, developing enough military strength to claim the entire land. (Kaplan, 2005)

The "Zionist Right" under, first Jabotinsky's leadership, in the mid-30s, followed by Menachem Begin's after 1943, influenced a movement that did not believe in nor support any form of compromise for the land.

> To Begin, the Jews were in constant battle against Amalek, the tribe who came to symbolize the archetypal enemy of the Jewish people in each generation. And after the Holocaust, it was the Arabs who were the modern-day Amalekites — the heirs of the Nazis, who were out to destroy the Jewish people ... it was the mythical struggle between the chosen people and its mortal enemies [an apocalyptic battle]. (ibid.)

Thus fear, itself, contributed much power to the establishment of the Israeli State. The ideals of power and place
became realities following the 1967 War and the Occupation
of the Mandatory Israel. This resulted in the emergence of
increasing numbers of settlements, all influenced by the
ideals that preceded them.

Since its early beginnings Judaism has represented some
sort of struggle over land itself. They've fought for it, owned it,
lost it, and had an identity of being "wanderers" until the opportunity arose for the Jewish State, and the development of
its policies, along with the expansion of its settlements.

According to the Israeli Interior Office there are over
250,000 Jewish settlers in the West Bank, and another
200,000 in East Jerusalem. The evacuation of four settlements was not as hopeful as portrayed, especially given the
fact that settlers in the West Bank had increased by 9,000 in
2004-2005. In reality, the withdrawal of Israeli troops from
the West Bank never occurred, and the separation wall
represents the largest prison ever built. In the meantime, the
Israeli government keeps its Jewish citizens in a state of fear
by assuring that its aggressive actions will protect them,
and in so doing, takes advantage of their fear of anti-
Semitism, while shielding them from the evidence of its
own violence against the Palestinian population.

The rising Palestinian population represents a threat to
the Israeli control of the land. One of the main arguments
many Israelis have against a bi-national state is that they
fear an Arab/Palestinian majority. High birth rates among
the Arab population, and low birth rates among the Israelis
(excluding the ultra-Orthodox population) will eventually
create a demographic situation in which the Jews will
become the minority. In an attempt to avoid this dilemma,
and to assure dominance over the Palestinian-Arab population and the land, the Israeli government has welcomed and
funded increasing immigration of American and European
Jews.[9] In fact, according to media reports, it

---

[9]   200 French Immigrants Arrive in Israel. Haaretz news, 7/29/04 by
       Amiram Barket and Yuval Azonlay.

offers loans of up to $25,000 to help with moving and absorption expenses, according to need, which becomes a grant if the newcomers stay three years. The average family receives $15,000 to $18,000 and a single from $5,000 to $8,000 ... in addition to the subsidized flight from the US.[10]

But Zionism and the far right Christian obsession with Armageddon are also behind these moves.

For an orthodox Jew, who views the state of Israel as part of the fulfillment of the Covenant, expressed in Ezekiel 36:24, a territorial compromise will violate that same Covenant. The mythical battle continues its influence, and actualized destruction for this position has led to the domination of Palestinians, and their own claims to the land. It has created the position of Palestinian extremists and suicide bombers justifying murder as a religious duty to protect what they believe to be their own rights. It has led the Israeli government to exercise collective punishment against the Palestinian population.

Politics and religion have both contributed to this ongoing nightmare; but religion itself is a potent mechanism behind the ideals that inspire and unite people, politicians, freedom-fighters, militants and terrorists to engage in destructive behaviors. Both Jews and Palestinians have historical reasons for understanding Arundhati Roy's commentary that

> They [fascists] have mobilized human beings using the lowest common denominator-religion. People who have lost control over their lives, people who have been uprooted from their homes and communities, who have lost their language, and being made to feel proud of *something* ... something they just happen to be. And the falseness, the emptiness, of the pride is fueling a gladiatorial anger that is then directed towards a simulated target that has been wheeled into the amphitheater. (Roy, 2003, p. 41)

The Israeli government has been influenced by the agenda of the Project for a New American Century, discussed in the

---

[10] Julie Stahl. (July 15, 2004). North American Jews Realize Dream to 'Come Home" to Israel. CNS News.com, Jerusalem Bureau Chief. http://www.cnsnews.com/ViewForeignBureaus.asp?Page=%5CF oreignBureaus%5Carchive%5C200407%5CFOR20040715c.html

previous chapter. A report was created in the late 1990s by the Institute for Advanced Strategic and Political Studies regarding plans for Israeli strategies they hoped to initiate in 2000. It was presented to the then Prime Minister Netanyahu, who had the wisdom to ignore it. The document "A Clean Break: A New Stratagem for Securing the Realm"[11] outlined a plan for the *new Middle East*.[12] Thus, just as the far Christian right has backed the plans of the PNAC and supported its ideals that violence and dominance will protect US borders, the far right Zionists have influenced a vast number of Israelis that violence and aggression will assure their safety. And, Islamic fundamentalists are responding to this paradigm. Each group believes that only power and violence will assure their goals are met. Religion and politics have melded without concern for the deaths of the innocent.

Like many Arab nations, Israel does not recognize a separation of religion and state, simply because it is the *Jewish* State. However, the country has also been torn by what can be defined as "civil war" between secular and religious Jews around social issues as well as political ones. Since the creation of Israel, the gap between secular and orthodox Jews has widened.

Regardless of religious beliefs and population issues, Asad Ghanem, an Arab scholar, sees the bi-national model as a necessity since "the two people have no choice but to live together in a single state" (Ghanem, 2001, p. 196.) Bi-nationalism will create a situation similar to that of the black majority of South Africa, as Ghanem describes,

> ... at the first stage, given the balance of power in the region, the Jews will continue to dominate the Palestinians and even intensify the conditions of control, discrimination, and repression. Nevertheless, with a new growing fragment among the Palestinians and a willingness to initi-

---

[11] Iraq is addressed and targeted in this document. It was considered to be a threat to Israel. This and its strategic position in the Middle Eastern oil market had much to do with the attacks to occur a few years later.

[12] The Institute for Advanced Strategic and Political Studies, Jerusalem and Washington. http://www.iasps.org/strat1.htm

ate violent action against Jewish control … one can antici-
pate the development of local as well as international
pressure to allow the Palestinians to participate … in managing the affairs in the country on an equal basis. (ibid.)

Needless to say, such a solution is not acceptable even
among most of the left-wing liberals in Israel. Israel was created as a Jewish state, and because of its ideals and its fears
related to the relentless history of anti-Semitism in the
world, it strives to maintain its identity. Also, Uri Avneri, an
Israeli peace activist, argues that both Israelis and Palestinians are not "ready to live together as supra-national citizens … two states are needed for two peoples. This will
direct the national feelings … into reasonable, constructive
channels".[13] Both groups have to release their historical
fears and defenses. They have to negotiate with respect for
one another's rights to live in peace. Obviously, this option
is not open for discussion at this time, and without the help
of the International community, it will not take place.

In reality, an even greater barrier stands between the Jewish population and the Palestinians. A large wall has been
created to separate, and one might say "to imprison", the
Palestinians from the Israelis. Israeli officials have used the
term "security fence," to describe this wall. The hope was to
prevent terrorists from entering Israel and massacring civilians in buses and cafes (although the "separation" has not
prevented the Israeli military from entering Palestinian territory, killing targeted militants and ordinary citizens in the
vicinity, and demolishing homes and orchards).[14] In fact,
the reason given for the summer 2006 kidnappings of Israeli
soldiers by Palestinian and Hezbollah militants was based
both on retaliation for Israeli aggression, with the intention
of negotiating the release of some of the 8,000 to 10,000 Palestinian prisoners held in Israeli prisons (many held without a formal charge).[15]

---

[13] Cited at *The Nation* (2003, December). p. 1.

[14] Mosaic: Daily News from the Middle East. LinkTV. San Rafael, CA.

[15] Israel has a long and bitter history with Hezbollah. In the late 1970s,
Lebanon was ruled by a radical Palestinian regime. The Israelis
attacked Lebanon and ousted the Palestinian leaders. At first the

This situation causes grief in the hearts of those people who love all human beings equally. Innocent citizens on both sides of the dispute over the land, and the separation wall, live in continuous fear. They simply want to earn a living through their work, enjoy their families and their lives. They want to move freely through their streets and cities without fear, but for the Palestinians, the separation fence causes immense suffering and hardship, as reported by the World Bank (cited in Ha'aretz newspaper).[16] In many cases, it splits villages in half, prevents children and teachers from access to schools, separates families, cuts off farmers from their lands, and limits employment options. The wall has intensified the hostility between the two populations. It stands as a glaring representation of human divisiveness, and has created a seedbed for retaliatory violence.

Military Action and Palestinian Rights

Prejudice, fear and hatred exists against the Palestinians. Being an Arab is not a moral reason for denying the Arab and Palestinian people the right to a sovereign state, including the right to a safe, decent life. The continuous insistence on long term evacuation of Palestinians from the occupied territories represents a continued threat to the very existence of the Palestinian people, and the policy only aggravates hatred and furthers violent activism. For example, Golda Meir (1898–1978) denied that Palestinian people existed,[17] implying that they should be incorporated into Arab countries, and leave the now "Israeli- owned" land forever. Even though Meir was a woman, her ideology and governance were patriarchal in nature.

Shi'ites were pleased, but then the Israelis began to attack them. Ariel Sharon was deemed to be responsible for assassinating hundreds of Palestinian civilians, and indicted for committing war crimes and crimes against humanity. Hezbollah emerged during this time as a military force to oust the Israeli occupation. So the enmity has a long history. The fact that Iran and Syria support Hezbollah could initiate further warring.

[16]   http://www.gush-shalom.org/thewall/worldbank.html
[17]   Meir quoted by Sarah Honig, Jerusalem Post, 25 November 1995

Arab nations have felt betrayed by the United States for the US continues to negate the plight of the Palestinians, literally ignoring reports from numerous Human Rights organizations. Amnesty International reported on May 15, 2004 that,

> For decades Israel has pursued a policy of forced eviction and demolition of homes of Palestinians living under occupation in the West Bank and Gaza Strip and the homes of Israeli Arabs in Israel. In the past three and a half years the scale of the destruction carried out by the Israeli army in the Occupied Territories has reached an unprecedented level.
>
> More than 3,000 homes, hundreds of public buildings and private commercial properties, and vast areas of agricultural land have been destroyed by the Israeli army and security forces in Israel and the Occupied Territories in the past three and a half years. Tens of thousands of men, women and children have been forcibly evicted from their homes and made homeless or have lost their source of livelihood. Thousands of other houses and properties have been damaged, many beyond repair. In addition, tens of thousands of other homes are under threat of demolition, their occupants living in fear of forced eviction and homelessness.

The mandatory Israeli military has attacked and killed demonstrators with rubber or plastic-coated metal bullets and live ammunition. Amnesty International reported that these weapons "were potentially lethal, suitable for combat situations, not for policing violent demonstrations." According to the US Report on Human Rights: "There are credible reports that police failed to protect Arab lives and property in several incidents in which Jewish citizens attacked Arab citizens".[18] Also, the media, in both the US and Israel, ignores the settlers' acts of violence against civilians in the occupied land and Jerusalem. And, these conditions have worsened, for as Palestinian militants retaliated, the Israeli responses increased in immensity. It is a patriarchal belief that if a nation increases its level of violence and fear, the nation will conquer its enemies — a very dangerous paradigm indeed.

---

[18] http://www.state.gov/g/drl/rls/hrrpt/2000/nea/794.htm

The majority of the International community (omitting the US) spoke out in opposition to Israeli's "disproportionate" response to the kidnapping of a few of its soldiers in that many innocent Palestinian civilians were killed following the incident, including children, and the water, electrical power and fuel were cut off for a large segment of the Palestinian population. The entire infrastructure of Lebanon has been decimated along with hundreds of its citizens. The death toll continues to rise both in Lebanon and Israel. The majority of victims include women and children. Likewise in Israel it is the innocent who die and suffer the cost of patriarchal ideologies.

We remind readers that many Israeli Jewish citizens are good people who do not support the demeaning and abuse of Palestinians at the checkpoints, or the Israeli military violence in the Palestinian territories. There are many peace movements taking place within the country. The problem is primarily with the politicians, religious fanatics and their followers. Also, many Israeli citizens have been indoctrinated and are not aware of the extent of Israeli violence against the Palestinian people by the Israeli government (just as many US citizens are ignorant of the true history of American foreign policy throughout the world).

But the above inequity does not justify suicide bombings, and the murder of innocent Israeli Jews. Violence on either side is unacceptable. But a closed system is in place, and negotiations are continually thwarted. The United States government tends to support Israeli policy at the expense of Palestinians' rights. In criticizing this general trend of American policy, Noam Chomsky notes how the

> US government has been, and continues to be, a major supporter of state-supported terrorism, favoring retaliatory or preemptive aggression over mediation in the world court, and avoiding accountability by excluding itself from the globally accepted definition of terrorism. (Chomsky, 2002)

In the Super-Power's (US) terminology, Israel is a success story. In a half century a population of what were predominantly immigrants came to an underdeveloped area and created a democratic nation with an advanced standard of living, a high-tech economy, and a sophisticated military. But from the perspective of the human condition, political interests and ethnocentrism imposed a hideous barrier between Jews and Arabs. For the two peoples, each of whom desires a safe haven, this region has become an increasingly dangerous place to be either Jewish or Palestinian. For the Israelis, the escalating US-supported war, with its Arab and Muslim neighbors, threatens the well-being of the entire world.

Separate Religions, Separate States: India and Pakistan

Politics and power are also behind the Hindu and Muslim conflict over Kashmir. Historically, Colonialism had spread into India, placing it under British rule for over a century. The British East India Company's hegemony was an established fact on the Indian continent; so much so that India was later absorbed into the world economy as a dependent of Great Britain, rather than on its own merits. However, overt British racism reinforced increasing awareness of an Indian identity; and in 1885, the Indian National Congress, the first all-Indian political organization, was founded in response. It soon developed an extremist wing that questioned the alien's right to rule India. In this struggle for independence Gandhi deployed his weapon of *satyagraha* (non-violent resistance), and initiated a massive non-violent movement. The political response was the Amritsar massacre of Indians, increasing racial bitterness.

Indian Muslims were active members of the British resistance forces. They were incensed by the allies' treatment of their spiritual leader, a Turkish sultan. The Non-Cooperation Movement (1920–1922), aimed at readdressing the "Khalifat wrong" and winning *swaraj* (self-rule), organized the first all-Indian mass movement. But the Hindu-Muslim movement unity was but a temporary one.

For the most part, Indian Muslims and Hindus lived together in friendship, and had done so for centuries. In August 1947 the subcontinent of India gained its independence from Britain, after 400 years of imperial rule, and long

held friendships would soon dissolve into terror and violence. Seven years earlier, the soon to be Pakistani leader,
Mohammad Ali Jinnah (1876–1948), had called for the partition of India and establishment of an independent Pakistan.
The Muslim League had gained a growing influence and it
backed up Jinnah. The partition solution was seen as a way
to resolve the Hindu-Muslim conflict.

Talks between Gandhi and Jinnah failed as plans continued. This eventually led to Lord Mountbatten's 1947
announcement of the partition of Pakistan from India. Gandhi was totally against this partition. He believed that Muslims and Hindus should remain in unity, for their past
relationship had been a positive one. Jinnah, as well, did not
initially favor the partition. Although he was a non-reli-
gious person, Jinnah was strongly influenced by extremists
at the Muslim League (Purcell, 2004). Both he and Gandhi
foresaw the human tragedy that would result from this partition. British India was partitioned into Pakistan and comprised of a Muslim majority. In that India was primarily
Hindu, religion and politics were deeply wedded in this
move. The Princely states,[19] including Kashmir, were free to
choose whether to join India or Pakistan. In this case, as in
the case of Israel and Palestine, Britain began to question its
rule of the Colonies in the midst of the increasing ethnic tension. When the Hindu-Muslim rioting was further aggra-
vated, British rule departed from India and endowed
Pakistan its independence.

The creation of the two states brought about a devastating, massive migration in which millions of Muslims fled to
the newly designated Pakistan, whereas millions of Hindus
segregated themselves into India's new borders. Never
before, in human history, had such a mass exodus of people
occurred in such a short time. Between August and November 1947, as many as 2,800,000 refugees crossed the border
in 673 refugee trains. The wealthy used the airways, and six
to seven planes flew every day between India and Pakistan.

---

[19]   The British ruled India with two administrative systems: Provinces
       (completely under British control) and Princely States (areas with
       local ruler or king with honorary titles like Maharaja, Raja, etc.).

The poorer had to leave by foot, in a massive human column known as *kafilas*. Muslims were traveling west to Pakistan while Hindus and Sikhs were roving east to India. Some large *kafilas*, consisting of over 400,000 people were so enormous that it took eight days for the foot column to cross a given spot. Urvashi Butalia, an Indian-born author, daughter to partition refugees, explains that everyone was subject to an attack on this treacherous journey. It did not matter if one was traveling by train, car, lorries or walking. It did not matter if one was Hindu or Muslim, or stricken with poverty. Every one was in danger as the kafilas passed one another (Butalia, 2000, p. 61).

Those who did not suffer direct violence endured other devastating affects. The madness of alienating millions of people was inconceivable, and apparently both governments were not prepared for its results. During the partition all administrative units were divided. This harmed all aspects of life: families were divided, homes destroyed, crops were left to rot, villages were abandoned, education was disrupted, and salaries, pensions and funds were lost. For years afterward the two governments attempted to find some sort of agreement in regard to what was owed and to whom it should be paid. Sadly, this entire devastating event was largely based upon religious identity.

Kashmir

In October 1947 India and Pakistan went to war over Kashmir for the first time. Kashmir consists of many different religions. The region of Jammu, for example, is largely Hindu; whereas Ladakh is a Buddhist–majority district; Mirpur and Muzzadarabad are Muslim-majority districts. The most desired and complex area, the Valley of Kashmir, contains most of the state's population and resources. The Valley's population is primarily Sunni Muslim. However, the Valley's Hindu minority includes the Kashmiri Brahmins (Pandits), one of the most important of Indian castes, to which many senior Indian politician and bureaucrats belong.

Thus, the chief conflict in Kashmir is over who controls the Valley. India and Pakistan have gone to war two times over Kashmir (in 1947, again in 1965, yet another major conflict in 1971 has not evolved into a war) and guerrilla fighting still continues. In 1948, the United Nations became involved in the dispute and Kashmir became the oldest conflict inscribed in its resolutions. China, as well, wanted a share in Kashmir. In 1962 China occupied a slice of eastern Kashmir, which it took during the war with India, while India and Pakistan fought over Kashmir. In 1972 Kashmir was divided into two sections along what is known as "the line of control": Pakistan controls the north whereas India controls the southern territories. The dispute, however, has not ceased, since the majority Muslim Valley was included in the Indian territories.

Pakistanis have long argued that the Kashmir problem stems from India's hegemonic aspiration and its refusal to accept the reality of rightful Pakistan. For the Pakistanis, Kashmir remains the "unfinished business" of the 1947 partition. Muslim guerrilla raids in Kashmir continue to this day. Their goal is to either include Kashmir as part of Pakistan or to create an independent Kashmiri state. Over a million Pakistani and Indian troops continually stand on the brink of war. Since 1947 the situation has grown exponentially more dangerous as each state deployed nuclear weapons. But the real problem began a long time ago, as patriarchal grabs for control of land, power and beliefs set the wheel of cause and effect into motion.

The violence between Hindus and Muslims continues. As of summer 2006, the world's largest Hindu organization, The World Hindu Council, has threatened another massacre similar to Gujarat against India's Islamic minority if the perpetrators of the Mumbai train incident are not brought to justice. The story just keeps repeating.

The People's Republic: Communism and Change

China is quickly gaining in economic and political power. Many believe that if its growth continues it may replace the

US as the world's greatest super power. It has a long, rich, and interesting history backing its recent emergence as a prominent world power.

China's patriarchal dynasties began under the Shang rule, (1700 to 1027 BCE) as a previously nomadic tribe rose and established its dominance. A succession of dynasties followed. The monarchal government was viewed as the earthly replica of its heavenly counterpart. Caste systems were substantiated accordingly, as even heavenly deities required warriors, merchants and servants to serve them. Thus, the Chinese style of patriarchal governance was put in place.

The great sage, Confucius (551–479 BCE) had a profound effect upon ideas of creating a proper balance between heaven and earth, ruler and citizens, parents and children. Various rituals, celebrations and sacrifices were performed to honor or appease the ancestors as it was believed that they maintained a profound influence upon earthly life. The philosophy of Confucianism emphasized knowing one's place in the hierarchy and assuring that proper decorum was met in order to assure a right harmony between heaven and earth. It contributed to a social moral code for proper behaviors within this hierarchy. The object of Chinese law was to ensure subordination to the ruler. Punishments for infractions were and remain unduly harsh (Werner, 1994).

Confucianism, Taoism and Buddhism have been the primary religious influences in China. In some ways Buddhism could have been considered a threat to Confucianism and Chinese government as it migrated from India into China for Buddhism bespoke of an enlightened state *beyond the beyond*[20] — and therefore beyond the heavenly-earthly political dyad that controlled the Chinese people. Irregardless, Buddhism was accepted as an integral part of Chinese life — until the onset of the People's Republic of China.

---

[20] This phrase is interpreted from the Buddhist Heart Sutra whereupon the disciple seeks to go beyond all thought, conceptions, sensations, feelings and so forth to attain the state of Nirvana — perfect peace.

The Chinese Communist Party (CCP) was formed in 1921 during the Chinese Civil War. The CCP, led by Mao Zedong, overthrew the Nationalist Government and ended the war in 1949. The Chinese had wanted independence from Western influences; so Lenin's beliefs that Western imperialism represented an evil influence caught the country's attention. The Chinese people rallied in support of this new government and its policies for economic development and social reform. Mao initiated a massive campaign for change proclaiming that "political power grows from the barrel of a gun," and forcibly repressed any and all opposition.

Domestically, Mao began to focus on massive campaigns for change. Old ideas, habits, customs and culture were to be eliminated. Another campaign was to abolish waste, corruption and excessive bureaucracy. The third was the *Five Antis* Campaign. Its focus was on eliminating tax evasion, bribery of any type, theft of state property, any form of cheating on government contracts and any theft related to economic information. Theoretically this was designed to destroy any remnants of what were considered capitalistic influences. The radio broadcasting company, Yan'an Xinhua, was renamed (as Central People's Broadcasting Station) in order to serve as an instrument of the CCP's economic and social reform policies. Land and wealth were taken away from previous owners and distributed evenly to Chinese peasants. Approximately three million landlords were also executed.

Intellectual pursuits were squelched and agriculturalists supported. For example, during Mao's *Hundred Flowers* Campaign, he invited intellectuals and artists to speak out. They did — and publicly affirmed opposition to Mao's policies. This resulted in banishment to hard labor camps and prison sentences.

Religious thought and affiliation became a primary target for reform. Communist China began a campaign to "free" its people from religious ideologies and rituals. The People's Liberation Army (PLA) invaded Tibet in 1950 to "liberate the working classes" (Kolas, 2003). Authority and wealth were taken from Llamas, monks and landowners. A re-classification of its citizens took place as wealth was taken from the wealthy and given to the agriculturists and other labor classes. This was the Chinese version of democratic reform (ibid.).

China had closed its doors to the rest of the world in order to initiate its reform plan. In 1975, under the rule of Deng Xiaoping, it extended its plan, known as the Four Modernizations, to allow for improvements in several areas namely, industry, science and technology agriculture, and national defense. In 1978 a dissident Red Guard noted that a fifth Modernization was needed, referring to *Democracy*. Within a year, he was arrested and jailed (for 15 years). In 1989 young modernizers demonstrated for political and economic reform. This resulted in the well-known massacre at Tiananmen Square as the government exercised its control.

Yet, despite the governmental suppression, China's inherent creativity, imagination and power are evidencing themselves in numerous ways. The Chinese government's attempts to annihilate religion have failed. China now allows five religions, namely Buddhism, Taoism, Judaism, Christianity, and Islam; although each one must be registered and approved by the State Administration of Religious Affairs. The inner spirit of its people could not be squelched. It seems global economics has had the largest influence on China as it reopened its borders to increase its economy by competing in the global market. Time will reveal how all this plays out in world relationships.

Islam: The Melding of Religion and Law

Despite the fact that our concern in this chapter is more historical than analytical, it is necessary to examine the origins of contemporary problems in relation to how Islam was politicized. Islam is unique in that its messenger (Prophet) was also a ruler, who was inspired with a legal system of a divine origin.

Historically, Islamic movements were motivated by the Prophet's model of establishing a state in Medina after the migration from Mecca (described in Chapter One). Due to various interpretations of holy texts, and different perspectives of the Prophet's life, a variety of Islamic political systems have been established throughout its history. As much as these regimes seem to echo the same rhetoric, their implementations of the Islamic principles vary. However, they share a closed system, and those situated outside their intellectual borders are considered deviants.

As explained briefly in earlier chapters, the emergence of the political system in Islam during the Prophet Muhammad's time was a result of complicated social processes. When the Prophet lived in Medina, he was compelled to firstly protect his people, and secondly to organize ways for dealing with legal and religious issues. However, the Prophet's policies were not patterned according to a closed system. He welcomed the Jews and Christians into Medina, integrating them into the *Ummah* (the nation). Non-Muslims were allowed their own way of settling disputes. The Jews were advised by the Prophet to follow the Torah, and the Christians the Gospel. In the Qur'an we read the following:

> To each among you have we prescribed a law and an open way. If Allah had so willed, He would have made you a single people, but (His plan is) to test you in what He hath given you: so strive as in a race in all virtues. The goal of you all is to Allah; it is He that will show you the truth of the matters in which ye dispute. (HQ 5:48)

Eventually, the emergence of radicalized Islamic sects would go against this policy, and declare "believers" to be only those who followed a strict idea of Islam.

The Rise and Fall of Islamic Civilizations

The growth of the Islamic civilization was a product of this open system. Muslims benefited from Greek, Indian, and Persian civilizations and many of the cultural heritages encountered at that time. They were enriched by other cultures as they likewise enriched others. They shared their many cultural, art, and scientific achievements with Europe.

The Islamic civilization went through a major crisis in the fifteenth century when the Ottoman Empire (a closed system) blocked the interaction necessary for further intellectual growth. The Ottoman Empire was named for Osman, a Turkish Muslim prince who founded his own ruling line 1300 CE. By 1453, the Ottoman had destroyed the Byzantine Empire and captured its capital Constantinople, which henceforth served as the Ottoman Capital. By the mid of the sixteenth century, the Ottoman Empire became the largest in the world. It controlled parts of Persia, most of Arabia and also large sections of Hungary and the Balkans. In the 18th century, wars with Russia, Austria and Poland weakened the Empire. In the 19th century, it was called the "sick man of Europe" as European Colonialism had taken over many parts of the Middle East, including countries that had previously been part of the Ottoman Empire. The political territories of the present Islamic world were defined through Colonialism. Islam in the Middle East was hidden behind walls of ignorance as a result of the dogmatic religious mind that dominated the religious approach of the Ottomans.

> The Ottomans remained oblivious to the intellectual, economic and technological transformations that were taking place in Europe. Great efforts were made to revive the governmental structure of earlier centuries. Not surprisingly, this strategy did not prevent the Empire from losing further ground, literally and metaphorically, to its adversaries. (Heper, 2000, p. 63)

As a result of the French invasion of Egypt (1798-1801), which was then part of the Ottoman Empire, the Egyptians awakened to Europe's advanced knowledge in the fields of science and military technology. They realized they had been lagging behind and that the restrictions imposed upon the Islamic countries had caused them to be isolated from the rest of the world. Thus began a new era. They opened their gates in order to catch up with the modern world. Pioneers such as Rifa'a aTahtawy affirmed that there were no contradictions between learning from the West and keeping with the Islamic faith.

Reforms and Setbacks

In the early part of the twentieth century, Ali Abdul Raziq's book, *Islam and the Origins of Governance (Al Islam wa Usul Al-Hukm* (Hourani, 1962, p. 183) created a wide circle of disputes. The author was severely attacked. Abdul Raziq argued that the system of caliphate was not sacred, and therefore not an essential part of the Shari'a (Muslims' legal system). He called for a separation between politics and religion. The publication of that book coincided with Mustafa Kemal Ataturk's political reform in Turkey whereupon he abolished the Caliphate system of governance in 1924. Although they both advocated for discerning the political aspects from the religious, the ideological principles of Abdul Raziq and Kemal Ataturk were markedly different. While Abdul Raziq established his argument on Islamic resources, and defended his position by asserting the importance of Islam as a base for ethical and social domains, Kemal Ataturk divorced himself completely from the Islamic background and minimized its use to the very limited personal aspects. He established modern Turkey on the principles of Western civilization, changing the calligraphy of the language to match Latin letters, and replacing the principles of Islamic law with European ones.

Kemal Ataturk's political reforms echoed throughout with different themes and rhythms. This was especially evidenced after the European colonization, following World War I, of the majority of the Islamic world in Asia and Africa. These imperialist countries focused on modernization, seeing it as a way to advance science and technology, while assuring principles of justice and freedom.

This resulted in a counter-reaction against the westernized ideas of modernization. People in this portion of the world perceived modernization as an imposition of a foreign culture. Hasan al-Banna in the late twentieth century, emphasized the political role of Islam, defending its position as a religion concerned with politics as a core principle. 'Islam is a religion and a state' was the slogan of that movement. It formed the root of the political Islamic movements with various degrees of extremism.

> Three broad types of Islamic orientation may be identified: radical, conservative and moderate or secular. A moderate wishes to preserve Islamic culture and norms, but without taking this to the political arena. He believes in reforming the Islamic society on modern lines and argues that religion should not to be invoked in political, legal and economic matters which should be conducted in the context of the present-day world. Islamic revival or fundamentalism in its radical aspect seeks to interpret Islam as a reform movement and is opposed to modernistic interpretations of Islamic teachings which are attempted by modernist and liberal-minded Muslims. A conservative interprets Islam in legalistic-ritualistic terms that helped the ruling elites to use Islam as a political instrument. (Ghazali, 1999/2004)

Islamic Law

An examination of the way in which Shari'a is used offers yet another means of understanding how much of Islam became a closed system. Shari'a was considered the divinely inspired way of organizing the society. The Shari'a covers a wide range of social relationships, from individuals' rights and duties within a given society to the relationship between nations. For example, Shari'a advises Muslim children to respect their parents irregardless of religious affiliation. On the national and international levels, Shari'a banned any aggression from one nation against another. War is only legitimized in the case of defense. On the other hand, Shari'a includes a system for social control based on the Islamic philosophy, and provides the essential principles for building political systems. Punishment was/is not seen as a tool of revenge within this philosophy, but rather as a tool of purification. The belief is that it would be better to punish the aggressor in this world than to be subject to a far greater punishment in the hereafter. Shari'a provides the guidelines for the relationship between the political leader and the people, where justice is the highest principle and it is the responsibility of the leader to make efforts to realize it.

Ideally, Shari'a is considered to be the source of all the legislation in an Islamic society. There were various schools of jurisprudence throughout Islamic history; the most famous of which are Shafi' Hanbali, Malki, Hanifi for Sunni and Jafari for Shi'is. Each of these schools has its own way of interpreting authentic Islamic resources and offers views accordingly. Unfortunately, fanatics tend to twist the meanings of original texts; justifying autocratic regimes, for example, by taking certain verses from the Holy Qur'an out of context.

For those who claim Shari'a as the main legal source, there is the problem of interpretation. This is still a source of confusion in Islamic countries. Sometimes institutions adhere to old jurisprudence rules, and refuse to face new situations with creative ideas. This can be problematic as explained later in the chapter. Fifteen centuries ago, the Prophet Muhammad foresaw the spirit of sectarianism that would come as a result of rigidity, so he encouraged people to use their minds and creativity when faced with new situations. That process is called *ijtihad*. Ijtihad (the mental efforts used to deduce an acceptable legal accord) was practiced with great courage. The second Caliph Omar Ibn el-Khattab banned cutting off hands as the punishment of theft. By today's standards, Caliph Omar would be blamed for his ijtihad.[21] As noted many Islamic nations have failed to come up with creative ideas in order to face modern situations. For example, in Egypt as elsewhere, due to fanatic conformation to Shari'a, it takes two women to bear witness in a legal case whereas it would take only one man's testimony to achieve the same conclusion. This way is no longer acceptable, or feasible, to evaluate credibility based upon gender. The Holy Qur'an had advised that two women be used to witness financial dealings because at that time women lacked business and commercial knowledge and experience.

Women throughout the Islamic world are deprived of basic human rights as a result of mixing the outdated tribal

---

[21] Ijtihad is the intellectual efforts that are made by legal and religious experts to introduce solutions to new situations. There is nothing particular in Qur'an about ijtihad in the legal sense of the word, but there is continuous advice for humankind to use their intellect.

spirit with misinterpreted holy texts. For example; although women in Egypt have become ministers, ambassadors, professors in different fields, they still suffer within their families. Many women have striven to improve their positions in Islamic society. Yet, family law still lags behind their efforts and advancements.

Women are not able to travel (even in official governmental tasks) without obtaining the consent of their husbands. Similarly, they cannot leave their marital home to visit families, friends, without receiving permission from their husbands. These norms are enforced by irrational laws. If a woman leaves her husband, she loses all her legal rights under divorce proceedings. The punishment of adultery for women is more severe than that of a man. In some Islamic ruled nations it can lead to execution. We cannot stereotype all Arab nations, but the situations in some Muslim countries are worse than in others. For instance, in Saudi Arabia, women are banned from driving their own cars, and have no choice in the way they dress. They are expected to cover their whole body and faces — hidden from the sight of others. This gender bias contradicts sharply with the main principles of Shari'a.

Ironically, people who advocate the existing family law, claim that it conforms to Shari'a. They depend on verses from the Qur'an, interpreted by males intending to weaken women's status. The translations of specific verses are clearly biased toward men as being superior. In a previous book, *Islam from Adam to Muhammad and Beyond*, co-authored by Ali, Aliaa and Aisha Rafea, it is said, that the

> Islamic Shari'a considers the oneness of man and woman in broad lines of how each can take care of the other and enjoy being cared for by the other in turn, in a way that values each person's role. The Shari'a does not impose rigid roles, to be literally and strictly followed, otherwise one is considered deviant from the Shari'a. The husband, for instance, is given the responsibility to provide for the family in order to allow his wife to rest during the rigors of pregnancy and, later, of nursing and caring for infants. As mothers, women enjoy the ability to give without limit and to love unconditionally. This division of labor between

> husband and wife is deliberated in the Qur'an primarily to
> encourage both man and woman to respond to their natu-
> ral roles, defined by biological differences, but not to
> imprison them in those roles or to humiliate either of them.
> (Rafea, 2004, p. 149)

The Prophet suggested men both revere women, as evidenced in his oft repeated saying, "Paradise is under the
feet of the mothers," and care for them. This was in keeping
with that era in that patriarchy was the dominant consciousness. It was also a response to the violence against women
that had been occurring in the culture prior to his message.
But the suppression of women grew following the
Prophet's passing. As fundamentalist movements grew, the
Shari'a became prey to rigid and dogmatic interpretations.

There are also other problematic issues. For example, the
question that has been repeatedly asked is whether Islamic
legal systems and the secular legal system of non Muslims
can reconcile. Is it possible to modernize the Islamic nations
without them becoming westernized or secularized? Such a
question assumes intrinsic contradictions between the principles of Islamic law and Western principles of democracy
and freedom. Scholars such as Karen Armstrong have
found that those contradictions are illusive noting that "The
reality is that Islam and the West share common traditions.
From the time of the Prophet Muhammad, Muslims have
recognized this, but the West cannot accept it" (Armstrong,
1992, p. 266).

This question took on another dimension as the phenomenon of globalization began to imply American dominance.
Islamic revivalist movements reacted by attacking in order
to defend against perceived encroachment upon their
philosophical ideals. America became Satan in the eyes of
those movements (Armstrong, 2000, p. 301).

These polarizations nourished the spirit of enmity, which
in turn bred terrorism. Islam as a religion of peace respects
variations and differentiations of cultures and calls for harmonious coexistence among nations. Each country in the
Islamic world can develop its legal system according to
Islamic principles without necessarily being completely

alike. The Islamic law provides guidelines for legal systems, and there is room for interpretation. As such, there is no way to be limited or bound by a specific model of implementation, past or present. Accordingly there should be no contradictions between the freedom of thought that is provided by secularism and the freedom of creativity that is encouraged through Muhammad's teachings. There may be different views in dealing with certain problems, but that would not necessarily bring Islamic nations to fight the West.

The politicization of Islam today has become synonymous with the struggle for political powers taking place in different parts of the world. The prime role of radical Islamists is to defeat Western encroachment. The previous Taliban regime in Afghanistan provides an obvious example. The Taliban were unable to hold the perspective that Islamic values can coexist with others' values. It is sad to see the once liberating power of Islam being used to oppress the masses. Worse still, and in the name of religion, people are banned from thinking for themselves — fearing being deviant from the "righteous path", they instead blindly obey religious authorities.

Certainly, changes are desperately needed in many Arab countries. Many of these nations have been, and still are, ruled by rigid, Islamic fundamentalist regimes. As discussed earlier, these regimes tightly control and suppress Arab women. Groups who build their existence on closed systems nurture superiority — whereupon close-minded beliefs, feelings and behaviors lead to discrimination, and justification of violence. If these groups do not find "the other" to fight, they start fighting among themselves. Civil wars in Algeria, Lebanon, Nigeria, and Eritrea represent a few examples.

Africa: The Clash of Religions, Politics and Culture

Africa is yet another powerful example of the destructive results of patriarchal political, economic and religious meddling. To begin with, religion and politics have played a significant role in keeping Africa in a state of poverty and religious discord. Christianity was brought in the first century (CE) into Alexandria by Saint Mark.[22] Christianity soon spread west across the northern part of Africa, then traveled into both southern and eastern lands until reaching the Horn of Africa (which now includes Ethiopia, Djibouti, Eritrea, and Somalia).

During the seventh century, Islam began to spread as Muslims sought refugee in Ethiopia to escape the persecution of the Quraysh. Islam soon replaced Christianity in many areas, including Somalia and the states of North Africa. However Christianity remained the majority in Ethiopia. In the 15th century, with the arrival of the Portuguese, Christianity came to Sub-Saharan Africa. The Dutch founded the beginnings of the Dutch Reform Church in 1652 in Africa's South continent. Missionaries began arriving from Europe during the 19th century, and Christianity began to replace indigenous religions as it spread across the land. However it proved difficult for them to take over the areas where Islam had already been established.

Today, we find that Islam covers the whole of the North Africa and Sahel region, and East Africa. Twenty-three African countries out of fifty seven are members of the Organization of Islamic Conference. Christianity is mostly found in the South. Indigenous religions have not disappeared completely; often blending their rituals and beliefs with those of Islam or Christianity, and each establishing its unique flavor. This is evidenced in various parts of Africa.

Ethiopia and Eritrea

Both the Qur'an and the Bible refer to Ethiopia as one of the great ancient civilizations. In this geographically wide spread country, the ethnic groups that make up the Empire are of diverse types. Of these groups, Amhara and Tigris claim authenticity and superiority over the others. They consider themselves "chosen people" as descendants from

---

[22]   According to the Coptic Church, Saint Mark witnessed the preaching of Jesus, and wrote the earliest Gospel. He arrived at Alexandria in 48 CE, and died in 68 CE.

Moses and Solomon. In the Constitution of 1955, it is documented that the imperial dynasty of the country originated
with Menelik I, the son of King Solomon and Queen of Saba.

The northern part of Ethiopia, which includes Eritrea, is
inhabited by a Muslim majority. In the early twentieth century, Eritrea was an Italian colony, but came under the British administration in 1941. Britain, however, sought to
divide Eritrea along religious lines, giving the coastal and
highland areas to Ethiopia and the Muslim-inhabited
northern section, including the lowlands, to British-ruled
Sudan. The trend to divide Colonies and create religious
conflicts was a common political line that ensured British
control over Colonies. "Divide and rule" become a well
known British strategy. In 1950, Eritrea was considered to
be an independent nation linked with Ethiopia through federation. However, in November 1962, the Emperor Haile
Selassie announced the end of the federation and considered Eritrea to be part of Ethiopia. In 1984, in order to
weaken the rebels of the Eritrean population, the government of Ethiopia launched a forced resettlement program,
relocating more than one million Muslim peasants to Ethiopia's central and southern regions. Many thousands died
and continue to die in these resettlement camps.

The Eritreans did not stop trying to gain their independence. They finally succeeded in 1993, but lacked a clear
demarcation of the borders between the two countries. This
eventually led to more violence. The 1998-2000 clashes
between Eritrea and Ethiopia over the disputed border is
estimated to have resulted in the death of over 100,000
people.[23] Although warring has stopped, tension remains.
A peace-keeping force is currently patrolling the security
zone between the two countries.

The conflict between Ethiopia and Eritrea is political and
economic, rather than religious and ideological. However,
religion is used as tool to inflame hatred in the hearts of the
two nations. There is much tension both at the borders and
within Eritrea.

---

[23] http://www.biddho.de/portal/article4219.html

Crises in Sudan

Although Sudan backed Eritrea in her 30 years struggle for independence (1961–1991), the relationship between these two countries quickly deteriorated when the Eritrean Islamic Jihad Movement (EIJM) began to compete for power. According to the Eritrean government's interpretation, the EIJM was created with the help of General Omar al-Bashir, who led a military coup in 1989. In 1992, the Eritrean People's Liberation Front (EPLF) fought fierce battles against armed EIJM.

Social instability continues in Eritrea, due to particular challenges imposed by rebel forces. Also, the tension between Eritrea and Ethiopia remains inflamed, with its deteriorating relation with Sudan adding to its problems.

Sudan is a complex society with many tribes, each with its own regional identity, yet they are overwhelmed by an Arabic culture. Southern Sudan is the only exception, where local identities are highlighted over the national one. Although Arabic is the official language, there are also more than one hundred spoken languages in Sudan. Islam forms the base of the dominant culture. Two thirds of the Sudanese are Muslims, 5 percent Christians, the remaining are animists who follow their tribal beliefs.

Islam entered the Sudan during the fourteenth century as traders from the north brought their religious ideologies to the native inhabitants. Later, mystic teachers of Islam (*Sufi Sheikhs*) migrated to Sudan and established their mystical orders. By the nineteenth century, a more politically-focused religious orientation manifested. The most famous of these was Mahdiyya. It attempted to establish an Islamic state, but was attacked by the British and Egyptians, and defeated in 1898. Christian organizations were established with the support of European missionaries. They were dominated by European clergies until after Sudan's independence in 1956.

During the first national government in Sudan, the South started to feel that it was marginalized and rebel movements began to take action. It was not until 1972 when president Nimeiri allowed the World Council of Churches to mediate peace with the Sudan Liberation Movement, a treaty was signed, giving the south regional autonomy.

While the situation in the south was calming, Nimeiri was facing challenges in the north. The Muslim Brotherhood, who originated in Egypt and whose ideology was becoming popular in many Arab countries, was gaining political power. In order to contend with the increasing popularity of the Muslim Brotherhood, Nimeiri declared Islamic Law to be the source of all legislation in the country, thereby assuring control over any opposition. Nimeiri was playing a political game, aimed at building popularity in northern Sudan while still facing problems in the south. He divided the south into three regions in order to settle the leadership disputes. But that solution didn't work. As a result, the regional government in the South was dissolved. Discontent among both Muslims and Christians regarding Nimeiri's Islamic laws resulted in his overthrow on April 5, 1985. The regime that followed did not last long, and was overthrown by Al-Bashir (1989).

The peoples of Eastern, Western and Southern Sudan felt politically and economically marginalized by the Islamic North. The turmoil between these regions continues. It has been estimated that 2 million people have lost their lives as a result of these conflicts. The Christian rebels in Southern Sudan have used at least 10 thousand children, between the ages of 8 and 18, as frontline soldiers. At least four million others have been forced from their homes.[24] Human Rights watch reported that the Janjaweed, an Arab Muslim militia group, commit ongoing genocide against the moderate Sufi Muslims in Darfur (in Western Sudan). It is estimated that as many as 50,000 people have been killed as this "ethnic cleansing" continues. Towns and villages are destroyed as civilians are executed. The Sudanese government has responsibility for these tragedies in that it has supplied the

---

[24] Center for Reduction of Religious based Conflict
      http://aps.naples.net/community/NFNWebpages/storyboard.cf
      m?StoryBoardNum=142&PageNum=170, accessed on Feb/11/2004

Janjaweed with weapons. It is a most destructive mix of politics and religion.

Nigeria: Problem of Implementing Shari'a

The story in Nigeria is yet another version of struggle, fear and dogmatism. In a country of 120 million people, where half the population is Muslim, the clashes between Muslims who follow a dogmatic and fundamentalist version of the Shari'a and Christians appears to be irresolvable. The BBC news (September 14, 2003) reported that,

> It's estimated that during President Obasanjo's first four years in office (from 1999-2003), well over 10,000 people died in clashes between the country's Muslim and Christian communities.

> Many observers see this unrest not as a result of the spontaneous eruption of religious tensions, but as being provoked by marginalized politicians, using cultural divisions and misunderstandings to destabilize parts of the country for their own ends.[25]

It presents a similar story of spreading fundamentalism, influencing a radical interpretation of Shari'a to take place. Christians are also well aware that they are not accepted by extremist Muslims.

Yet, Muslims, are also dissatisfied. They had believed that Shari'a would provide justice for all and reform the social order, but have since learned that the radical implementation of Shari'a has, instead, constrained their freedom. In practice, people ended up being controlled by the powerful and elite because they demand that their translation of a holy text and its historical beginnings be accepted as the only one. Their version is deemed to be sacred, and opposition is silenced. So we find similar stories in different parts of the world with different actors and players. When hierarchy is stressed, there becomes only one voice, one authority, and all others are silenced. This results in both oppression and injustice.

---

[25] BBC News, September 14, 2003

These are but small examples, as many innocent groups of black peoples throughout the African continent are living in poverty, starving, suffering and dying from the AIDS epidemic, being raped and/or killed, and so forth. One cannot ignore the immense disservice to the native inhabitants of Africa as the West mines its diamonds, robs its natural resources while allowing its indigenous people to live in poverty, fueling discontent. What evil force convinces people to dominate another group's land, using its native inhabitants as cheap labor to mine diamonds (Sierra Leone is a good example of this) and other resources, while forcing them to live in poverty? There was no poverty when these indigenous Africans lived naturally, in harmony with the land. Poverty was the result of exploitation by the rich seeking to get richer—the ongoing saga of the haves and the have-nots.

Conclusions

In his research into the rise and fall of civilizations, historian Arnold Toynbee made significant contributions to the study of the process of societal decline. Toynbee noted that "an increasing command over environments is a concomitant of disintegration rather than of growth" and that,

> Militarism, a common feature of breakdown and disintegration, is frequently effective in increasing a society's command both over other living societies and over inanimate forces of nature. In the downward course of a broken-down civilization's career there may be truth in the Ionian philosopher Heracleitus's estimates that "war is the father of all things", and since the vulgar estimates of human prosperity are reckoned in terms of power and wealth, it thus often happens that the opening chapters of a society's tragic decline are popularly hailed as the culminating chapters of a magnificent growth. Sooner or later, however, disillusionment is bound to follow; for a society that has become incurably divided against itself is almost certain to "put back into the business" of war the greater part of those additional resources, human and material, which the same business has incidentally brought into its hands. (Toynbee, 1946/1974, p. 364)

Toynbee noted leading criteria for a great nation's fall: namely, that there arises a schism in class distinctions and inter-state oppositional forces; and the leading minority loses its faculty for creativity along with its ability to attract the majority by charisma rather than by aggression. In so doing, the leading minority attempts to hold its privileged position by force.

Toynbee's research both examined and rejected the idea that there is an "innately superior race, e.g., the Nordic Race, in the world which is responsible for the creation of civilizations" (ibid., p. 568). This means the idea of manifest destiny and the "white man's burden" are illusionary concepts. In short, these ideas have created more harm than good. Each culture, race and religion has its own unique value, and these are undermined when a dominant culture steps in and takes over.

It also appears that humanity continually attempts to create (or enforce) a right balance between religious beliefs, social governance and political life — with limited success. Motivations of greed and destructive power eventually fail as they erode our attempts to create a truly democratic society, continued evidence of the damage wrought by gender imbalance for the feminine energy would temper these inclinations. Closed systems and ethnocentric isolation are no longer tolerable. Globalization appears to be the next step in social evolution, but it is best that it is undergirded with respect for all. The ominous spread of the US Empire threatens humanity's future — in that it doesn't represent respect for all; instead, it reflects an extremist patriarchal model seeking to dominate the world based upon fear of threat and desire for the world's resources. International activist and author Arundhati Roy noted this threat in her keynote speech to the World Social Forum in Mumbai,

> Poor countries that are geopolitically of strategic value to Empire, or have a "market" of any size, or infrastructure that can be privatized, or, God forbid, natural resources of value oil, gold, diamonds, cobalt, coal must do as they're told or become military targets. Those with the greatest reserves of natural wealth are most at risk. Unless they surrender their resources willingly to the corporate

machine, civil unrest will be fomented or war will be waged. (Roy, 2004)

In his introduction to *Jihad vs. McWorld*, Barber explains that "True politics can never take a step without rendering homage to morality" (quoting Kant, 1957, p. 46). This morality includes respect for all members of the human family. Democracy can only succeed if it does not disdain cultural or gender differences.

In our research, we discovered numerous examples of governments and religious institutions dominated by patriarchal ideals leading to the diminishment of *the other* — all sad tales of prejudice against women and people of color. Religious ideals advising us to love and honor one another and to live in harmony have failed time and time again. Political ideals for democratic societies have likewise failed. Perhaps it is time for a major change — a change that recognizes the role of women in helping to create a healthy balance between political governance and religious life. Einstein believed that problems could not be solved at the same level of thinking in which they were created (Covey, 1994). We must reach for new understanding, before we create further destruction. Surely, given the above history, we are ripe for new perspectives.

But women, who know the price of conflict so well, are also often better equipped than men to prevent or resolve it. For generations, women have served as peace educators, both in their families and in their societies. They have proved instrumental in building bridges rather than walls. They have been crucial in preserving social order when communities have collapsed.

We in the United Nations know, at first hand, the invaluable support women provide to our peacekeepers — by organizing committees, non-governmental organizations and church groups that help ease tensions, and by persuading their menfolk to accept peace.

Kofi Annan, Secretary General

United Nations, October 24, 2000

Chapter Six

Armageddon or a New Paradigm?

*Horizontal and Vertical
Perspectives*

Are war and violence inevitable expressions in life? Some people claim this to be the case; but if we accept this worldview, humanity is doomed. We can continue to develop advanced warfare technologies, and experience the consequences of violence begetting violence, or we can take another path—one that holds a greater respect for all life. We are at a threshold, and the decisions we make will affect not only ourselves, but also the future of all humanity! This is why we chose to examine patriarchal history and its influence in the arenas of religion, political regime and corporate power. Can we learn from our mistakes and move into a new paradigm? Or will we choose another world war?

Although we have primarily focused on patriarchy's shadow side, we are clearly aware that this evolutionary stage has brought numerous achievements, and also created much beauty. It is obvious, when one studies the great historical achievements in art, music, philosophy and science, that the masculine side of humanity has brought forth both wisdom and beauty. But, as we have pointed out, these patriarchal ideals and accomplishments have, for the most part, failed to make the world a better place due to gender imbalance.

Women are equally capable instruments in the arenas of art, science, philosophical thought and spiritual understanding, and the suppression of women has allowed men to take the primary credit for human advancements. Even at this stage of our human development, the majority of women, worldwide, are given few educational opportunities. Poorer nations consider education and the like to be more important for the male. Knowledge is power; therefore educating women has not been a high-level priority in many countries. As long as women are kept in ignorance or isolation, males remain in control. Perhaps this is why patriarchal religious beliefs denounced the woman's intellectual and leadership capabilities, for it assured the primacy of the male. Misogynist influences supporting this enormous human error are more than abundant. For example, early Vedic teachings taught that "Lord Indra himself has said that woman has very little intelligence" and that "She cannot be taught" (Rig Veda 8.33.17). The Confucian Marriage Manual explained that "'One hundred women are not worth a single testicle." Gregory the Great (although how great might be debatable) told others that a "Woman is slow in understanding and her unstable and naïve mind renders her by way of natural weakness to the necessity of a strong hand in her husband" for "Her 'use' is two-fold: animal sex and motherhood" (Chittister, 1983, p. 3), whereas Aristotle philosophized that "The female is a female by virtue of a certain lack of qualities—a natural defectiveness" (Mills, 1989).

A gathering known, as the Council of Macon, was held in the year 584 CE, in Lyons, France, to determine if women "were human" (or beasts). The decision group was comprised of 66 men (many of them Catholic bishops). Thirty-one of the men voted against women's humanity. Likewise, family laws in many societies in Islamic nations treat women in a discriminative manner, considering them irrational, irresponsible, and needing guardianship. Each of these examples provides a clearly defined illustration of the great lie that undermined women's equality.

We have noted the wide abuses of women and people of color. In all honesty, although we have presented many images of the dark side of patriarchy's chronicles, we have addressed but a small portion of its numerous abuses of *the other*. So where do we go from here? How can we change the tide?

We cannot allow patriarchal governance and greed to destroy nature. It is time to return to a felt connection with our earth — to work together to heal the human caused pollution of land, water and air, and to reduce, if not fully eliminate, our contributions to global warming. Early cultures, and this is still evidenced in modern indigenous groups, respected the natural world — the relationship with nature was and still is perceived to be one of *stewardship* as opposed to *dominion over*. Plundering the land, using it to test nuclear bombs and so forth represents gross negligence, for true stewardship and caretaking requires recognition of the natural relationship and equality of spirit and form (matter) — with an inherent reverence for both. Even though it seems inevitable that our evolution may move us to explore the further reaches of the cosmos, we must first heal our relationship to the ground upon which we stand.

We need to work together to create gender-balanced governance, motivated by the desire and intention to heal our human relationships. In his excellent book, *The Fourth Power — A Grand Strategy for the United States in the Twenty-First Century*, author Gary Hart describes the difference between a *republic*, based upon a "commitment to civic virtue and citizen duty, the centrality of popular sovereignty, resistance to corruption, and a sense of the commonwealth" (Hart, 2004, p. 138) and an *empire*, based upon military might, occupation of foreign land and exploitation of its resources. As discussed in Chapter Four, the founders of the United States, following the ideals of the European enlightenment, sought to create an ideal nation — a republic that offered opportunities for all (particularly if you were an Anglo-Saxon male). This patriarchal ideal failed as we see its shadow side — the policies of preemptive violence, economic and corporate corruption, and increasing control of other nations — spreading across the globe. This ideal could become an embodied reality if we had gender balanced governments and equal rights for all.

The patriarchal era will eventually end. Its final grasp for power is but the last throes of its dying era. A more egalitarian world is inevitable, prompted by globalization, the rise of the internet, and easy travel. Satellites can be found hooked to roofs of primitive jungle huts in remote regions of Mexico, South America, Africa and other lands. Images of other cultural paradigms are abundant. *The other* is becoming known! Humanity is ripe for this needed change, even though patriarchal governance and ideologies are apt to create much harm before the needed transition. Part of this transition also requires an integration of the ideals we've *talked about*, but have yet to *embody*. The topic of "democracy" is a primary topic on news stations around the world. The idea that democracy can be forced upon other nations is ludicrous, for it goes against its very nature. The ideal of democracy needs to be more deeply understood in order to be successfully employed.

From a systems perspective, one can say that hypocrisy itself has evoked the emergent threat of increasing terrorism. Iraqis were told they were being rescued from their tyrannical dictator. Many innocent Iraqi people were, and continue to be, killed by bombs (from both military and insurgents), as we occupy their land and claim their oil. The sectarian violence that has led to the ongoing deaths of numerous Iraqis was initiated by US maneuvers, and the instability they caused to the region. The US applauds and supports the disproportionate violence by the Israelis against the Palestinians (and Lebanese civilians) while talking about "freedom loving" peoples. Indigenous Africans are robbed of their natural resources (for example, diamonds and other precious gems and minerals) while at the same time we attempt to help them with food rations, medicines and loans. These hypocritical acts are also supported by the ethnocentric premise that one nation's racial preference, ideals or religious beliefs are superior to another's. It is quite evident that war and related violence simply beget

more war and related violence. The limitations implied by
the patriarchal ideal have failed to serve humanity, as a
whole, simply because someone always has to be better
than another; whereas *gender-based politics* ask us to consider all of humanity as one human family embracing the
realization that our decisions and our behaviors have an
effect upon all.

As we reconsider our political policies, we are also asked
to re-examine our interpretations of religious teachings and
practices, for these have been founded upon patriarchal
interpretations and utilization of religious dogmas for controlling purposes. The increasing relationship of extremist
religious and political ideologies represents a significant
threat to humanity and its future. We must reach out to one
another and join in our efforts to create a better world.

Gender-balanced leadership, in both religion and parliament, will take a significant role in this changing era. It is
time for women to take their place — to step forward into
leadership positions in religious, political and corporate
arenas. We believe this is the evolutionary development
that will assure humanity's survival. Men and women concerned with equality, respect for all life and for our environment need to form an alliance that builds upon these values.
Numerous egalitarian groups have developed in the last
few decades, heartfully and wisely responding to our current challenges. Some examples are Human Rights Watch,
Amnesty International, the National Association for the
Advancement of Colored People (a civil rights organization
for ethnic minorities in the US), Greenpeace, the Sierra Club
(a prominent environmental organization in the US), the
Global Peace Initiative of Religious and Spiritual Women,
and numerous other world-wide Non-Governmental Organizations committed to equality and healing. A more recent
phenomenon is that of increasing numbers of rock groups
influenced by Bono's humanitarian endeavors, and business leaders such as Bill and Melinda Gates, using their
riches to help the less fortunate societies, such as African
people suffering with AIDS and poverty. Our future is supported by these important institutions and movements —

for they seek to eradicate prejudice and related abuses wherever they are found. This caring behavior is founded in our political ideals of equality for all, and is likewise at the heart of our religious institutions.

Although the founders of our religious traditions modeled intra-psychic gender-balance (an internal balancing of masculine and feminine qualities), our religious institutions have been rather schizophrenic in the images presented of the divine feminine.

On the one hand traditional Jews welcome the Sabbath "bride" each Friday as Shabbat begins, but the living woman is considered unholy during her sacred menstrual cycle, and laws requiring purification rituals subtly tell her that her natural processes are deemed unholy.

Conservative Christians revere the sanctity of Mary, the mother of Jesus, yet follow the Apostle Paul's epistles that a woman's role is secondary to that of the male. She was created to serve her husband, and bear children. Both Judaism and Christianity adopted the ill-fated story scapegoating Eve for the loss of Unity with the Divine (metaphor of loss of paradise).

Muslims honor the saintly Fatima, the Prophet's daughter, yet follow practices that dishonor, and often endanger, the well-being of the living female. The Qur'an stresses that men should take good care of women, it also says "The Believers, men and women, are protectors one of another: they enjoin what is just, and forbid what is evil; they observe regular prayers, practice regular charity, and obey Allah and His Messenger. On them will Allah pour His Mercy: for Allah is Exalted in power ..." (Sura 9, verse 71). Later additions to the Qur'an presented an understanding that "men are superior to women on account of the qualities in which Allah has given them preeminence." This ill-interpreted passage has led to the denigration of the female as fundamentalist Arab nations hide women under burkas, enact honor killings for victims of rape, and control women under numerous contrived religious edicts. (Likewise the Bible, both new and old Testaments have committed great crimes against the female due to similar passages proclaiming male superiority.)

Chinese religious philosophy depicts the I Ching symbol, a blatant image of masculine and feminine balance — yet Confucius himself clearly stated that the female was subservient to the male.

Hindus have numerous feminine deities and temples dedicated to the Goddess Kali Durga, yet women are used as pawns in the marriage market and beaten if their parents are unable to meet the material goals of the in-laws and spouse.

The goddess is still revered in Africa. But in reality untold numbers of women are beaten, sexually mutilated and raped throughout the continent.

Considering these atrocities and the gross disparity represented, our final chapter will explore paths for healing and promoting gender balance. Whereas the previous chapters were descriptive of the results of patriarchal interpretations of religion and social-political governance, we are eager to present images of a more egalitarian future. Let us face the truth: men were the ones who interpreted and wrote down the teachings of the Prophets, usually years after their death. In stating these were the words or recordings of a male God, they affirmed that any challenges would be considered evil. Unlike their Prophets, they disparaged the personage and role of women — the other half of humanity, *and also the other half of their own psyches.* Each human being contains potential strengths and capacities evidenced in both genders. Their integration leads us to wholeness.

Thus we suggest that the next step in our human evolution is that of gender balance. The inherent relational qualities within the female are needed. This balance will ground our spiritual ideologies and greater potentials and allow us to embody the real guidance of our Prophets. As we address the role of women in grounding spirituality and transforming leadership styles in both religious and political realms, we offer a vision for a significantly healthier psychological relationship to life, and also a new found view of spiritual teachings based upon the findings of Quantum Physics.

Healthy Psychology

We are each endowed with *will*. In other words, we have the ability to choose whether we act with integrity and compassion, or follow paths laden with destructive attitudes and behaviors. In order to recognize the subtle and oftentimes overt forces of hidden prejudice lurking behind our thoughts, words and deeds, it is necessary to fine-tune our inner awareness. Much of our violence in thought and deed is really a lack of self-acceptance, projected outward on "the other". This allows us to not fully acknowledge our own pain, shame, anger, fear and sadness. We have learned to disown these feelings because of social disapproval. Men are taught to never express pain or sadness and women are deemed as unfeminine if they show anger. This kind of tight, cultural control over our emotional life serves the patriarchal powers well. It keeps us from the full force of our vitality. Male violence is conditioned, for anger is the socially accepted emotion for men. Conversely, since women's anger has been deemed unacceptable, they've been shackled to patriarchal subjugation. The patriarchal negation of the body encouraged a negation of the full range of our emotional awareness and developed senses. All emotions are felt through the body, so awareness of the body's subtle cues needs to be included. Changes in our breathing patterns, muscular tension and neurological sensations help to alert us when we are on the brink of negative projections. This requires a finely tuned state of inner awareness. Taking responsibility for our feeling states facilitates the clearing of projections. In doing so, we can begin to rid our inner beings of erroneous patterns and beliefs that were often founded in fear. This healing process brings with it many gifts — opening our hearts and our "eyes" to the beauty inherent within each of us, and experiencing that beauty in ourselves as we recognize it in others.

Thus, on a societal level, we are called to move away from closed systems and cultivate open systems of communication — whereupon all people, nations and religions have a voice and a place. Increasing numbers of religious teachers are recognizing that our understanding and practice of religious segregation is changing. No doubt religion will look quite differently in the future; women will play a major and positive part in these changes, and it will be a change for the better (Buehler, 2004). The beginnings of this change are evidenced in increasing media dialogues, the internet and the emergence of numerous interfaith groups manifesting around the globe. If we deny one nation or religion within the human system, it will create a dark pocket of hatred that will eventually erupt in violence because it was isolated and not acknowledged.

Integrating the Shadow

Humanity's shadow side must be acknowledged. This is why we have included numerous examples of patriarchy's destructive behaviors. This archetypal[1] force has great creative potential—once we recognize it. Our consciousness evolves as our inner and outer worlds are illuminated. This requires attentiveness to the various presences acting within consciousness. This was well illustrated in an old Star Trek episode in which Captain Kirk was split in two. Each of the two versions of Captain Kirk represented an opposite side of his character. The benevolent Captain Kirk became a nice but ineffective leader for he lacked the power and will to govern the Enterprise. He was kindly and well-motivated, but weak and ineffective. Captain Kirk's shadow/dark side was violent and unconcerned regarding his effects upon others. He attempted to rape the women, fight the men and overall represented egotistic viciousness with a lack of concern for others—a prominent feature of evil. The moral of the story was that both sides are needed for human wholeness. The dark side needs to be illuminated, accepted, and integrated through awareness of repressed emotion in the body-mind. This will bring back

---

[1] Archetypes are primordial instinctive forces shared by all human beings on an intra-psychic level. They are strongly motivating forces, such as the hero who sacrifices him/herself for a cause, the shadow/dark side of a human being represented in the struggle between good and evil discussed in Chapter One.

the vital will and energy present in his dark side in order to have *effective beneficence*. Without this integrative awareness, dark energies act out destructively — unchecked.

In particular, Buddhist and Taoist teachings,[2] as well as ancient Sufi and Kabbalist alchemists,[3] emphasized the integration of light and dark sides of human development. As noted earlier, alchemists' drawings contained images of both dark and light sides of the anima (feminine archetype) and dark and light sides of the animus (masculine archetype), indicating that these archetypes were evolving within both genders. Awareness and recognition of these differing motivating forces brings us to a greater human responsibility for our behaviors. Carl Jung taught that the shadow contained vital, creative energy available for transformation. When we unleash the shadow's destructive forces against *the other*, we waste the potent energy available for human development.

The systemic world view explains how one nation or religious group will act out destructively when other nations or religions are creating and maintaining some form of imbalance within the system. If there is a destructive pattern within the larger field of human relationship, its unconscious, dark energy will take some form of retaliatory or destructive behavior in a misguided attempt to establish equilibrium. The initial imbalance could be evidenced as deceit, oppression, hypocrisy and so forth. At the deepest level the resultant, destructive behaviors are the movements of an energy field attempting to heal the rift. If the system remains closed to change, the shadowed energies will simply rise again. We have to rise to a new level of

[2]   In Buddhism there is the path of the Middle Way, whereupon the individual holds the tension between the opposites. These opposites are also portrayed in the Taoist symbol of two forms enclosed in a circle representing wholeness. One form is black with a white dot in the center and the other white with a black dot in the center

[3]   Alchemy is most often described as an ancient science focused on turning mercury and other essences into gold. But its deeper work denoted the process of illuminating the divine within the human being (Shah, 1964).

understanding and dialogue in order to open the power of creativity and transformation within the field.

If we acknowledge our own participation in the human drama rather than projecting the shadow upon others, this creative life force could empower our journey into a new era of humankind. The story of Lucifer (In Arabic, Iblis), the light bearer, becoming Satan, the prince of darkness, having fallen from the grace of heaven's light, also represents this restorative work. As human beings begin to honor one another and all creation—they heal the split between heaven and earth. The final sentence of the Marie Corelli quote, at the beginning of this book, expresses this intention. *"When the world rejects thee, I will pardon and again receive thee, but not till then"* (Corelli, 1895, pp. 65–66). Humanity is consciously restored to its oneness with the Divine once it rejects is prejudicial stance.

Healing the Past

Ignorance of the roots of our contemporary civilization has encouraged us to see the "other" as our enemy. Anthropological perspectives indicate that Homo-sapiens originated in the center of Africa. Racial discrimination, a culturally created phenomenon, crumbles when presented with the knowledge that there is but one root beginning for all. Sudanese Muslims would be unable to perceive themselves to be superior to other African groups. Americans, who have violated their own principles of human rights by an unjust war and their cruel treatment of Iraqi prisoners, would no longer act out such inhumane behaviors. Anti-Semites would no longer hate or mistreat Jews. Israeli politicians would be psychically unable to call Palestinian Arabs vermin, or kill them indiscriminately. Our human relationships would have to be reconsidered. The realization that our humanity stems from one common physical origin (not to mention the metaphysical unity), asks us to reconsider our relationship with one another. DNA research by molecular biologists suggests we all share a common ancestry.

Part of the evidence to support this theory comes from molecular biology, especially studies of the diversity and mutation rate of nuclear DNA and mitochondrial DNA in living human cells. From these studies an approximate time of divergence from the common ancestor of all modern human populations can be calculated. This research has typically yielded dates around 200,000 years ago." Molecular methods have also tended to point to an African origin for all modern humans, implying that the ancestral population of all living people migrated from Africa to other parts of the world — thus the name of this interpretation: the "Out of Africa Hypothesis."[4]

From the ethnological point of view, each human civilization has contributed to the one that followed. If we widen our scope to include the dawn of civilization, which started in Egypt and eventually led to the modern American civilization, we can clearly see how each civilization has contributed its revelations and developments to the modern world. The ancient Egyptian civilization had its impact on Hellenistic civilization, and the Islamic civilization that followed incorporated the distinct characteristics of Greek, Persian, and Indian cultures. Europe benefited from the Islamic advancements in philosophy, science, art and culture during its renaissance period. This holistic view of history allows us to see all cultural variations as part of an integrated picture.

Unfortunately many perceive themselves as isolated islands overlooking the underlying links to humankind on both physical and cultural levels. Exploring our roots in other civilizations and cultures helps us to remove these imaginary barriers.

Our premise stems from our conviction that hidden racist feelings stand in the way of establishing dialogues between cultures. Lack of respectful communication contributes to conflict, and feelings of enmity are inflamed. We are also convinced that the many wars around the globe reveal a deeper level of conflict within the human psyche. The imbalance between feminine and masculine aspects within

---

[4] http://www.mnh.si.edu/anthro/humanorigins/ha/sap.htm
     Accessed on 5/8/2004

ourselves, our religions and our cultures affects the way we view others and the universe itself. We are challenging the view of a unilinear evolution that has, and still, influences many intellectuals' and politicians' choices — for this view by its very nature proposes that one culture or religion is superior to others.

Interpretative anthropology emphasizes the uniqueness and individuality of each culture. It stresses the meanings behind actions, and encourages anthropologists to look deeply into the cultures they study, and to uncover the mysteries and beauty of each one. One culture is not considered to be superior to another. This practice can be applied by all. As discussed in Chapters One and Two, humankind has been advised by its many Prophets not to judge others, and to recognize a unity beyond diversity. This unity does not imply uniformity, but rather emphasizes our common aspirations. In the words of Clifford Geertz:

> ... anthropology has attempted to find its way to a more viable concept of man, one in which culture, and the variability of culture, would be taken into account rather than written off as caprice and prejudice, and yet, at the same time, one in which the governing principle of the field, "the basic unity of mankind," would not be turned into an empty phrase. (Geertz, 1973, p. 37)

The "basic unit of humankind" is used to specify ideals which are given absolute values as basic. What we have learned from social sciences in general, and anthropology in particular is to respect variations of human experience in the search for values, and to understand that there are multiple angles in defining "reality". As a result, communication is possible through active listening, empathy, and a recognition of others needs.

As much as modern civilization has transformed the world through science and technology, it has also created a psychological imbalance, and therefore needs the nourishment of its ancient past. This past can reconstruct and renew our future. This does not mean we create yet another fundamentalist approach by viewing the past as more divine than the present or the future, but rather that we can aspire to learn its lessons, and examine how a greater balance can be achieved. Humanity will heal much of its current problems by enabling a greater sense of our unity with all peoples everywhere and with all of life.

Anthropological learning has conveyed an important message to humankind for it demonstrates how history contains layers of accumulated human experiences. It teaches that without the hard work of our ancestors, we would not be able to enjoy the luxurious technological life of today. The progress we have achieved today came as processes of attempts to discover the world and to make sense of human existence. The learning gleaned allows us to envision our past, enabling it to come alive in the present. Awareness of the continuum of history brings to consciousness the oneness of humanity beyond all diversities, and makes of diversities a mosaic rich with the beauty of experience. We are part of one another. As our present is a continuation of the past, our future world is being created at this time. Either we contribute to the coming generations, making the world a better place, or we leave a legacy of conflict, destruction, and misery. During the process of writing this book, the authors realized that many human stories are not being told in many parts of the world. With a degree of unease, we conscientiously examined our cultural paradigms, and the stories we have been told through our culture and its media resources. For example, some stories about Iraq are unknown to the American people; some stories about Jewish refugees from Muslim countries are unknown to many Arab people and some stories about abuse in Gaza checkpoints and Palestinian villages are unknown to many Israelis. These are only a few examples.

Yet, awareness of past-present-future continuity alone is not sufficient, for it is shaped by our individual and cultural history. We define ourselves into groups that are influenced by ideas about cultural integrity, national affiliation, and religious identity. This enculturation process is important, as it provides us with a sense of belonging and identification. Patterns of thinking and behavior are formed within our group identity, and this new information is analyzed within this context. However, a strong sense of belonging is often followed by feelings of differentiation, individuality, and superiority. When people are highly embedded in their *in-group* identity, ignorance toward others tends to grow, even unconsciously. Our environment of upbringing creates an underlying paradigm of comprehension, which is hard to challenge. We learn to accept certain axioms. It might take a lifetime to unlearn and free ourselves from some of the beliefs assimilated into our life philosophy. It takes great effort, courage and humility to question our axioms and see the world through one another's eyes.

Listening to previously unknown stories is an essential process for all of us, in order to create a better future. Unbiased and non-defensive listening reveals other possible points of view, while it instructs us on the shadowed areas of our own cultural beliefs. We can then go beyond compassion and understanding to the realm of a shared destiny. Healing of the past can only occur when we challenge our own axioms and expose ourselves to the *untold stories* of our culture.

Consider the implications of the word *history* (*HIS* story). It subtly implies the dominance of patriarchal history, and ignores any validity in its horizontally oriented, egalitarian past. Patriarchy has historically suppressed the feminine side of humanity and highlighted its vertical perspective, using religious stories and assuring conformity to them. This divisiveness isolated humankind from its natural environment. It is in our best interests to rediscover the older (often dismissed as pagan) world view of ourselves and the universe, in which humanity and the natural world are extensions of one another as well as manifestations of the divine in life. We need the feminine aspects of personality, qualities emphasizing empathy, compassion, and integration to fuel our dialogues and create healthier communities in the 21st century. We also need to listen to everyone's stories, for each one is of value.

Balancing History: Creating Gender Balanced Culture

As humanity moved from this horizontal perspective (egalitarian, matriarchal with an earth/nature based spirituality) to the vertical one (concerned with an increase in
intellectual development, abstract thought, production,
and transcendent spiritual ideologies), we began an era that
enabled great developments in religion, philosophy, science and art. The other side of this phenomenon was the dis-
connection from and irreverence for the body, our emotions
and our environment (nature). This imbalance has brought
us to a point of necessary transformation — a transformation
that bespeaks of gender equality and healthful living. If earlier myths spoke of the separation of heaven and
earth — than our current task is one of reuniting them. On a
practical level this means utilizing both feminine and masculine characteristics with the purpose of co-creating a
better world.

Historical accounts affirm that the Buddha, Jesus, and
Muhammad embodied a gender balanced perspective.
They exemplified qualities of tenderness and compassion,
and were concerned with the well being of all humanity.
They manifested a way of wholeness and Self-realization
that included receptivity to spiritual influences as well as
the ability to reveal them in actualized behaviors. Their ideals were embodied in action. The psychologist Carl Jung
referred to this evolutionary path toward wholeness as
individuation. It is the place where the authentic self comes
into being.

Jung noted that the journey included an inner unity of
male and female archetypal forces. He paid particular attention to the writings of ancient alchemists, who revered such
wholeness. Their illustrations depicted both masculine and
feminine archetypes, alluding to their presence as an important element of the spiritual journey.

Many religious and philosophical practitioners, includ-
ing Jewish Kabbalists, Jungian-based Christians, Islamic
Sufis, Taoists, indigenous cultures, (and followers of
Transpersonal Psychology) believe the spiritual journey

requires evolutionary development and a balancing of
these divine emanations (spirit and matter, lightness and
darkness, male and female). This is why Alchemists drawings and writings especially appealed to Carl Jung, for his
research and psychological theory were related to the
human journey of individuation—the unfolding of the
divine nature within (Storr, 1983). Influenced by his studies
of Jewish Kabbalistic, Gnostic and Sufi teachings, he called
the culmination of this transformational process, *Mysterium
Coniunctionis* (the mystic marriage).

Religion and Gender

A vast number of religious institutions forbid women in
leadership positions even though the Book of Thomas, Book
of Phillip and the Book of Mary, three of the Gnostic scriptures compiled in the Nag Hammadi Library, reveal that
Christianity was egalitarian in its beginnings. These books
affirm that Jesus left Mary Magdalene in a position of
leadership. The following passage from the Book of Mary
clearly relates the story of Mary being asked to share what
Jesus had taught her and her authoritative position. Peter
had asked her to share what Jesus had taught her and then
negated her response. Levi confronted him saying,

> Peter, you have always been hot-tempered. Now I see you
> contending against the woman like the adversaries. But if
> the Savior made her worthy, who are you to reject her?
> Surely the Savior knows her very well. That is why he
> loved her more than us. Rather let us be ashamed and put
> on the perfect man and acquire him for ourselves. (Parrot,
> 1988)

Despite this, males have officially dominated Christianity since the establishment of the Catholic Church and the
development of the Nicene Creed (see Chapter 3). While it is
true that Mary, the mother of Jesus, along with many female
saints, have been officially recognized, authority has been
held by males. Where does the Catholic Church stand today
regarding female priests? The answer is given in the BBC's
coverage (2002) of the late Pope John Paul II's excommuni-
cation of seven women ordained as priests by a controver-

sial Argentinean priest, Romulo Antonio Braschi. The Vatican was especially concerned that these women did not demonstrate *"any repentance"* for their crime in that women *cannot* be ordained in the Catholic Church![5] The late Pope's statement follows St. Augustine's (354-430 CE) proclamation that "Any woman who acts in such a way that she cannot give birth to as many children as she is capable of, makes herself guilty of that many murders ..." And as this church demeans a women's authority, and sexual relationships with them by its bishops and priests, we hear ongoing stories of the church's representatives sexual abuse of young boys.

The Catholic Church, Eastern Orthodox Churches, and the Church of Jesus Christ of the Latter-day Saints (Mormons) and several fundamentalist and evangelical denominations refuse ordination of women. Their primary premise is that religious leadership is reserved for men alone; women are meant to have children and maintain the family. In 2000 the Southern Baptist Convention (SBC) debated this issue and its Baptist Faith and Message Study Committee announced in May of 2000 that "While both men and women are gifted for service in the church, the office of pastor is limited to man as qualified by Scripture."[6] The SBC has approximately 16 million members and represents the United States largest Protestant denomination perpetuating this blight (gender imbalance). Obviously these groups have not explored in-depth scriptural history and are unaware of, or have established a rationale for disclaiming, the Book of Mary. Instead they focus on St. Paul's determination that

> you [the woman] must learn to adapt yourselves to your husbands. The husband is the head of the wife,

and another of his proclamations,

> Let the woman learn in silence with all subjection. But I suffer not a woman to teach or to usurp authority over the man; but to be in silence ... for Adam was first formed, then

---

[5]   http://news.bbc.co.uk/2/hi/europe/2173868.stm
[6]   http://www.religioustolerance.org/femclrg13.htm

Eve. And Adam was not deceived, but the woman being
deceived as in the transgression. Notwithstanding she
shall be saved in childbearing, if they continue in faith, and
charity and holiness with sobriety (I Timothy 2:11–15).

The effects of these ill-fated inclusions in the Bible have
added to patriarchy's crimes against women.

Numerous civil rights laws have been developed in Can-
ada and the United States. Interestingly, although these
laws particularly apply to discrimination in regards to race,
gender, disabilities, etc., for the most part they have not
been enacted in areas of religious discrimination against
women. Section 702 of the Civil Rights Act of 1964
exempted religious groups and organizations. *This allows
any church to discriminate against women.*

However, there is hope. Regardless of the above, the
advancing evolutionary energies are opening doors for
women to emerge as religious leaders. Protestant, Episco-
palian and other Christian denominations have ordained
and provided equal rights for women, and Buddhism, Hinduism, Judaism, non-denominational and protestant Christianity are evidencing an increasing number of female
teachers, pastors, gurus and rabbis.

According to the Ontario Consultants on Religious Tolerance, one out of every eight clergy and approximately 50%
of graduate students in North American Christian-based
theological schools are women. This is a rise from approximately 10% in 1972.[7] The Society of Friends (Quakers) first
began to allow female ministers in the early 1800s. Between
1853 and 1970 a variety of Christian affiliations also began
to ordain women (albeit very slowly), and the number of
women being ordained continues to rise.

Although Buddhism might appear to have been slow to
acknowledge women with equal rights and ordination, the
dialogue between patriarchal and more egalitarian ways of
being has been included from its beginning. Early Buddhist
history reveals that Mahapajapati Gotami, the Buddha's
foster-mother (who nursed the Siddhartha in his infancy),
was ordained along with 500 other women by the Bodhi-

[7]   http://www.religioustolerance.org

sattva (enlightened one) himself. Apparently Mahapajapati had made this request three times beforehand and had been turned down because they were women. The 500 women were the wives of the monks (early followers of the Buddha) who had relinquished their positions as husbands in preference of the monastic life. These women felt they had no other recourse than to follow the monastic life themselves. Their arduous journey by foot and determined requests had proved their commitment. The response was that they were to live the same eight special rules expected of the male followers (although they were still relegated to an inferior position because they were women).

Tibetan Buddhism has both female nuns and lamas. Many women are presented to the monastic life as young girls (as young as three) because their families could not afford to keep them. In Japan, the heart of Zen Buddhism, women can be nuns, but cannot be priests. However, the value of the feminine presence is recognized. A significant contribution of female dharma teachers is that they are more open to emotional expression and value the importance of relatedness. Nevertheless, a nun can only become a Sensei (priest or teacher) if her male teacher feels she is ready.

Buddhism has taken on a different flavor in the Western world as Buddhist teachings blend with cultural differences. American Buddhism has numerous female teachers representing a variety of Zen and Tibetan sects. Many of these dharma teachers are also married. There are many female priests, however there are few female Senseis (teachers). The first American female Zen teacher was Ruth Fuller Everett Sasaki. She received a rare honor in that she was ordained in Japan in 1958, following many years of Zen training. One can see in the slow increase of female entry into the realm of religious leadership, an affirmation of the rising evolutionary trend.

There are numerous popular female Gurus representing the Hindu/Vedic religion. Yogic teacher and author, B.V. Tripurari, founder of the Sadhu Sangha nonsectarian on-line discussion, believes that "the number of women gurus has reached new heights. The popularity of women gurus is in part also a reaction to well-documented abuses on the part of male gurus and the belief that women are less prone to exploiting others than men are."[8] Although the Vedic religion is well grounded in patriarchy, its deeper teachings hold that the soul is neither male nor female. Swami Tripurari explains that if a female guru "represents a tradition or lineage with a scriptural canon, and whose words and actions conform to that canon and standards of that lineage (albeit dynamically applied in terms of today's world)" (ibid.), her teachings are recognized and as valid as any male Guru's.

Mother Maya (Swamini Mayatitananda) is one example of a modern female Guru. Traditionally Vedic meditative practices have focused away from life as the devotee seeks inner peace, but this female Guru's teachings differ in that the focus is to better life itself. Mother Maya specifically focuses on healing and balancing oneself in order to heal and balance our environment and world. It is this focus that repeatedly emerges from female leaders — regardless of religious affiliation.

All branches of Judaism, except the Orthodox, value the female role in Jewish rituals. Orthodox Jews do not allow women to take leadership positions in the Synagogue nor to participate in rabbinical studies. Orthodox Jews maintain strict rules enforcing their ideas of modesty, which requires a separation of men and women during religious rituals. Women attend the Synagogue, but remain in a separate area — hidden from men's eyes. Orthodox Jews also reject the ordainment of women as rabbis. In the Orthodox view, such an act would be an unacceptable deviation from the expectations derived from tradition. In traditional Judaism, women are seen as separate but equal; their primary role is as wives and mothers, irrespective of the fact that many Jewish scholars believed that the matriarchs (Sarah, Rebecca, Rachel, and Leah) were superior to the patriarchs (Abraham, Isaac, and Jacob) in prophecy. Instead, women are expected to hide themselves in men's presence (e.g.,

[8]   http://www.swami.org/sanga/archives/pages/volume_five/m2 28.html

cover their bodies and hair) and to only socialize with other women. All public prayers are done by men alone. In fact, a common prayer of orthodox Jewish men is "Blessed art Thou, O Lord, our God, King of the Universe, that Thou didst not make me a woman."

Other branches of Judaism, however, are more receptive to change. For example, in an attempt to achieve equality for Jewish women, Regina Jonas wrote an elaborate polemical analysis of Jewish law in 1930 to prove that women could become Rabbis. Jonas finally received her rabbinical diploma in 1942 in Berlin, but was, tragically, murdered by the Nazis a few years later. Also, Sally Priesand was the first Jewish woman to be ordained as a Rabbi in the United States by the Reform movement in 1972. Today, many Jewish females can celebrate Bat Mitzvah, and also serve as Rabbis, cantors, and community leaders.

Islam's beginnings were gender balanced. In fact, Khadija was the Prophet's partner in his message, whereas his daughter Fatima is considered to be Islam's first religious teacher. For Muslims, whether Sunni or Shi'is, Fatima az-Zahra and her daughter Zayinab represent the feminine archetype. They refer to Fatima as Az-Zahra'a. The word Az-Zahra'a denotes the quality of radiant light, and the one who manifests beauty, the similitude of that quality beheld in a tree, which blossoms and brings forth fruits continuously. To acknowledge Fatima's special qualities, the title of Al-Azhar university in Egypt (971 CE) was derived from her nickname (A-z-ha-ra is the root of Al-Azhar and Fatima's nickname Az-Zahra).

In the early Islamic period, it was a natural occurrence for women to have authority in religious education, and it is well known that the famous jurisprudent Al-Shafi studied under Sayyedah Nafisa (a great granddaughter of the Prophet Muhammad). She was called the "jewel of knowledge" (Helminski, 2003). Given this history, it is sad that in the modern Islamic world, most key positions are designated to men, such as the presidency of religious institutions, or jurisprudence. This type of discrimination against women is perceived and justified as religious. Women, used to giving up their rights, believe they would be breaking religious rules if they rebelled against these norms. They were not provided with the knowledge about their women predecessors. But this is changing; for example, Camille Helminski recently collected the life stories of Sufi women from Islam's early history through the contemporary period in her book *Women of Sufism*. The impressive list of women includes educators, healers, reformers, poets, and saints, pioneering the betterment of humanity (Helminski, 2003).

In many Islamic countries, there have been women's movements, which are based ideologically on Islamic principles, and aimed at liberating women from false Islamic ideologies. When given the chance, unhampered by masculine authority, women provide a needed balance to stereotypical male views. This is occurring throughout the world, including Islamic nations. For example, an American female scholar, Amina Wadud,[9] has introduced a way of reading and interpreting the Qur'an from a feminine perspective. Her interpretation is harmonious with the basic tenets of Islam while assuring that all human beings receive its riches irrespective of gender differences. In her book, *Qur'an and Women: Reading The Sacred Text From a Woman's Perspective* (Wadud, 1999), Wadud presents polemical issues in a clear, harmonious way, providing convincing and well-established conclusions that contradict male biased interpretations that have defamed the Islamic view and treatment of women for centuries. Although gender imbalance is evidenced throughout the globe, many extremist Islamic groups (for example, the Taliban and the Wahhabis of Saudi Arabia) have brought it to public attention in the light of recent world events. There are many Muslim women both quietly and overtly taking steps to

---

[9]   Amina Wadud was the first Muslim woman in the world to lead a prayer in a mixed congregation of both male and female in New York. This historic event evoked massive criticism from the orthodox Islamic groups who believe that a Muslim woman should never lead prayer in a mixed gender congregation.

help others become socially active, and this development is occurring throughout the Muslim world (ibid.).

In every religion, female religious leaders, concerned with healing the human family, are gathering around the planet. Dena Merriam and Christian leader, Reverend Joan Brown Campbell (USA) have formed the *Global Peace Initiative of Women Religious and Spiritual Leaders* gathering female religious, business and governmental leaders from all faiths and religions who are focused on building peace and a better world for all. This group emerged from the Millennium World Peace Summit convened at the United Nations in New York in 2000 — an immense effort aimed at uniting representatives of all faiths. The Global Peace Initiative is just one example of the emergence of feminine presence in religious and political domains. They have taken up the project of educating children around the globe towards peaceful ways of living with one another. It is significant that two women in a row have won the Nobel Peace Prize in recent years. Shirin Ebadi, an Iranian attorney, won this acknowledgement in 2003 as a result of her dedication to human rights and the plights of children. Wangari Maathai, from Kenya, was awarded the Nobel Peace Prize for her work with our environment. Her commitment is one of protecting the environment as a means of improving governance.

Politics and Gender

The presence of equal representation of women in government in sorely needed. The Policy Research Report on Gender and Development examined the relationship between women, corruption and government. The findings, published by the World Bank, reported that,

> Numerous behavioral studies have found women to be more trust-worthy and public-spirited than men. These results suggest that women should be particularly effective in promoting honest government. Consistent with this hypothesis, we find that the greater the representation of women in parliament, the lower the level of corruption. We find this association in a large cross-section of countries;

the result is robust to a wide range of specifications. (Dollar et al., 1999)

The above research was one of several papers in a series on Gender and Development. The findings were published in *Engendering Development: Through Gender Equality in Rights, Resources, and Voice*. Researchers noted that "Gender inequality hinders development" adding that "Inequalities in rights, resources, and political voice generally disadvantage women, but they also disadvantage the rest of society and impede development" (The World Bank, 2001, p. 73) Thus a rigorous movement towards gender equality is spreading around the globe.[10]

Leadership and governmental positions have long been deemed the domain of men. Therefore, for the few women who have dared to enter political realms, the tendency has been to repress their femininity and adopt masculine behaviors in order to obtain any status of power. This is no longer necessary. In fact, the unique qualities of the feminine are needed in order to create positive change. For example, (as noted in Chapter Three) increasing research in this area suggests that women do not respond to stressors in the same manner as males. The presence of hormonal factors, such as testosterone in males and oxytocin in females, supports these differences. Women are more apt to respond to discord or challenges in ways that reach out to those involved. (At the same time, the capacity to act with compassion or aggression is within each human being — regardless of gender.)

In their book, *Women, Gender, and World Politics*, Peter Beckman and Francine D'Amico note that even though biological differences exist between males and females, "gender characteristics are cultural creations, passed on to new members of a society [or religion] through a process

---

[10]   Many people tend to stereotype Middle Eastern, India and other nations as examples of female repression, forgetting that less than 100 years ago American activists Lucy Burn, Dora Lewis, Alice Cosu, Dorothy Day and others were imprisoned and viciously beaten for the crime of picketing the White House — in their demand for female equality and the right to vote.

called socialization" (Beckman & D'Amico, 1994, pp. 3–4). The premise is that biological sex and the topic of gender are separate issues in regard to what constitutes a man or a woman, and that these differ when comparing one culture with another.[11] Beckman and D'Amico also note the obvious variations in each sex. For example, one male can be totally focused on power over others whereas another may lack the strength needed for leadership, but exhibit nurturing qualities. The female could manifest total reliance on others for decision-making or evidence combative characteristics, or at a more developed level emanate both strength and concern for others.

These descriptions can be seen as levels of alchemical maturity (described earlier in the chapter), whereupon human development includes an integrative relationship between the archetypal anima (female) and animus (male) within the evolving individual. This development enables nurturing qualities balanced with strength and results in an egalitarian leadership style focused upon bettering life for the entire society rather than sacrificing numerous members of humanity in one's unilateral grasp for wealth and power. There is much hypocritical talk about democracy these days, but in reality true democratic leadership is by its inherent nature egalitarian.

Frene Ginwala, Speaker of the National Assembly of South Africa, notes that "The seed of democracy lies in the principle that the legitimacy of the power to make decisions about peoples' lives, their society and their country should derive from a choice by those who will be effected" (Ginwala, 1998, p. 1). This statement represents a more feminine perspective—one recognizing the relevance of the human beings comprising the culture. In fact, research reveals that women, in particular, tend to especially focus on "issues of justice, equity and human rights" (ibid., p. 2).

The idea and practice of gender-balanced leadership and government has reaped significant changes in Nordic soci-

---

[11] Social and anthropological studies affirm that social roles given to men and women do not belong to a natural order, but rather are culturally and socially developed.

eties. In addressing gender-balanced government, Birgetta
Dahl, Speaker of Parliament in Sweden, notes that,

> The most interesting aspect of the Swedish Parliament is
> not that we have 45 per cent representation of women, but
> that a majority of women and men bring relevant social
> experience to the business of parliament. This is what
> makes a difference. Men bring with them experience of real
> life issues, of raising children, of running a home. They
> have broad perspectives and greater understanding. And
> women are allowed to be what we are, and to act according
> to our unique personalities. Neither men nor women have
> to conform to a traditional role. Women do not have to
> behave like men to have power; men do not have to behave
> like women to be allowed to care for their children. When
> this pattern becomes the norm, then we will see real
> change. (Shvedova, 1998, p. 28)

The practice of sponsoring women to help them take leadership positions in a feminine way is especially meaningful.
Many people have experienced female supervisors or man-
agers who were insensitive, dominating and punitive—
oftentimes acting out a patriarchal style of governance.
Most likely, they simply had not been exposed to non-
patriarchal role models for feminine leadership. But
women are now finding their own way and supporting one
another, as increasing numbers of women are feeling compelled to step into significant leadership positions.

The succession of the arduous journey towards women's
right began in 1893 when New Zealand's women were
given the right to vote. Soon other countries followed suit.
Finland was the first to allow women both to vote and to
stand for elections. Now one-hundred and eleven years
later, almost every nation allows its women the right to participate in decisions regarding local and national leadership, although few and far between are the women who
stand in elected positions of leadership. This means that
women to a large degree are still omitted from policy-mak-
ing. However, this too is changing. Statistically, women
currently represent approximately "11.7 of legislative
members worldwide" (Lovenduski and Karan, 1998, p. 126)
with Nordic countries representing 36.4 % (the highest),
Americas about 13% and Arab states a little over 3% (the

lowest). Earlier US history reveals that, "Native American governments may have been more democratic in some respects [than the US government], particularly in the extent to which they permitted women to participate in governmental affairs" prior to the spread of US government's intrusion into tribal life (Alschuler, 1994, p. 867). In fact, Native American women continue to be active in tribal affairs. Even though the *Chiefs* are traditionally male, women often give a final word on major tribal decisions.

A spectacular event occurred in 1983 when Norway made the decision that both males and females must be included in 40% of all elections and nominations. The Swedish Social Democratic Party proclaimed in 1994 that every other electoral candidate was to be one of the opposite gender (assuring the possibility of equal representation). On the average, women now fill slightly over one-third of its governmental positions (Karan, 1998). Birgitta Dahl, Speaker of Parliament in Sweden, explains that a quota system in itself does not make the difference. Swedish women "laid the groundwork to facilitate women's entry into politics. We prepared the women to ensure they were competent ... we prepared the system, which made it a little less shameful for men to step aside" (Dahlerup, 1998, p. 93). They opened the door for women and men to work together, with each sex utilizing the unique facets of their gender along with the contributions of their individual personalities. The presence of women in parliament has influenced decision-making policies on education, health, social services and care of children and elders. Women leaders are, by nature, more concerned with gender equality, promoting rights for women, ending domestic violence and creating egalitarian societies. They are less concerned with war, and the development of greater and more powerful weaponry, and therefore focused on improving life for all.

It is not surprising that female representation is limited in the Middle East (with women constituting 3% of parliament). Muslim men have long ignored Islamic history in regard to the political influence of women in its beginnings. Few pay attention to the fact Aisha, the second wife of the

Prophet, exercised political leadership when she led an army to drive back the attacking forces of Ali Ibn Abi Taleb. Although she later regretted taking a military stance, her martial knowledge and strength nevertheless provided a model for future generations demonstrating that women can take charge of political leadership. Modern Muslims use Aisha's regret to validate their beliefs that women's leadership would be a failure. They have forgotten that her decision to fight Ali was later deemed to be a mistake that had nothing to do with gender.

In more recent times, women have been elected as heads of state in both Bangladish and Pakistan. For example, Khaleda Zia was a prime minister of Bangladesh from 1991 to 1996 and was succeeded by Sheikh[12] Hasina Wajed. Benazir Bhutto was Prime Minister of Pakistan from 1988 to 1990 and again from 1993 to 1996. Tansu Ciller was chosen to become the Prime Minister of Turkey in 1993 and remained in office for three years. Israel's Golda Meir also became a well-known political figure in the Middle East. She began her career as a minister of foreign affairs (1956–1969) and eventually became Israel's prime minister serving in this position from 1969 till January 1974. In the 80s, the people of Malta elected Agatha Barbara as their president (1982–1986). Although it is little known, the first female Vice President in the history of the Middle East was a US educated Iranian physician, Dr. Masume Ebtekar. She was appointed in President Khatami's administration, and has been very involved with Iranian women's rights.In short, although it appears to be a slow journey, women are steadily taking leadership positions in Middle Eastern countries.

Some of the above women followed a patriarchal leadership style. Women are recognizing that it is important to maintain their innate feminine nature when exercising leadership, otherwise there will be little, if any, change in patriarchal structures.

---

[12]   The term *Sheikh* is used for both women and men in Bangladesh, whereas in Arabic-speaking countries *Sheikha* is used to denote the feminine and to differentiate it from the masculine.

The beginning of the twentieth century witnessed conflicts between traditional ways of thinking and a progressive approach that is commonly classified as modernization (and we must note here that many Islamic nations are suspicious of westernization because of its secular and oftentimes irreverent approach to life).[13] Ironically, the main idealistic principles of modernization (equality, justice and human rights) are also embedded in the authentic culture of Islam.[14] A confusion occurs because Middle Eastern and Islamic nations express these same principles in a language and style that befits their own cultural identity, thereby Islamic and Arab nations perceive western democracy to be alien in comparison to their own style.

Egypt was a pioneer in unraveling these contradictions. Bold men went against the majority and initiated campaigns for defending women's right to education and work. Courageous women have encouraged political participation on the grass root level. This increased social awareness among Egyptian women. During the 1919 revolution in Egypt, women participated positively and expressed their solidarity with national leadership against British occupation. Figures such as Houda Sha'rawy, Nabaweyya Musa, early in the twentieth century and later Duriyya Shafique and Amina As-Said opened the doors for many women to join the women's liberation movement. Their ideas echoed throughout the Arab world.

> At the Arab Feminist Congress in Cairo in December 1944 Huda Sha'rawi and other Egyptian feminists made a strong case for political rights, this time not just for their

---

[13] The Harem culture was created during the Ottoman and Mamulak periods in the sixteenth century. This pseudo religious notion isolated women. Radical Islamists were also opposed to the women's liberation movement as they believed it to be a western imposition. An argument can be made that western ideals have the potential to motivate new ways of thinking and to deconstruct pseudo religious ideals. Slowly, these new ideas are establishing roots within Islamic nations.

[14] Muhammad was elected by the majority of Medina citizens to take the leadership of the first Ummah (community). He consulted his companions on any decisions to be made, and opposition was allowed.

> compatriots but for all Arab women. As president of the
> Egyptian Feminist Union and head of the Arab Feminist
> Conference Sha'rawi declared in her keynote address,
> "The Arab woman also demands with her loudest voice the
> regaining of political rights, rights that have been granted
> to her by the shari'ah." Sha'rawi, we notice, legitimized her
> call for women's political rights in the discourse of Islam
> rather than the language of secular democracy. (Badran,
> 1995, p. 216)

Throughout the Middle East and Africa, women have
struggled for and been given the right to vote and to be
members in parliaments.

Jewish women represent many of the more influential
feminist leaders of the past century. Gloria Steinem, for
example, was a major feminist leader in the US during the
1960s. She had a life long career as a writer and a journalist,
drawing attention to political and social issues of women's
rights, and encouraging women to acknowledge their
empowerment resources. She was the founder of *Ms.* Magazine, the first American national women's magazine run by
women and remains an impressive and dedicated woman
at the forefront of human rights.

In Israel, however, women are under-represented in all
areas of public life. Few women have been involved in the
nation's leadership since the resignation of the powerful
Prime Minister Golda Meir in 1973. Moreover, in recent
years, small religious parties, that generally opposed participation of women in public life, have gained increasing
political influence. The Israeli mandatory army service is
another arena of discrimination. Many politicians have
paved their way to public service through a military career.
Although the service is mandatory for both men and
women, women are excused more easily, and also banned
from some positions. Only a few women have been able to
rise to a high rank in the Israeli army. The story of Alice
Miller's petition to volunteer for a pilot-training course
exemplifies the inequality in the Israeli military. Ms. Miller
became the first female combat jet pilot after a landmark
decision of the Israeli High Court. But these are examples of
women following male-dominated paradigms as increas-

ing numbers of women are gathering to represent more humane examples of female leadership in Israel and throughout the world. For example, many Israeli women are active in the Israeli-Palestinian conflict over the occupied territories. On one hand religious women from Jewish settlements fiercely claim their right over the land, and on the other hand groups such as *Women in Black* protest against Israel's occupation of the West Bank and Gaza.

Women in Black has evolved into a worldwide network, committed to peace and justice, actively opposed to war and other forms of violence. It is not an organization, but rather a means of mobilization and a formula for action. They claim:

> Women-only peace activism does not suggest that women, any more than men, are "natural born peacemakers". But women have a particular experience of life, being disproportionately involved in caring work. Women are often at the receiving end of gendered violence in both peace and war, and women are the majority of refugees. A feminist view sees masculine cultures as especially prone to violence, and so feminist women tend to have a particular perspective on security and something unique to say about war.[15]

Dr. Nurit Peled-Elhanan is an Israeli peace activist bereaving the loss of her only daughter, 13 year-old Smadar, killed by a Palestinian suicide bomber in Jerusalem in 1997. Despite her personal bereavement, Nurit likewise understood the pain of Palestinian mothers. She recognized that her enemies were not the Palestinian people, but rather those who perpetuate wars. She avowed that "wars are waged for no other reason than the insanity and megalomania of the so-called leaders and heads of state."[16] Nurit, who won a peace award (Sakharov prize laureate, 2001) from the European parliament, represents a compassionate woman, one capable of seeing the grief endured by both sides of this sad conflict. She suggests a new propaganda for those who want to be free and safe in this world. In her speech to Women in Black, Nurit proclaimed, "... a cry must rise, a

[15] http://www.womeninblack.net/
[16] http://www.nimn.org/jewishper/npe1.html

cry that is as ancient as man and woman, a cry that is beyond
all differences of race or religion or language, the cry of
motherhood: Save our children" (ibid.).

This is a cry we must all listen and respond to, for all
nations would benefit by following the example established
in the Nordic gender-balanced ideals for government (even
though it still needs to achieve a 50-50 balance). Education
and preparation of women while encouraging and utilizing
both masculine and feminine characteristics could help to
bring our world into needed equilibrium, a balanced position
whereupon men are willing to relinquish dominance and
stand alongside of women, supporting them as co-leaders.
This applied alchemical effort of gender balance will move
us towards wholeness, and spiritual unity.

A group of 200 women, representing a cross-section of
Israeli society, joined in the creation of "Women, Peace and
Security — An Index of Women for Peace Negotiation
Teams." It is based upon UN Resolution 1325 created in
2000, which noted that since women are affected by war
they should be involved in negotiation and conflict resolu-
tion. According to an article in the Israeli newspaper
Ha'aretz on July 12, 2006:

> Their goal is to help negotiate peace talks between Palestin-
> ian and Israeli representatives. "Men make war, they
> should let women contribute to making peace," says Reuya
> Abu-Rabia, a social worker and law student who directs
> the Yedid advocacy group's center in Rahat. The index lists
> her as a group facilitator who deals with empowering
> women and developing political and social leadership
> through public campaigns to realize rights.[17]

Perhaps this index of Israeli women, can help to negotiate
peace between Palestinians and Israelis if and when given
the chance. According to Ha'aretz reporter Ruth Sinai, it
includes lawyers, security experts, representatives from
"health, human and civil rights, education, economics,
trade, environment, planning, communications and even

---

[17] Sadly, the meeting with the Israeli President was scheduled on the
same day the Israelis attacked Lebanon. Hopefully, these women
will pursue their intention.

culture and art." This cross section of Israeli women includes, "Jews and Arabs, Mizrahim and Ashkenazim, veterans and new immigrants, heterosexuals and lesbians, women who belong to the mainstream and more radical representatives."

Admittedly, these women are following the example provided by Visaka Dharmadasa of Sri Lanka, the mother of a soldier who had been killed in combat. Her response was to enter Tamil territory accompanied by a group of seven other mothers to negotiate a cease fire with the leaders of its terrorist organization. She created ties with them that led to a cease-fire in 2002.

Healing Religion

Imagine the changes that could occur if religious practitioners were to focus their meditations and love of the divine in the present moment, where it can be felt and expressed in life. After all, love and compassion are to be found at the heart of all religious teachings. As we move away from dogmatic translations and apply the dynamic principles of Midrash and Ta'wil, allowing ever fresh and ever deepening understanding to influence consciousness, we will move into a new era.

The Heart Sutra, a Buddhist prayer, tells followers to move beyond all ideas, thoughts, and beliefs in order to have a direct experience of that presence that is beyond human words. This same truth may well be the reason why Jews have a scriptural ruling saying that the name of the divine cannot be spoken. Reverence for the sacred is one thing, but the belief that we can mentally articulate that which is beyond the human mind may well be ludicrous — let alone a most egotistical venture. Fundamentalist and dogmatic renditions of scripture lack the life force that opens the heart to the divine. In such environments, religious theology, beset with rules, rarely, if ever, awakens the heart. Mystics of all religious traditions recognize that true spirituality enters with direct experience. This is why the very appearance of our Prophets initiated such strong responses in that they reflected a direct encounter of the divine. It is a waste of effort to argue over mental conceptions of the divine. And yet, much grief, madness and death has resulted over this extensive human error.

Earlier in the book we noted the words of the great Sufi master, Hazrat Inayat Khan, who had imaged each religion as a musical note, emphasizing that each one came from the same source and that great music was the result of all notes being combined (Khan, 1979, p. 19) – a symphony to the cosmos. When one begins to perceive each religion as yet another distinct expression of the Unlimited Divine, one can only appreciate the power and creativity of God. As humanity learns to honor the distinctions and differences that divide us, we can move beyond prejudice, ignorance and the limitations of fundamentalist thinking. We will be able to understand and follow the prayerful example from another great Sufi master, Ibn al'Arabi (1164–1240), who provided a formula for transforming this human evil when he proclaimed,

> My heart is capable of every form:
>
> A cloister for the monk, a fane for idols,
> A pasture for gazelles, the votary's Ka'ba [temple],
> The tables of the Torah, the Qur'an.
> Love is the creed I hold: wherever turn
> His camels, Love is still my creed and faith.
>
> (Shah,1964, p. 165)

Ibn al'Arabi was speaking of the open heart that rejoices in reverence and beauty wherever it is expressed. The problem with the patriarchal influence in religion is the fact that it has made its sacred texts and rulings more important than human beings – and life itself. They have ignored the message to be found at the heart of all religions. This message is called the Golden Rule in Christianity, but its universal significance is expressed in every religious tradition. The following examples evidence this archetypal message:[18]

---

[18]   The Golden Rule. Poster created by Scarboro Missions. A Canadian Catholic community of priest and laypeople (2000. Paul McKenna).

Hinduism: This is the sum of duty: do not do to others what would cause pain if done to you (Mahabbarata 5:1517).

Buddhism: Treat not others in ways that you yourself would find hurtful (The Buddha, Udana-Varga 5:18).

Confucianism: One word which sums up the basis of all good conduct ... loving kindness. Do not do to others what you do not want done to yourself (Confucious, Analects 15:23).

Taoism: Regard your neighbor's gain as your own gain, and your neighbor's loss as your own loss (Lao Tzu, T'ai Shang Kan Ying P'ien, 213-218).

Zoroastrianism: Do not do unto others what is injurious to yourself (Shayast-na-Shayast 13.29).

Sikhism: I am a stranger to no one; and no one is a stranger to me. Indeed, I am a friend to all (Guru Granth Sahib, pg. 1299).

Judaism: What is hateful to you, do not do to your neighbor. This is the whole Torah; all the rest is commentary (Hillel, Tahmud, Shabbat 31a).

Christianity: In everything, do to others as you would have them do to you; for this is the law and the prophets (Jesus, Matthew 7:12).

Islam: Not one of you truly believes until you wish for others what you wish for yourself (The Prophet Muhammad, Hadith).

Only a gender-balanced, egalitarian society has the potential to provide the sacred container in which to make these ideals a reality. This will ready us for our next stage of human evolution for we are on the brink of a new realization of spirituality. This evolutionary step will both embrace the horizontal honoring of sacredness of life itself evidenced in nomadic spirituality as well as the vertical ideal of the sacred central to the patriarchal religions.

Our stories about divine creation may well change as our new story will be supported by the ongoing findings of Quantum Physics and other sciences. If we embody the true message of the love, wisdom and compassion inherent within the open heart, as we explore the inner and outer depths of the cosmos — we hold this possibility of expanding into a new evolutionary stage of Self Realization. Fundamentalists fear the language of science. They believe it to be anti-God — but they are wrong. Science will ultimately evidence the magnificence of the universe and divine creation. It will take us beyond the limiting stories that have both contributed to and initiated abuse of *the other*.

Human Transcendence and the New Story

Scientific research and findings have also enhanced our understanding of human behaviors. Studies of the three levels of evolutionary brain development (reptilian, old and new mammalian), reveal the human motivation toward aggressive and defensive behaviors, but there is a fourth level associated with the enlargement of the pre-frontal lobes. This more recent evolutionary brain development allows for heightened intellectual and creative abilities. It is also associated with compassion, love and other virtuous human capacities. Its, oftentimes dormant, faculties offer an entirely new world view — one that can harness and redirect the interdependent forces of our earlier developed triune brain (Pearce, 2002). Research done through the HeartMath Institute reveal this higher faculty has a relationship with the heart, itself. Their work reflects the potential evolutionary effects that the heart and mind have upon one another. This is a potential result of the balance of masculine (ideals) and feminine (caring) characteristics.

Scientists have also been able to measure brain waves for some time now. A more recent measurement is that of the heart's electromagnetic field. Using a magnetic imaging device, the University of Utah has been able to measure an arc (torus) of magnetic waves emanating several feet from and returning to the heart. Pearce explains that

> ... according to physicists, a torus is a very stable form for energy, which, once generated and set in motion, tends to self-perpetuate. Some scientists conjecture that all energy systems from the atomic to the universal level are toroid in form. This leads to the possibility that there is only one universal torus encompassing an infinite number of interacting, holographic tori within its spectrum ... One implication of this is that each of us centered within our heart

torus is as much the center of the universe as any other creature or point, with equal access to all that exists. (ibid.,
p. 59)

Thus, science and mystics are arriving at the same
place — the center of the cosmos can be known through the
heart.

In his book, *The Hidden Heart of the Cosmos*, Brian
Swimme, who holds a degree in Mathematical Cosmology,
explains that science itself goes through a process of Midrash
/Ta'wil in its contemplation of the universe. For instance,
Swimme notes how science tests and rejects hypotheses,
and describes how it "offers a hypothetical story of reality
that is constantly revised, but stronger and more depend-
able with each generation for the simple reason that an ever
larger body of experience is appropriated into its intellectual framework" (Swimme, 1996, p. 77). Our understanding
of the divine in all of its manifestations is an ongoing
process of discovery and integration leading us to an ever
deepening relationship with God.

Science is making vital discoveries. Its findings can transform our understanding of Creation and our relationship
with the divine. It has its own contribution towards the
development of an egalitarian world. When one considers
the obvious damage caused by rigid religious theologies,
the discoveries taking place in Quantum Physics and other
scientific traditions offer a fresh reorganization of how we
perceive and manifest our spirituality. The mysteries made
known by Quantum Physicists suggest that we can co-cre-
ate a new reality — one that moves humanity beyond limited egoic religious interpretations into infinite possibilities
within the divine (Wolf, 2000). This new scientific revelation is unconcerned with religious dogmas, racial, cultural,
class and gender differences. Instead, its fundamental tenets reveal that at the subatomic level we are all one, verify-
ing the experience long proclaimed by mystics of all
traditions.

Swimme explains that Albert Einstein didn't simply discover gravitational effects and the dynamics of the universe
when he defined the theory of relativity; but that something

much deeper was occurring as "shattering truths dropped from his fingertips," for "through these symbols the universe whispered that it was expanding in all directions" (Swimme, 1996, p. 71). Galaxies were increasing and yet every single point was the center of the universe.

This means that we are each at the center of the universe. Swimme asks of us, "When we picture the cosmic birth as some kind of explosion taking place away from where we are observing, just where we are standing? How can we stand outside the universe if from the beginning we are woven into this birth?" (ibid., p. 82). If each one of us is manifesting from the center of the cosmos, a unique creation of the most sacred, how can we dishonor or harm another — for in reality we are harming ourselves — in that we are each an expression of the unifying fabric of the universe.

We are all following our great Prophets in a human procession "a caravan of creation" (Douglas-Klotz, 2003, p. 103) toward the center of our hearts — the center of the Universe. In the Hadith Qudsi (divine illuminations presented to Muhammad), it is written that God declared, "I was a hidden Treasure, I yearned to be known. That is why I produced creatures, in order to be known by them" (Corbin, 1958/1969, p. 183). As the great Jewish-Dutch philosopher Spinoza believed, "… lasting happiness can ultimately be attained only in the knowledge of God. Each of us however, must travel this road by ourselves. While the final destination is the same for all, each existence is unique and individual. Each of us must come to know God in our individual way" (Schipper, 1993, p. 123). The realization of the divine is the great treasure to be discovered within life. As we move beyond rigid belief structures and open our hearts, we can follow Jesus' advice, "*Ask, and it shall be given you; seek, and ye shall find; knock, and it shall be opened unto you: For every one that asketh receiveth; and he that seeketh findeth; and to him that knocketh it shall be opened*" (Matthew, 7:7–8). Everything we desire is here, right now. All we have to do is to make a choice to enter into humanity's *New Story*.

Imagine a world in which human communities contribute to one another and bring the vision of spiritual love and compassionate wisdom into being. Imagine a world in which each person feels supported by the whole human family — encouraged to develop creatively the unique gifts we all bring. What kind of, as yet inconceivable blooming could take place? Problems cannot be solved on the level on which they were created, states Einstein's oft-quoted observation. We have to allow for the shattering of the patriarchal mind-set and its absolute authority, if we are to embrace a larger, more inclusive vision. We grow by discarding what no longer fits us, by letting go of what we have outgrown. We can, if we so choose, create a new, heart-centered world together. Together, we can create this world and gift our descendants with peace.

If ever the world sees a time when women shall come together purely and simply for the benefit of [Hu]mankind, it will be a power such as the world has never known.

Matthew Arnold
British poet (1822-1888)

Epilogue

A Place Where the Authors Share their Process and Ideals

Changes in gender balance have begun. In January 2006 two women were elected to presidency, one in West Africa and the other in South America. A New York Times article[1] noted that "unlike Margaret Thatcher and Golda Meir, the strong women of the previous generation, Ms. Bachelet [Chile] and Ms. Johnson Sirleaf [Liberia], have embraced what they have both called feminine virtues and offered them as precisely what countries emerging from the heartbreak of tyranny and strife need." This is an amazing achievement, for the majority of humanity has all been deeply influenced by the patriarchal paradigm. Even in the United States there is talk that Hillary Clinton and Condaliza Rice may compete for presidency. Sadly, both of these women represent a patriarchal political paradigm whereas Ms. Bachelet and Ms. Sirleaf are more concerned with the people they serve. They represent a feminine model. A paradigmatic shift in how we deal with neighboring countries, health, education and the like, may occur as increasing nations accept these changes — the inclusion of feminine leadership.[2]

---

[1]　Lydia Polgreen and Larry Rohter (January 22, 2006). *Where Political Clout Demands a Maternal touch.*

[2]　Since coming into office, Michelle Bachelet has appointed 50% women in all governmental positions. Her government allocates 64% of its budget to social programs.

Four women, each differing in culture and religious expression, have openly discussed political and religious regimes, including their present and historical failures. Given the current state of this world, this is not necessarily a "safe" thing to do. We have made a case for a humanitarian ideal, possible through a shift in gender balance. Each of the authors in this book have also had to check our personal biases, clear our hearts, and choose to support what we truly believe in. We have steadily progressed despite the troubling events taking place in each of our nations, our personal lives, and even in the writing of this book. The ongoing Israeli-Palestinian conflict, Israel's attack on Lebanon in retaliation for the killing and kidnapping of soldiers stationed at its border, and the US's so-called "war on terror" were areas that evoked deep emotional responses in each of us. In fact, they prompted the writing, and oftentimes re-writing, of this book.

In the following pages, we will each share our personal stories, including the difficulties that were encountered in dealing with some of the material in the book as we wrote it, along with our responses to the current escalation of war in the Middle East and troubled spots around the globe. This will allow each of us to voice the thoughts most deeply held within our hearts.

Aliaa first suggested the Epilogue, because she recognized that it would give an opportunity to individually express our views. She also believed that the disclosures of any personal struggles and the ways we individually resolved them would support the intention inherent in this book. Rachel had the idea of the initial format, by suggesting we tell our experience in the same spirit used in the biographical stories contained in the Introduction. Both Aliaa and Rachel had the idea that we write separately, and then respond to one another's statements. Sharon and Jenny added to this process by suggesting that we spend some time meditating on one another's contributions, before responding. We believed this way of feeling the words and listening to one another from a deeper place, would enable us to respond from our hearts, thereby demonstrating a truly feminine paradigm. Therefore the Epilogue has two parts. Part I was written separately and Part II was then written as a response to what had been evoked in each one of us.

Our first section begins with Jenny's experience. Jenny had joined the team towards the end of the book. She provided a very important balance as she read through the manuscript and added her voice.

Part I

Jenny Eda Schipper

It is difficult to process the Arab-Israeli conflict, both as a Jew and as a humanitarian. As a Jew, I am on high alert whenever the Israeli-Palestinian issue comes up. I immediately ask the question in myself and of others: where was the world when the whole of European Jewry (including my grandparents, aunts, uncles) were taken from their homes, sent to concentration (not refugee) camps and murdered by the millions?

If I am to be in integrity with my humanitarian ideals, I need to first express my outrage at the numb, callous response of the world to the horrific fate of my people under the Nazis. Had I been born a mere five years earlier, I most likely would not be alive to contribute to this book.

Because of this, and the history of persecution the Jews have suffered in this world, I empathize with the attitude that says "never again!" This mentality legitimizes doing whatever is necessary to secure the state of Israel which exists in a sea of hostility, surrounded by nations set to destroy it. This is a gut response on a survival level that most Jews share, including myself.

However, I am more than a Jew. I have always felt that being part of humanity encompassed far more than being defined simply as a Jew. The shared experience of heart and mind is, for me, far more significant than external traits such as skin color or the shape of one's nose. It would be laughable, were it not so tragic, that such distinctions are the basis of hatred by one group for another.

After seeing Steven Spielberg's movie, Munich, whose main theme is revenge begets revenge, I was left with a gut-wrenching feeling of the futility of men's testosterone-driven violence. There is a poignant moment in the film when both the Israeli and the Palestinian stand in a doorway, and there is this recognition that Palestinians are caught in a similar plight, longing for a land of their own. As I processed my response to the film's theme, it brought back a childhood memory. My younger brother and I would argue, and we sometimes came to blows. Every time I hit him, he returned the blow, with greater ferocity. I soon realized the ineffectiveness of our struggle, recognizing the possibility of injury. In order to end our sibling violence, I let go of the desire to win, and chose peace instead. I think that this example says something important, namely that someone has to stop the violence first.

As a human being who happens to be both a woman and a Jew, it is hard for me to observe the inequalities and violence in our world. It is imperative that we identify with our common humanity. We have all been wounded and we all need healing. It is my greatest desire that all people, including Palestinians and Jews, in particular, focus on what we have in common as a basis on which to interact, rather than on what separates us.

I had a Palestinian friend, Yanni , when living in New York City's East Village. Our cultural and religious backgrounds did not impair our relationship. We respected each others' creativity and intelligence. We were able to communicate, even when we didn't agree. As a Jew, it is my deep wish that Palestinians and Israelis would get to know each other, both individually and collectively. When one is accepted as a human being, rather than seen as *the other*, the opportunity for appreciating our common humanity increases. I hope that Israel will recognize the Palestinian plight. I would hope that Israel, having proved itself as a formidable military power, could allow itself to understand the suffering that a people without a country endure. Of all the peoples in the world, Israel knows well this experience. Let this be the basis of opening the heart to others rather than sealing it off only for ones own kind. As for the Palestinians, I hope they can come to appreciate the necessity of a state of Israel, given the horror- filled history of persecution the Jewish people have experienced. They have shared this land in the past, and therefore the possibility exists that they could do it again. If Israel could begin to open its heart in a way that could be felt by the Palestinians, I believe it would encourage them to release their bitterness and hatred.

In particular, this book has focused on the damage done by the imbalance of patriarchy. No one has escaped its influence. Even as a child, I recognized that women were not taken seriously in the way that men were. Actually, I did not like the word "woman" and in my heart, I also did not want to be a girl. It did not feel fair, in that I recognized that this was a man's world. I resisted and resented any message that I learn to cook, sew, and take part in women's domestic work. I passionately hated the implication that it was my job to do these things.

Eventually I would find I could enjoy doing some of these more traditionally feminine tasks, but what I wouldn't accept was the assumption that I had no choice. I resisted being narrowly defined in any way; as a Jew, as a girl, even as an American.

First and foremost I felt myself to be human. It is this perspective that opened my life to a variety of experience. The world was fascinating, and I wanted to know it directly. I didn't want to fit anyone else's stereotype, and I didn't want to stereotype others. Instead, I wanted to know others for who they were, and to be known for myself. I was curious about what was true from my own experience. I was curious and eager to meet people from all over the world. My heart was open to embracing cultural differences. In fact, I sought them out.

My awareness of prejudice and power regarding gender imbalance, has greatly increased through the years. I didn't understand the women's movement in the sixties, nor did I feel drawn to the feminist activism of the seventies. I had an unconscious anger and resentment against women, for I embodied the patriarchal male's condemnation of women. I felt influenced by men's impulses and desires in ways that constantly violated my soul and the soul of all women.

Co-writing this book has been a very powerful, positive way of seeing clearly into the roots of prejudice, domination and control. My awareness of the suppression of women has deepened, blended with an awareness of the role of women in the future. I feel an urgent necessity to claim and proclaim my own feminine nature and embody it in a world that has brazenly opposed gender equality.

Rachel Falik

In his movie, *Live and Become*, Romanian director Radu Mihaileanu initiated a discussion about religious affiliation and rightfully claimed that *"people are too often judged by old and dated stereotypes: Arabs, Jews, Algerians, Romanians, French and Germans... Such identities are restrictive and approx-imate. They are wrong. They fail to show how cultures interact, how individual paths and destinies cross each other."*

The movie tells the story of an Ethiopian Christian child escaping the deadly famine of 1984 passing off as a Jew. The Israeli government arranged a large-scale covert operation known as "Operation Moses" in order to smuggle the Afri-can Jewish tribe into Israel and save thousands of people from inhumane conditions. The child's only chance to sur-vive was pretending to be the son of a recently bereaved Jewish mother. In Israel, the child learns Hebrew, receives Jewish education and excels as a bible scholar. He later serves in the Israeli army and even marries his Jewish sweetheart in a religious ceremony. He is not different than any other Ethiopian-Israeli child. Does it matter that he was not born to a Jewish mother? In the movie, as often in real life, it did not matter to the people that knew him as an indi-vidual, and to those who loved him. But it did matter to the Israeli authorities.

In Israel there is no separation between religion and state (although the amount of state involvement in religion and vice versa is constantly challenged). The Ethiopian child would not have been saved had he not pretended to be Jewish. Ironically enough, less than half a century earlier in Europe, during the Nazi occupation, claiming to be a Jew meant a death sentence.

But even though one's religious or national identity is completely arbitrary, it has the potential power to shape one's life. As the movie suggests, it might be the difference between life and death. It is true for Americans in Iraq; it is true for Israelis in the Palestinian Gaza; it is true for non-Janjaweeds in Darfur and so forth.

Such realization is terrifying but eye opening at the same time. I did not choose to be Jewish and I did not decide to be an Israeli. Can anyone choose? Don't we already have an identity by the time we have learned enough to choose? The "accidental" elements that shaped my being include the society into which I was born, my culture, my race. (The race question is particularly puzzling for me. What is it, really, my race? Does it have to do with my olive skin color?) I had no control over the religion of my birth or my birth nationality. Those I cannot change; but I had to question their significance. Are they important to me? What should be their effect on the way I perceive myself? And maybe, the real question is not how *I* perceive myself but how *society* perceives me.

I was born to a Jewish mother. According to the Jewish practice, that is sufficient reason to be considered Jewish. My family's religiousness swayed between "secular" and "traditional," but as any Israeli child I was exposed to Jewish mythology (studying the bible is mandatory in public school), Jewish traditions (ah! the wonderful yet exhausting ceremony of Passover and the stories of our ancestors fighting for their freedom) and Israeli legacies (the Independence war, the heroes that sacrificed their lives to allow ME a better life). Those stories and rituals were a great source of pride. But at the same time the seed of fear was instilled: my people were persecuted throughout history for their faith and for their appearance (the antithesis to the Arian perfection). My people were also persecuted for their peculiar customs, costumes, and for living in other nations without assimilating their cultures—and always belonging else-where, dreaming of Jerusalem. And this exclusive cocktail of pride, patriotism and fear shaped my identity.

As I left my homeland and moved to this diverse, multi-cultural environment outside of Israel, I wished to see myself more open-minded and tolerant. When Sharon shared her vision for this book I imagined myself fit and unbiased for a dialogue that stresses our commonalities. I saw the unique esthetics of feminine collaboration repre-senting three different religions and cultures. But aestheti-cism doesn't mean simplicity, and it did not come without effort. Such beauty has to do with bringing different ele-ments to blend in original harmony. For that to happen, I had to define what I would be able to contribute to the book and then, once again, question my own identity.

I wanted to think that my national identity was less rele-vant in the new context of my life abroad. For example, after a few years in America, I received my Green Card. In a few more years I might even obtain dual citizenship. Will that make me less Israeli than I am now? I am reminded that Albert Einstein once said that "nationalism [was] an infan-tile disease." And apparently it is a hard disease from which to recover. Oddly enough, the process of writing has high-lighted the fact that my culture/religion/nationality plays a bigger role in my life than I was initially willing to admit. Writing with wonderful open-minded women was an enriching experience. Sharon, I knew, had abundant curios-ity and openness, and she never feared to question her own "truths." Getting to know Aliaa was another inspiring expe-rience. Aliaa lives and works in Egypt, a country that for many years was Israel's fiercest enemy. We had the oppor-tunity to examine historical events and compare our differ-ent perspectives and interpretation. We reached for each other with such tenderness that I was often very moved.

But, with tenderness, we expressed attitudes that at times were not harmonious. I found myself disagreeing with Aliaa about the necessity of a specific armed operation that took place in Israel, because of my own perspective on these historical events. To some extent I felt that I was representing the Israelis, and that it was my duty to show the complexity of the Israeli-Palestinian conflict. I also felt that the book over-stressed that conflict, especially when we reviewed atrocious clashes around the globe that seemed to be of greater magnitude. I thought I had an important role in explaining *my* truth. It was easy to criticize Israel's foreign policy while in Israel, but once abroad, once among those who see Israel as the assailant abusing the helpless, I became very protective of my country. What I said to my friend and co-author sounded very apologetic, defensive and at times even aggressive.

In discussing prejudice, Edward R. Murrow, the late American journalist, said that "many people think they are thinking when they are really rearranging their prejudices." Was that what I was doing? Fear, I had to acknowledge, was part of me, part of the archetypal notion of Jews living in the Diaspora. It is our fear that separates us into "we" and "they" that contributes to the inability to trust others after long history of persecution and anti-Semitism, and I saw how I had also integrated that fear. But I was lucky to work it out in a supportive and tolerant environment, with Sharon, Aliaa, and Jenny. Each bringing maternal wisdom and patience that proved to be essential and therapeutic.

The harmony has to do with the seemingly effortless combination of the different elements. It wasn't simple, it wasn't effortless, but if it seemed to be so, we did well.

Aliaa Rafea

We tend to identify ourselves with our affiliation to our families, our social status, our creeds, our nationalities or other entities. Deep in my heart, I realized that the sense of "I" is a core that is experienced, but cannot be defined by any of the above images. I tend to ask myself "who I am", that is, not to answer that question, but to get continuously purified from "illusive images of the self".

This process has guided me throughout the writing of this book. However, it was not easy for me to separate between my "Muslim" identity and my core "Self". For me to be a Muslim is to engage in the same process of purifying oneself from "illusive images of self". Therefore, it was not difficult for me to distance myself from my cultural identity in order to observe Muslims' behavior and study history. However, I struggled to explain the path of Islam in a way that would not be defensive or a claim of absolute truth. I have tried my best, but I am not sure that I have succeeded in fully conveying my intention. I will leave this to the reader to judge.

As these pages were being written, many events occurred that threaten the world with a clash of civilizations wherein religion plays a most important part. The cartoons of the Prophet Mohammad, which were published first in a Danish newspaper, and then included by other European media, caused an explosion of anger among the populace Muslims. I have been a participant and an observer at the same time. I took this event, not as something that happened "out there", but as something that is happening right here within my heart. I asked myself once more who am I in the midst of this conflict? The answer came from the depths of my heart. I am a human being who can understand both the situation of furious Muslims and critical westerners.

As some one who comes from an Islamic country and who also has an understanding of the western world, I can see clearly where the problem lies. It is simply related to the difference in cultural paradigms.

In general, Muslims see their religion as their only glimpse of hope in a cruel and dark world. To them for someone to take that in vain is like destroying a large part, if not all, of their identity. Of course their reactions to this were at the same time problematic, in that the violence they inflicted was the exact opposite of Islamic teachings. At the same time the level of provocation from the Danish prime minister did not decline, he stood firmly on the position that, "this was freedom of speech".

Those who do not understand the fury of Muslims fail to understand the sacredness of this issue in Islam, and are therefore unable to empathize with Muslim emotions. On the other hand, such violent behaviors failed to make the "other" understand the Muslim stance. From an Islamic perspective, insulting the Prophet of Islam does not fall under freedom of speech; the same way as making racists statements or anti Semitic statements would be rejected in the west. Who is to judge where to draw that line, the Muslims or the West? Both parties need to stop judging the "other" according to their own paradigm, and need to respect the "other". Gradually, barriers may be removed.

I experienced conflicting thoughts when Hamas won the Palestinian election. While I could understand the fear of the average Israeli, hearing that Hamas' long term strategy is to liberate the whole occupied land of Palestine, I could also understand the need of the Palestinians for a strong leadership that can stand in the face of the continuous assaults of Israel's army. As much as I am aware of the possible determination of ending Israel's existence among some zealot Palestinians and Arabs, I am also aware that Israel is a state without defined borders, and it expands according to the demographic needs. Each party knows of the other's hidden intention, and deals with it as reality without trying sincerely to create long lasting peaceful solutions. I cannot claim that I equally sympathize with the Palestinians and Israelis. I depict the Palestinians as those who just try to defend their right to survive as a nation in a limited area of what was previously their land. They have less power, and are subject to continuous humiliation, and constant assaults. At the moment they are deprived of basic human rights, that is, to live as a self –determined nation with dignity and integrity.

On the other hand, Israel has become a developed nation in a very short period of time, and has one of the strongest armies in the area. Moreover, Israel enjoys the support of the United States, the most powerful country in the world, and continues to gain cooperation and support from the rest of the world. I still sympathize with the young Israeli generation who identify themselves with the land of Israel where they live, and feel that they face a continuous threat from their neighbors, not only the Palestinians but also the countries around them. Their need of security is not satisfied by the State's strength, and its continuous hyper-vigilance in the hopes of avoiding attacks. The election of Hamas on top of the Palestinian authority must feel terrifying to them.

I don't see a resolution to these fears and insecurities from either side through mere talks and negotiations. Unless each group sees the "other" as part of themselves, identifying with their mutual struggle, fear will remain part of their own existence. The crisis of July 2006 when Israeli troops invaded Lebanon proves that the way to realize peace in this area still has a long way to go. Like peoples all over the world who were watching the death of innocent children, mothers, and old people, my heart was aching. I asked myself will Lebanese be able to build a good relationship with the Israelis in the near future? For how long shall we suffer from violence in the Holy Land where calls of peace came through our prophets? In the wake of the Qana Massacre, I watched the angry people attacking the UN building in Beirut, expressing their fury against the international community that is sided towards Israel's interests alone, forgetting that there are also other people who deserve to live in peace, and security. The massive destruction of Lebanon, the killing of children, and the continuous use of the American veto in the Security Council, left people dispirited and angry.

I worry about the growing rejection and hatred in the area. If Hezbollah is a terrorist group (I consider it a resistance movement for liberation), it should be left to the Lebanese government to deal with, not a foreign power. As explained elsewhere in this book, the Israeli attack was a response to Hezbollah abducting two soldiers (not two civilians). One million Lebanese paid the price, as well as thousands of Israeli citizens — all experiencing fear and insecurity. One million people left their homes and became refugees, living in parks, schools, and mosques. Nearly 1000 Lebanese (at least 95% of them are civilians) were killed, compared to 120 Israelis, wherein 70% are soldiers.

My agony increased when I was hearing some irresponsible voices threatening Israelis and cursing them. I cannot accept calling people who defend their land as terrorists. Hezbollah never targeted civilians before this war. The pull of polarization is strong, yet I recognize even despite these statistics and explanations, I will not help the cause of peace if I demonize the other.

In war there are no winners, everyone loses. Fear prevents many Israeli people from seeing the consequences of using extensive power over others. Yet, I am sure there are many people who see beyond this veil of fear, and I count on them for help in the future

Now, we can see clearly that the spirit of motherhood is missing in this world. By nature, mothers and women are compassionate. The true female spirit would not allow this insane war to occur.

It is my hope that this book provides hope, and that it finds its way to a world wide audience. It is a demonstration of four women from different backgrounds working together and accepting the challenge of criticizing their own cultures, and extending their hand to the "other" to embrace them with love. Jenny joined us late in the project, but she has become very close to my heart. The process of writing this book has been valuable, not because it was easy, but because we faced challenges and we could get over them.

Sharon Mijares

If I am going to speak from my heart, I must admit to both my fear and my hopefulness. I am frightened because the world news seems to worsen by the day. Those in charge of the financial decisions seem to be unconcerned with the pollution of air, water and land, and its effects upon future generations. Hurricanes, such as Katrina, flooding, heat waves and other natural disasters appear to be gaining in ferocity. Many believe this to be the result of global warming, but the Bush administration ignores the evidence. It is dismaying to know that George Bush stated the United States would never sign the Kyoto treaty, an agreement made among other nations as a means of controlling destructive emissions.

The destruction of Lebanon, and the killing of so many innocent people in Lebanon, Israel, and the Palestinian territories has caused me great grief. It is hard not to fall into the pull to take sides, especially when I see the disproportionate amount of deaths on the Arab side of the violence. I cannot imagine what it is like to have one's entire country devastated, and to be surrounded by bombs and death. I can also conceive of the fear of the innocent Israeli citizen, who simply wants to live his or her life as peacefully as possible, and yet is overcome by fear of being hit by katushas or other weaponry.

Daily news programs disclose the latest bombings and deaths in the Middle East and other countries. Approximately 100 Iraqis die daily as a result of this ill begotten war. The bombings of Mosques and Synagogues, the numerous civilian and military deaths throughout the world, and increasing threats to human wellbeing, the Israeli domination and abuse of Palestinians, the fear of an Israeli citizen to ride a bus or enter a market—all of these events are felt within my heart.

Wrongful wars are endangering the safety of innocent people throughout the world. The persons making these enormously influential decisions have little, if any, caring for the ordinary human being and the planet upon which we live. It is up to the women, the mothers of the human race, to come forward and bring balance to our world.

This gives me hope. As I see increasing numbers of women voicing their concerns and taking leadership, I feel a stirring of change—a shift from the demise of gender imbalance. Women's peace groups are increasing around the globe. I also see the many men who understand equality, and who care about the earth and its children. These people provide hope for future generations. It may well be the destiny of women to help restore well-being and ongoing life, after much destruction and death.

Our book represents our own deep caring. This project has not been an easy journey. I had the vision for the book, but then had to find the right co-authors. My criterions were that each author had to be able to stand aside and criticize both their nation and religion. If we can't face its shadows, we're limited in our ability to truly love and understand what takes place outside our limited cultural perspective. We also had to be able to deal frankly with the problems taking place, and not be defensive, or the book would not have been possible. At times I was very aware that we were dealing with sensitive issues, for example, Jenny is a Jew, Rachel, is as an Israeli Jew, and Aliaa, an Egyptian Muslim. I didn't want to offend anyone. Therefore I strove to find a place to listen, support, and yet speak what I believed with sincerity as opposed to defensiveness. I strove to listen from the other person's point of view, respecting her history and her feelings.

So much can be written on the numerous ways in which prejudice, hatred or fear of *the other* manifests, but we had to narrow our scope. Hopefully, we have not offended any one group that feels we could have spent far more time and effort on their cause. Believe me, we were and are more than aware of the numerous offences against people of color, and sexual orientation. But we chose to focus on the root cause of the problem, patriarchal dominance and gender imbalance. Our intention is that this focus embraces the need for respect and inclusiveness, which all groups deserve as all people are manifestations of one human family.

The Palestinian-Israeli conflict was the one issue that evoked differing responses within each one of us, but we separated this from our personal relationship with one another. We did not let it intrude upon our friendship. I had met many Palestinians on a trip to Israel in May of 2001. The Palestinians, both Muslims and Christians, were very kind and hospitable to our group. My heart had been deeply affected. I saw their oppression, and my heart was opened to the Palestinian plight. Upon my return I began to watch LinkTV's news program, *Mosaic*, on a daily basis. The various news media in the Middle East videotaped Israeli bulldozers taking down olive orchards and crushing whole streets of houses into rubbish, as their previous inhabitants stood nearby in grief and helplessness. I felt deep grief for the people. This was because a "human connection" had been made. I now knew these people, and this made quite a difference in my heart's response. Jewish friends explained the fears Israelis felt living in a small country surrounded by its enemies. Yet, it was obvious the Israelis were the ones with the greater power, and they were not using it for the good.

I also saw the news when Palestinian suicide bombers killed innocent Israelis. Like many others I recognized that the tribal mentality of "an eye for an eye and a tooth for a tooth" governed this land, and that both Jews and Arabs had blood on their hands. Revenge and fear are ineffective motivators for change. Stephen Spielberg's 2006 film, *Munich*, illustrated this fact as he portrayed the ongoing acts of revenge, showing how it simply begets more revenge. His film also portrayed a poignant moment demonstrating the longing of Palestinians for a land they once knew as their own. Both Jews and Arabs share this longing.

As a Sufi Christian, and a person who cares equally for all people, I find it very sad that this drama has continued for so long in the so-called Holy Land. Its inhabitants truly fail to understand the way one responds to sacred ground. But then I am reminded that the entire world is sacred ground, as is every spark of life within it.

Part II

After reading one another's writings, Rachel, Jenny and I gathered for lunch to discuss our responses to one another's contributions to the beginning Epilogue. Aliaa telephoned a few days later. She had been unable to call us during the meeting, as she was traveling with her husband, and en route from Egypt to Washington DC.

In response to Part I we all agreed that it was important to go ahead and share any places of disagreement, and to acknowledge the areas that had been problematic. We had worked on this book for the last three years, and given the nature of the project and our own cultural differences, we didn't always concur with one another. Sometimes, we agreed to disagree, sometimes we simply came to a consen-

sus, and other times we simply found a way to re-state
something in a way that encompassed both sides of the discussion. The escalation of war between Israel and Lebanon
then brought up all our differences at a yet deeper level. We
had to meet more than once to listen with an open heart to
all sides of the story. We found areas of disagreement, and
we listened to one another as friends— *the person and the
relationship had more value than our differences.* In Part II of the
Epilogue we discuss these areas, and how we resolved them
to the best of our ability.

We also share why and how we moved beyond these
spaces, for we had agreed upon on a mutually shared goal.
As women, the mothers of the human race, our hearts were,
and are, filled with concern for the entire human family,
and all other life. We've probably said this before, but it's
worth saying again in that, it was, and is, this caring and
intention that fuels every sentence, word and page of this
book. As we end this book, we share our deep intentions.

Jenny Eda Schipper

I felt a strong response in my own heart, to each of my
co-author's writing throughout this book, and, especially,
the first part of our Epilogue. I resonated with Sharon's contribution as she expressed my own deep anguish at the
on-going pain and suffering that continues to grow in massive proportions on a daily basis throughout the world.

The Israeli war against Hezbollah, and the country of
Lebanon, compromised Israel's heart and soul. Peace will
never be secured by such appalling killing, especially of
women and children. Israel might remember that they
themselves used terrorism against the British to help them
gain the state of Israel. The question being begged is: what
are the ultimate aims of the Israeli government and whom
do they really serve?

That being said, I have come to keenly recognize how the
taking of sides fuels conflict. Each side becomes isolated in
its own story and there is no hope of finding common
ground. The current Israeli offensive triggered the four of

us into this type of behavior. At one point I was afraid to open my e-mails as I felt threatened as a Jew by Sharon and Aliaa's sympathy for the history behind Hezbollah's actions. One by one, we each saw the futility of getting swept up in such polarization and what became clear to us all was the need to hold a space larger than the story that each side tells.

Alongside the horrors of war, there is the more accepted fact of massive poverty and starvation on much of the planet. The cruelty wreaked by humanity seems to be endless, driven by a pathological demand for power. The corporate mentality with its compulsive hunger to consume the world as if it were one big market-place, is compromising both our environment and humanity itself with its negligent disregard for anything other than monetary profits. This patriarchal influence is hoodwinking us all.

Rachel beautifully brings up a point that has puzzled me throughout my life; namely, how can a human life be rejected, simply because he or she was born, without choice, into a cultural and national identity. If we really thought about this as individuals, rather than blindly accepting our cultural assumptions, we would be inclined to release these kinds of prejudices, and actively practice what our religions preach. There is no ethical reason for prejudice against any human being, simply because he or she is born into a different culture or race.

I also deeply appreciated Aliaa's ability to understand two sides of a polarized conflict. This is an essential quality that is vital for everyone to cultivate now. We need to develop it in ourselves as much as work for it on the global level. It boils down to a practice of finding inclusiveness, looking for the widest vision in which what we share is larger than what we fear and differ about. The truth is that what we share is vastly greater than the variations that make us different. What we share is basic; we all have hearts and minds that think and feel. What separates us, is relative; the color of our skin, the slant of our eyes. Why have we made what is relative (minor) so much more important than what is basic to us all? We need to each honestly ask and answer this question.

Many years ago, I began to experience a sense of inner connection with my deceased mother, whose early death in 1974, had deeply affected me. My mother, Rose Schipper, was a charismatic, outspoken, and high-spirited woman. Born in Vienna, to a German-Jewish family, she was the youngest of six children, and the only one who escaped the Nazi Holocaust.

She was the first woman to receive a doctoral degree in German Literature from Wayne State University. She had to fight the all-male department who didn't want to give this advanced degree to a woman (and a Jewish one at that)! In fact her doctoral thesis was on "The Image of the Jew in German Literature". Although like many other women of her era, she had to follow the patriarchal model to achieve a position, she still modeled a spirit of feminine strength in her accomplishments.

In the years following her death, I felt an on-going sense of her presence. One day, while pondering the question, "would there ever be peace in the world," I received the following strange and unexpected response. "There will be peace in the world when the Jews accept Christ. *Read* Romans, Chapter 11, verse 12!" My attention was riveted, because both my mother and I were unfamiliar with the Christian New Testament. I located one and immediately looked up the verse, surprised by the words: "Now if the fall of them [Jews] be the riches of the world, and the diminishing of them [Jews] the riches of the Gentiles; how much more their [Jews] fullness?" What I understood this to mean at the time was; were the Jewish religion to recognize the teaching of Yeshua (in English, Jesus), a new, unknown harmony among peoples and nations might be birthed, but I didn't understand why or how.

Although my mother was a free-thinking woman, she was also firmly established in her Jewish identity, and would never, while alive, have endorsed such a thought, let alone articulate it. I have never shared this response with anyone, until now, because it is so open to misinterpretation. I have puzzled over this simple verse for the last twenty years, trying to understand its full meaning.

It led me into an investigation of the teachings of Yeshua. I came to understand that his teaching was completely heart-centered, emphasizing love and respect for all people, all races. This instruction of goodwill and love toward all peoples, irrespective of hierarchical ranking, was revolutionary because it was unprecedented in the world of that time. The Christian Church, as it developed, did not manifest this teaching in the world. On the contrary, it cultivated hatred, especially of the Jews, which is ironic given the fact that Jesus was a Jew and Christianity birthed itself out of Judaism.

I asked my father what Jews thought of Yeshua, the man, and his teachings. His answer was rather abrupt, and two-fold. The first part he expressed with visible disgust. His words went something like this: "For thousands of years, Jews have experienced Christianity as something ugly, violent and persecuting. There has been nothing good for them since Christianity's inception. It has brought only suffering to the Jews, all in the name of a man who was himself a Jew."

As to what Yeshua taught, my father said: "He taught something that is impossible for human beings to follow, the goal of perfection! It goes against human nature. The Jewish religion is something that can be practiced *in* this world. The Christian ideal is unachievable." Judaism focuses more on life on earth, and how we act in community.

For years I thought about his response. I had to admit he was right. For example, the instruction to "Be ye therefore perfect, even as is your Father which is in Heaven is perfect" (Matthew 5:48), is a precept, not consistent with the human condition. The desire for it often prevents people from owning their shadow side. In fact, the prejudice created when people's shadow side is disowned and projected onto others, has been covered throughout this book. The literal interpretation of perfection, as something outside oneself that must be attained, stems from a hierarchal world view – a patriarchal characteristic.

On the other hand, perfection seen from a feminine stand-point generates loving acceptance of all parts of oneself and others. This in itself is transformational, leading to the perfection of wholeness, or what is called oneness with God.

What I have come to understand is that the union of body and mind, of masculine and feminine, of heaven and earth, as emphasized by Eastern traditions, allows for an experience of unconditional love for, and a felt connection to everything. This vibrant flow of energy through the body opens the heart, releasing the ego's need to be separate and prove oneself as better (or worse), than another. The nobler human qualities, exemplified by Moses, Yeshua, the Buddha and others, become natural to us, when we embody them. Step by step, by embracing the disowned feminine (through experiencing our feelings), we can heal the split between body and mind and open our hearts to universal love.

I suspect Yeshua, the man, understood this. He fulfilled the law by bringing forth the feminine qualities of love and compassion in himself, and in others. In being able to see others for who they were, he brought them into greater wholeness. I believe we need to come to this concept of universal love, and to energetically integrate it mentally, emotionally and physically. The embodiment of this universal love leads us to wholeness and peace.

Yeshua (Jesus) came (as he said), to fulfill the law, not to destroy it. His emphasis on law was the commandment that we love one another. So the fulfillment of this law is one of compassionate caring for one another, as emphasized in the Beatitudes. The recognition of the fundamental value of every life on earth is still a revolutionary idea, far from being practiced. Perhaps the Pharisees, representatives of the patriarchal way, were unable to accept the feminine teaching of love that Jesus brought to the Jewish religion.

Were the Jewish people to separate Jesus' message from the Christian Church, and recognize him as someone whose teaching is most appropriate today in a world on the verge of self-destruction, they could have enormous influence by setting the precedent of embracing a larger whole, deeply challenging Christians and Moslems to let go their special claims. By transcending their deep-seated, historically inculcated fear of being persecuted and killed, Jews all over the world, including Israel, could initiate a heart-felt peace process with the Palestinians.

I recognize how this idea can be seen as an affront to Judaism. It is not easy for me to share this belief, one I have pondered over for so many years. As a child of holocaust survivors, I do not take my Jewish heritage lightly and my intention is in no way to slight it. What I am suggesting, for Judaism, and for all other groups, is that we need to expand beyond our limited ideas of identity in order to survive as humanity. When I consider the aftermath of the holocaust, and at the same time recognize the monumental suffering of all peoples throughout the ages, I am led to embrace this more inclusive understanding.

It has long been recognized that suffering is a way that opens the heart. The Jewish people, having suffered so much as an exiled people, are in a unique position, at this crucial point in history, to fulfill their concept of "a chosen people". By paradoxically releasing the idea that makes them, "God's chosen people", and choosing, instead, to embrace the universality of all humanity, they could set an example for other religions and nations, to drop fiercely held identities, and come together as one human family with common interests for the good of all. This would be a fulfillment of the Jewish heritage. It is the meaning, I believe, behind my mother's surprising message.

Rachel Falik

Wars are not new to humanity. But even if we are not becoming more aggressive, we are surely becoming more destructive. The machine gun was invented only 122 years ago; since then we learned how to separate uranium isotopes and bombed Hiroshima. We learned to enrich plutonium, and Nagasaki was then covered with deadly radiation. Modern industrial societies are caught in an arms race, accumulating deadly weapons, and the rest of the world tries to catch up with their alarming pace. And the numbers are terrifying! The United States has about 6,000 active warheads of nuclear weapons. Russia, formerly the Soviet Union, has even more. China has at least 400 warheads.

India tested its nuclear power for the first time in 1974; the fission explosion code name was, ironically, "The Smiling Buddha." Britain, France, and Pakistan are also armed with nuclear weapons. North Korea is suspected to be a nuclear state, and Israel, although never admitted, also has its own nuclear arsenal. And there are several other countries that have initiated nuclear weapon programs and who also possess substantial nuclear technology. But ever since Nagasaki the sky has been clear from atomic bombs, but awash with combat aircraft. For example, there are 570 combat jets in Israel, 680 in Egypt, 2,100 in Russia, and 400 in Germany. The United States holds an impressive record of 7,600 such jets in its air force.

There are armored fighting vehicles such as tanks and other combat support vehicles: 7,400 in Egypt, 8,500 in Syria, 1,200 in Angola, 14,500 in China, 2,800 in Vietnam, and the ongoing list is tediously long. Of course, it takes an active military personnel to operate all those machines. It is a fact that 1.5 million people do active military service in the United States alone. More than 10 percent of the Israelis are either doing mandatory service or employed by the IDF (Israeli Defense Force). Close to 300,000 people are relegated to Brazil's military manpower; almost 200,000 people in Mexico; there are about half a million soldiers in Turkey and surprisingly enough, more than 350,000 citizens of the so-called neutral country Switzerland are being paid for contributing to combat or support units. This is how nations maintain their balance of terror.

And here we are, the authors of this book, talking about love and tolerance. I can't help from feeling small and insignificant, overwhelmed by those figures, and these destructive forces that we view as our protection and as a deterrent force. At times I feel that writing about our effort to communicate is meaningless. I am afraid that inspecting our own biases, prejudice, blind spots, fears and dogmas is an important personal journey, but has little effect on the world. My innate skepticism beats me.

I recognize that Sharon, has been active in women and peace organizations for many years, and therefore set the optimistic and prophetic tone of the book. I was carried by Sharon's enthusiasm and conviction but all along took a cynical stance. I asked Sharon and myself: Who would read us? Who would listen? Are we trying to convince the already convinced about non-violent solutions? Will it stop the next suicide bomber in Tel Aviv? Does it really matter what we say and write or is it the all-powerful Secretary of Defense, Donald Rumsfeld to call the shots? Is there a value to our work? And now, more than before, it seems to me that when dealing with fanatic violent extremists there isn't always a peaceful solution. We, the authors, reside comfortably in different continents, we do not have conflicting interests and we were able to find a common ground and uphold a civilized dialogue. But I find it hard to believe that fundamentalist and terrorist groups have the aptitude and the desire to do so.

I disagreed with Aliaa and Sharon. As an Israeli, I believe that Hezbollah is a terrorist organization because of its guerrilla tactics, use of civilians, and ultimate goal of destroying the Israeli nation. It initially sought to transform Lebanon into an Islamic republic and today calls for the elimination of the "Zionist Entity." These lines are being written in Israel before a cease-fire with Lebanon and the Hezbollah had been achieved (Israel endorsed the UN resolution but Nasrallah, Hezbollah's leader, would not commit unless the Israelis left Lebanon). The pain and the devastation of the war were much more palpable here than in San Diego. I have just met with two good friends who live in Haifa, doctors in their occupation, who described how they spent the last month in shelters. They described their attempts to work between the wail of one siren to the next, alerted by the warnings that a katyusha missile had been shot in their direction. They cared for the overwhelming number of wounded and traumatized patients, some of whom were Israeli Arabs. The wounded were often the elderly and those without means to flee Northern Israel. Yes, just as it is in Lebanon.

At first I disagreed with what I considered to be a compulsive discussion regarding this crisis. As I stated in Part One of this Epilogue, I feel we emphasize issues that engage the Western media and public opinion much more than we give attention to the poverty, hunger and violence in Africa or women's oppression in the Muslim world. But I realized the Israeli vast defensive operation in Lebanon is an opportunity to see if we practice what we preach. It became a moment of truth for us, the authors, to communicate in the midst of differences. Even my mere definition of the conflict (defense rather than assault) was hard for my author friends to accept. However, we did agree to disagree, and we are aware of the differences in our political stance.

Here in Israel, I see images that are not being seen in the Arab world. For example, testimonies of Lebanese describing how the Hezbollah built underground fortified bunkers in their villages and above them raised apartment buildings for the poor to reside. Is it a humanitarian gesture or a ruthless use of those villagers as a human shield? When Sharon condemned the Israeli intention of destroying Hezbollah one might think that the Israeli attack was not in any way provoked by the Hezbollah. The Israelis have never attempted ethnic cleansing (to eradicate another nationality), but rather to eliminate the means that are constantly being used for terrorizing Israel, which have been accompanied by clear messages articulating the intention to destroy "the Zionist enemy". I doubt that Israel pulling out of Lebanon and Gaza will eliminate terrorism.

In this book we try to create a bridge between religions, cultures, perceptions, and choose not to demonize the "other." I realize, however, that the "other" can be sometimes aggressive, cruel, and even inhuman but luckily there are many of us that are communicative, compassionate, open-minded, and peace-seekers. We might not change the world with our words but we can become ambassadors of tolerance and thus counterbalance the belligerent mindset.

Aliaa Rafea

I got to know Dr Sharon Mijares through the online Sufi Women Dialogue,[3] and then met her in person at the International Association of Sufism Symposia as we were both scheduled to speak at this annual gathering. In August 2003, I received an email from Dr. Mijares, describing her vision for this book, and asking me if I would like to participate. The idea of the book fascinated me. It harmonized with my plan of work whereby I wanted to find out the base on which humankind can come to a common term. I accepted co-authoring this book because it responded to an urgent need of disentangling the misunderstanding among nations and civilizations, and to search for the "roots of these evils". At the outset of the project, I was curious to know more about Rachel. I read her biography and felt great relief and appreciation when I read the following paragraph,

> My perception of the *other* as a human being allows me to hope that there will be increasing communication between various nations and religions rather than continued fear, bloodshed and violence. In this global chaos, it is up to us to touch the *other*, it is our personal responsibility to transform this chaotic condition with open hearts and open minds.[4]

It became clear to me that writing this book was a responsibility, rather than a choice. I felt obliged to share in this project as conflicts between so called religious groups around the world and world politics were rapidly increasing. I considered that sharing this work would take the three of us to a far horizon, beyond fragmented problems. From that perspective, I felt responsible not only for what I was writing, but also for what Sharon and Rachel were writing. They shared the same feeling and responsibility. We used to comment, edit and add to each other's writings, and we got into deep discussions, and in most cases we were able to resolve

---

[3] This dialogue was initiated by Dr. Nahid Angha who established Sufi Women Organization (SWO) as a side activity of the International Association of Sufism (IAS).

[4] Quoted from the Introduction (pp. 11–12 above).

our differences. In one of our discussions, we felt that it would be better if we agreed to disagree. That is why I suggested we write an epilogue to give the reader an honest presentation of each author, and to acknowledge Sharon's role as an originator and planner of the work. Jenny joined us in the last episode of writing this book. The work would not have been complete without her contribution.

We worked very hard to bring this book to its final shape. In the pre-final phase, Sharon reorganized the manuscript to clarify the main thesis of the book, and I shared the task by re-editing and collecting other material. We enjoyed the procedure, and it opened new avenues to re-examine the book's theme from different angles.

Although, I did not want this epilogue to focus much on the Israeli–Palestinian conflict, because its subject is wider than can be covered thoroughly here, I have to stress the fact that the four authors of this book have come to a consensus whereby we acknowledge the Palestinians' and Israelis' rights to continue to exist as two nations who respect each other. There should not be any hidden agenda in the minds of politicians from either side, or plans to destroy the other, or to create an environment and justification for continued assaults. We agreed that peace should be implanted in the heart of people before it materializes on the factual ground. Politicians need to balance their feminine side, and let the spirit of motherhood inspire them in their decision-making. Mothers are wise enough to understand that it is peace rather than war; compassion, but not revenge, which will provide security for their children. Building a great wall, or using violence will not provide security, or solve problems. Quite the contrary, it increases the feeling of insecurity and complicates the situation. The July 2006 crisis in Lebanon and Israel motivated us to work harder and to get closer. Although I live in Cairo, and my co-authors live in the US where they can see one other, I was able to communicate with the three of them through emails as we supported one another.

Although the authors of this book share a common goal and agreed upon the main premises of the book, we are uniquely different. Our differences are not something to be ashamed of, or hide. Quite the contrary we cherish them, and we have made the best out of "being different". When I read the final version of our book, I was thrilled by the changes that took place as a result. For example, I intended to write about my disagreement on calling Abraham "a Hebrew" prophet in this epilogue. This expression lasted in the book script till the pre-final version. To my amazement, I did not find it in the final version. I had to express my respect that the change had taken place. In my understanding, all prophets came to guide humankind, and they should be acknowledged by their messages, not by their ethnical background. Equally, I would not agree with people who call Prophet Muhammad the "Arab" Prophet.

I feel a responsibility to explain some aspects of my own way of thinking. I don't claim to hold a monopoly on the truth, yet I stand firm in what I believe to be just and right. For example, I could not take homosexuality as "normal" behavior, and I wanted to avoid mentioning it in our book; because I thought it was a culturally sensitive issue. Sharon felt uncomfortable about ignoring it completely. Through writing this book I had to consider my co-authors different perspectives. Despite the fact that I still hold the same view, we agreed to widen our scope and to respect people who have different values regardless of any personal views.

> Regardless of differing views based upon our own cultural upbringing, each of us agreed that any prejudice against those who differed because of religion, class, ethnicity, race or sexual behavior (for example, homosexuality, polygamy, and so on) violated the respect each human being deserves.[5]

In the first part of the epilogue, Rachel was extremely honest and honorable when she mentioned her sensitivity in relation to criticism to Israel's politics. I thought I wrote honestly and objectively; I was sure also that I sought reconciliation and coexistence in this area. I was not aware of my harshness. I learned an important lesson here, and that is,

---

[5]   Quoted from the Introduction (p. 14 above).

one should be tactful and not hurt people, yet be clear and obvious in relation to what one believes. I tried to see the world from Rachel's eyes. That is what anthropologists are trying to do all the time (I am one), but they also realize that there is no way to completely remove the gaps between one's own culture and others'. Maybe that is the reason why we agreed to disagree. The epilogue is the place that narrates our story as four women who were determined to consult their hearts, and to come together. Because of this we were able to come to consensus despite our differences. Along these lines, there are some remaining points that I would like to raise here.

First, as far as I am concerned, I am aware that we cannot consider Muslims as one group. I mainly try to be honest with myself and with my readers and talk about Islam out of experience. I experience Islam as a dynamic process for attaining peace with oneself and with the whole world. That is why I cannot understand why there is such a polarization between Islam and the West. Unfortunately, extremists from both sides stereotype each other, and build their enmity on false generalizations.

For me a Muslim[6] is an attribute to any one, of any religion, who surrenders to the Divine Order, and who searches for right balance in a dynamic way, regardless of any given religious name. When I read the Qur'an and studied the Prophet's life, I become more aware of that dimension in Islam as revealed to Prophet Muhammad.[7] Therefore it breaks my heart to see some Muslims violate the very essence of Islam. Why should Muslims, Jews, Christians, Buddhists, and Hindus compare one religion to the other? Why can't we learn from each other?

When I read Jenny's part 2 of the epilogue, her writings echoed deeply in my soul. Her tool to decode the Bible's words, was not her knowledge of a language or history.

---

[6]   Muslim literally means the one who "surrenders".
[7]   This vision is included and explained in one of my published works :
      Islam from Adam to Muhammad and Beyond, Book Foundation, 2004,
      UK., and an article "Universalism in Islam" in R. Hangloo (edit),
      Approaching Islam, Sundeep Books, India, 2005.

Through her pure heart she gradually interpreted the message given to her from the spiritual realm, realizing that Jesus' words fulfilled the Jewish message. When our hearts are purified, we can see, understand, and decode religious symbols.

Muslims have no problems acknowledging the messages of all prophets, yet they are completely convinced that others should follow the path and rituals of Islam. I have offered in this book a different perspective, and I am so grateful that Jenny's experience materializes my hope of how we can see the message of unconditional love beyond all names, so we can recognize it in all the great teachers of humanity, as each new revelation fulfills the message of a previous one. I wonder, as did Sharon, Rachel and Jenny, why can't we see beyond names, colors, features, and places?

As this book discusses, it is likely that heart blindness is due to a spiritual emptiness wherein people tend to hold on to false images. I consider every self-image that stands in the way of finding our human roots as a false image, be it cultures, religions, nationalities, races, or gender. For the four of us, writing this book was not only a scholarly work, but also a spiritual process. I hope I am not exaggerating when I say that we got into a deeper level of our different cultures, and at the same time we were able to see beyond them. I consider this part of our epilogue as a culmination of our human unity.

The barrier to true spirituality is translated in this book as an imbalance. It is found in individuals, social structures, and it also affects the global world relationship. Gender imbalance is a manifestation of a spiritual imbalance in our world. In a discussion with a dear friend about our book, he thought that we were reducing a great issue into male-female conflicts. I would like to stress that our thesis is not about the biological formation of the two sexes, but the traits that are related to feminine –masculine as two integrative aspects within the universe and within the individual human psyche, be it a man or a woman. Our history has been dominated by male traits, even with some women's leadership styles (for example, Margaret Thatcher and Golda Meir).

Aside from our Prophets, we find Gandhi to be an example of a gender-balanced leadership as he did not adopt a style of domination and control, but instead supported East Indians to find their way toward independence and freedom through non violence. His style expresses a spirituality wherein humanness prevailed over racism, caste, religion and gender. With sincerity and honor he disclosed:

> I learned the lesson of nonviolence from my wife, when I tried to bend her to my will. Her determined resistance to my will, on the one hand, and her quiet submission to the suffering my stupidity involved, on the other, ultimately made me ashamed of myself and cured me of my stupidity in thinking that I was born to rule over her and, in the end, she became my teacher in nonviolence.[8]

When humans (men or women) respond to the inner urge of moving towards a higher level of their fuller potential, they ultimately move towards spiritual balance. Masculine and feminine characteristics merge as part of this inner balance, and the core of our humanness manifests. A spiritually balanced person is known by this integration. The imbalance has been discussed throughout this book.

Releasing women from the invisible chains that society and fanatical "religion" have created for them by entrapping them in a narrowly defined set of roles, will create unprecedented harmony and balance in our world. This will open our humanity to a new era wherein our societies harmonize with the same balance manifest in nature and the cosmos.

This cosmic balance is revealed in the integration of the opposites that form the whole; day and night, heaven and earth, darkness and light. Therefore, when women stand in equality to males, they balance our world and harmonize it with the divine order of the universe. As a matter of fact I am repeating and emphasizing the message that the whole book has emphasized in a few words. We are not fanatical

[8]   http://www.mkgandhi.org/nonviolence/index.htm
       Accessed 3/27/06

feminists, but rather we are deeply humanistic, seeking the wellness of the world as one big family.

Initially I suggested writing this epilogue (among other reasons) to highlight each of our contributions to the book, but this could not be clearly defined because of the way in which the project was accomplished. Unlike other projects where authors write separate chapters, we shared the writing of each chapter. The detailed plan of the book was in Sharon's mind, and she designed and began the writing of each chapter. We then started working together chapter by chapter, and all contributed according to the pre-prepared outline and goal.

The four of us were pleased to join the lists of the many people helping to move segregated groups from isolation into community. As women representing differing religions and cultural backgrounds, we believe that we have and are offering a positive and hopeful example.

Last but not least, I cherish the intimate and warm relationship with my co-authors. Sharon is a very special person, and my co-authoring this book with her gave me a real chance to appreciate her openness and her pure heart. Although I have never met Rachel or Jenny, we have come to know one another, and I am looking forward to seeing them in person one day. We can build a better place for all our children and grandchildren to live in. This goal is shared by pure hearts around the world.

Sharon Mijares

My own heart was also deeply moved as I read through my co-authors' words. This has been quite an adventure. Everyone's concern for the human condition is obvious. It shows in Jenny's denouncing of prejudice, domination and control, her dedication to support her own feminine emergence process and in her understanding of Jesus' role in Judaism. It is evident in Rachel's recognition that we must find and release any roots of fear and prejudice from within our own hearts; and also in Aliaa's acknowledgement of the need for gender balance and the reminder that we have to see *the other* as part of ourselves, and in so doing, recognize our mutual struggle for respect and co-existence. We realize these issues are not confined to one area, such as the Israeli-Palestinian conflict; rather they represent an historical patriarchal drama that appears over and over again, in different lands, with different faces. At one moment a group of people may be the victims, at the next they may well be the victimizers. We must all release these roots from our own hearts, for the first place to begin is within ourselves.

This three-year writing adventure did have its problems, for we did not always agree with one another. As an American who is very cognizant of the violence and abuse against gays and lesbians, and who has gay and lesbian friends, I wanted to assure this issue was also mentioned in our book. This was troubling to Aliaa, as Muslims believe that sexual contacts are designated solely for male-female relationships. Therefore, she preferred I not add this topic to the list of abused minorities. I did not feel comfortable with this, and was trying to figure out how to resolve it. Then came the day when Aliaa wrote something about the Prophet Muhammad, noting his kindness toward all of his wives. I had an immediate negative response. As a Westerner, and a feminist, I was unable to accept polygamy in a positive light. This caused me to examine my cultural bias. It turned into a "win-win" deal, as we decided that each should include what is important to us; and, we did. For me, it was a lesson in *listening and respecting* others, while *speaking up and honoring* my own beliefs, and, in the process, finding a *compromise*.

Another major glitch for me was when Rachel lost faith that the book would be published. This occurred right after we had completed the first draft. She told me she would not contribute any further work, until we had a contract. This was difficult! It was a challenge of *faith* on all of our parts. I remained steadfast in my belief that Rachel was the right person to co-author this book. I knew it when I asked her, and I remained with this feeling throughout the project. The belief was not ill-placed. I began this journey with her, as she had begun before I asked Aliaa to join us. Rachel's contributions are evidenced throughout the book, and they represent a very important voice in the dialogue. And, once she had "proof" that our ideas were being accepted, she immediately re-joined the project. For me, it was a lesson on *patience* in a person's process.

As Rachel so rightly pointed out, the war on Lebanon provided the occasion to see "if we really practiced what we preached." I was deeply disturbed when the Israeli government began its bombing campaign on Lebanon, with the proclaimed intention of destroying Hezbollah. Demolishing a nation, and killing women and children, when Hezbollah represents but one portion of its citizenry is unacceptable to me. It made sense from the Lebanese history that they would not accept Israeli occupation of their land. I wanted to take sides, as I am very aware of the fact that many Arab nations have been targeted for destruction one by one as part of the "redesigning of the Middle East." I had to separate my love for the "Jewish" people from my knowledge of and feelings about the intention to dominate the Middle East, regardless of any human toll. I also felt ashamed to be an American, as the US gave its blessing to continue the violence despite the protests of the larger world. I also became more aware of the fear of the innocent Israeli people, caught in the throes of this violence.

In a phone conversation with Rachel, I pointed out that the deaths and destruction in Israel were simply the results of war. Everyone involved is going to suffer. I then went beyond the controlled media, and did the research, discovering that the PNAC, and its affiliates, had a much larger plan for war and destruction. It left me with much fear for the future of our humanity, and anger at the perpetrators of violence.

I recognized that my spiritual practices would help me avoid the patriarchal pitfall of defenses that led to bitterness and separation. It required a fine balance of doing my research, speaking what I knew to be correct, and holding it all with caring for the entire human family, and hope for a greater future. We are all defensive, and this defensiveness manifests in many ways. It takes dedication to a greater cause to change this pattern. One might say that the field of psychology is a gift of Grace for the world. We have all held ideals for positive relationships, but few have been able to apply them when defenses are triggered. The value of psychological understanding, and related self-exploration, is that it provides a deeper opportunity to both see and release the blocks to positive relationship. It allows for forgiveness, of self and other.

Along these lines, I find myself thinking a lot about the African Truth and Reconciliation process, for there has been so much wounding throughout our world, and we will all have a great need for such healing processes in the future if we continue in the current direction. Untold numbers have lost, and continue to lose, their lives, as victims in the quest for power over others, or in the name of revenge. Much damage has been perpetrated in the name of national boundaries, and falsely-held religious identities, not to consider the insults and atrocities committed on a daily one-to one basis.

The South African Truth and Reconciliation Commission (TRC) is not based upon a patriarchal ideal that perpetuates revenge, rather it is gender-balanced in that it combines a sense of justice with compassion and understanding. It is based upon recognition of our common humanity.

The TRC was a process for justice established by the Government of National Unity, following the end of apartheid, and the election of Nelson Mandela as president. The TRC recognized that violence and human rights abuses were suffered on all sides of the conflict, and that "no section of society escaped these abuses."[9]

The commission mandate accorded a structure for bearing witness to, recording and, in some cases, granting amnesty to the perpetrators of crimes relating to human rights violations. It encouraged reparation and rehabilitation. Archbishop Desmond Tutu, chaired its construction with the help of many dedicated peace-builders. One clause

---

[9]   http://www.doj.gov.za/trc/

of the Promotion of National Unity and Reconciliation Acts states,

> AND SINCE it is deemed necessary to establish the truth in relation to past events as well as the motives for and circumstances in which gross violations of human rights have occurred, and to make the findings known in order to prevent a repetition of such acts in future; AND SINCE the Constitution states that the pursuit of national unity, the well-being of all South African citizens and peace require reconciliation between the people of South Africa and the reconstruction of society; AND SINCE the Constitution states that there is a need for understanding but not for vengeance, a need for reparation but not for retaliation, a need for *ubuntu* [my italics] but not for victimization …

Ubuntu is an African concept, stemming from Zulu and Xhosa languages. It recognizes the common thread in which all human beings are unified. According to Archbishop Desmond Tutu, "A person with ubuntu is open and available to others, affirming of others, does not feel threatened that others are able and good, for he or she has a proper self-assurance that comes from knowing that he or she belongs in a greater whole and is diminished when others are humiliated or diminished, when others are tortured or oppressed."[10] The idea of ubuntu provided the motivation for the reconciliation movement.

Certainly Africans have suffered, through slavery, and the violence and abuses associated with the colonization movement. It seems right to include the TRC in the Epilogue, for it represents a positive model for world-wide reconciliation. There are numerous stories of the ways these unique tribunals were held. For example, an aged woman, whose son had been brutally murdered during apartheid, stood before the murderer during his trial; having been granted the right of retribution. Her retribution was to ask him to take the place of her son — to become her son — and, thereby, fill the void his loss had created! The man was so overtaken by her choice that he fainted on the spot.

---

[10] http://speakingoffaith.publicradio.org/programs/2004/01/01_truth/

A young American scholar, Amy Biehl, living in Cape-
town while working against apartheid, was stabbed to
death on August 25, 1993, by four youths. These same
young men served five years in prison, and were then
released on amnesty in 1998. The sentence had been
decided upon by Amy's parents. Two of these young men,
Easy Nofemela and Ntobeko Peni, now work for the *Amy
Biehl Foundation*, a Trust established in Amy's name, with
the intention of deterring further violence. Amy's mother,
Linda, believes wholeheartedly in "ubuntu." She refuses to
consider herself as a victim, and likewise recognizes that the
young men do not want to see themselves as killers. From
their point of view, they believed they were fighting for
their liberation.

In Easy's words "I am not a killer, I have never thought of
myself as such, but I will never belong to a political organization again because such organizations dictate your
thoughts and actions. I now passionately believe that things
will only change through dialogue. People are shocked I
work for the Amy Biehl Foundation Trust. I tell them that I
work here because Peter and Linda came to South Africa to
talk about forgiveness."[11]

The United Nations and Human Rights groups could
hold a place for Israelis and Palestinians, even militias such
as Hezbollah, to follow in these footsteps. The forces that
prosper financially through the creation of further wars
must be stopped. Love, generosity and caring must take
their place.

Human relationship was the core message of Jesus' teachings. Mainstream Christianity has forgotten this message,
expressed in Jesus' double commandment, that we love our
God with all of our being, and that we love one another as
ourselves. The rise and onset of Protestantism, at a time
when Catholicism had fallen prey to wealth and power, was
an attempt to return to Jesus' simple message, to care for the
poor and the needy, and to know that this caring was the

[11]   http://www.theforgivenessproject.com/stories/linda-biehl-easy-
       nofemela

way to God. This message has been largely replaced by a church in unison with large corporations and governments who have failed to care about the many needs of our brothers and sisters around the world. Our future is dependent upon the realization of Ubuntu. I grieve that my own country and my religion have been largely taken over by a false god.

It is no wonder that unseen forces have led to recovery of the once hidden Gnostic Gospels, especially the Gospels of Mary and Phillip, for these texts have not been tampered with. They clearly depict Jesus' gender-balanced teachings, and his honoring of Mary Magdalene. I place my hope in the progressive scientists, environmentalists, spiritual teachers and clear-intentioned people around this planet. All of these favor a gender-balanced planet — a paradigm of peace and good-will.

Buddhists pray that their actions have merit, and ask that they benefit the good of all living beings. We end our book with this prayer. We each play a part in the process of human transformation. It is imperative that we all search our own hearts, to root out prejudice, and defensive and destructive attitudes, moment by moment, thought by thought, until our behaviors are in harmony with our highest ideals. In closure, we want to say that we are grateful that we can speak for the coming paradigm — a time in which women take their place and help restore our world.

References

Adam, K. (1951). *The Roots of the Reformation*. New York: Sheed & Ward.

Ahmad, Syed Nesar (1991). *Origins of Muslim Consciousness in India : A World-System Perspective*. New York: Greenwood Press.

Alschuler, Albert W. (1994). *A Brief History of Criminal Jury in the United States*. University of Chicago Law.

Angha. Nahid (1995). *Deliverance: Words from the Prophet Mohammad*. San Rafael, CA: International Association of Sufism.

Armstrong, Karen (1992). *Muhammad: A Biography of the Prophet*. New York: Harper Collins.

Armstrong, Karen (1993). *A History of God: The 4000-Year Quest of Judaism, Christianity and Islam*. New York: Ballantine Books.

Armstrong, Karen (2000). *The Battle for God*. New York: Ballantine Publishing Group, Random House.

Armstrong, Karen (2004). The Battle for God. Panel presentation. Parliament of the World's Religions. Barcelona, Spain. July 12, 2004.

Asaeed, Ameena (2001). "Media as a Partisan Messenger." *The Times of India*. Oct. 24, 2001. http://www1.timesofindia.indiatimes.com/cms.dll/articleshow?art_id=909154110

Badran, Margot (1995). *Feminists, Islam, and Nation: Gender and the Making of Modern Egypt*. Princeton, NJ: Princeton University Press.

Banerjee, Partha (1998). *In the Belly of the Beast: The Hindu Supremacist RSS and BJP of India. An Insider's Story*. Delhi: Ajanta Books International.

Barber, Benjamin R. (1995/2001). *Jihad vs. McWorld*. New York: Ballentine Books. Back cover.

Barnstone, W. (Ed.) (1984). *The Other Bible*. New York: HarperCollins Publishers.

Barnstone, W. (Ed.) (1984a). Haggadah. In Barnstone (1984).

Barraclough, Geoffrey (Ed.) (2003). *Harper Collins Atlas of World History*. Ann Arbor, MI: Borders Press.

Beckman, Peter R. & D'Amico, Francine (Ed.) (1994). *Women, Gender, and World Politics: Perspectives, Policies and Prospects*. Westport, CT: Bergin & Garvey.

Berman, Morris (2000). *Wandering God: A Study in Nomadic Spirituality*. New York: State University of New York Press.

Black, J. & Green, A. (1992). *Gods, Demons and Symbols of Ancient Mesopotamia.* Austin: University of Texas Press.

Bond, M.H. (Ed.) (1986). *The Psychology of the Chinese People.* NY: Oxford University Press.

Boyarin, Daniel (2004). *Border Lines: The Partition of Judaeo-Christianity.* Philadelphia, PA: University of Pennsylvania Press.

Brinkley, Alan (1995). *American History: A Survey. Volume I.* 9th Ed. New York: McGraw-Hill.

Brownell, Charles de Wolf (1985). *The Indian Races of America: A General View.* Boston: Dayton and Wentworth.

Buber, Martin & Schmidt, Gilya Gerda (1999). *The First Buber: Youthful Zionist Writings of Martin Buber.* Syracuse, NY: Syracuse University Press.

Budge E.A. Wallace (1967). *The Egyptian Book of the Dead: The Papyrus of Ani.* NY: Dover Publications. This is an unabridged republication of the work originally published in1895 by order of the Trustees of the British Museum.

Buehler, Arthur (2004). Spiritual Practice For a Better World. Conference: *Peace: Universal Message of the World's Religions.* International Association of Sufism Symposium. San Jose, CA.

Butalia, Urvashi (2000). *The Other Side of Silence: Voices from the Partition of India.* Durham, NC: Duke University Press.

Chacour, Elias (1984). *Blood Brothers.* Grand Rapid, MI: Chosen Books.

Chakravati, Uma (1993). "Conceptualizing Brahmanical Patriarchy in Early India: Gender, Caste, Class and State," in *Economic and Political Weekly (EPW),* April 3rd, p. 579.
http://www.wsu.edu:8080/~dee/ANCINDIA/GITA2.HTM.

Champagne, Duane (Ed.) (1994). *The Native North American Almanac.* Detroit: Gale Research.

Chittister, Joan (1983). *Women, Ministry and the Church.* Paulist Press.

Chittister, J., Chishti, M.S.S. and Waskow, A. (2007). *The Tent of Abraham: Stories of Hope and Peace for Jews, Christians, and Muslims.* Boston: Beacon Book Press.

Chomsky, Noam (1983). *The Fateful Triangle: The United States, Israel and the Palestinians.* South End Press.

Chomsky, Noam (1999). *Profit Over People: Neoliberalism and Global Order.* New York: Seven Stories Press.

Chomsky, Noam (2002). *Distorted Morality: America's War on Terror?* DVD. Director John Junkerman. ASIN: B00008AOW1

Columbia Encyclopedia (2000). Sixth Edition. New York: Columbia University Press.

Corbin, Henry (1958/1969). *Creative Imagination in the Sufism of Ibn'Arabi,* translated by Ralph Manheim. Princeton, NJ: Bollingen Series, Princeton University Press.

Corelli, M. (1895). *The Sorrows of Satan.* New York: Grosset & Dunlap.

Coulter, Ann (2002). "Why We Hate Them." Universal Press Syndicate. 25 September, 2002.

Covey, Stephen R. (1994). *First Things First*. ew York: Simon and Schuster.

Dahlerup, Drude (1998). Using Quotas to Increase Women's Representation. In Karan (1998).

Dalglish, Cass (1996). *Moist Wind from the North*. Dissertation novel and companion essay submitted to The Union Institute, Cincinnati, Ohio. UMI 9623650. Ann Arbor, MI: UMI.

D'Andrade, R.G. (1995) *The Development of Cognitive Anthropology*, Cambridge University Press.

Daryle, Mark Erickson, Goldberg, Joseph E., Gotowicki, Stephen H. et al. (Eds) (1996). *Encyclopedia of the Arab-Israeli Conflict*. Westport, CT: Greenwood.

de Bary, T. (1958). *The Rig-Veda*, 10.90, in *Sources of Indian Tradition*. NY: Columbia University Press. Also on http://www.people.memphis. edu/~kenichls/1301HinduCreationCaste.html

Deschner, Karlheinz (1962). *Abermals krähte der Hahn: Eine kritische Kirchengeschichte*. Germany: btb bei Goldmann (btb. Bd. 72025).

Dollar, D., Fisman, R. & Gatti, R. (1999). "Are Women Really the 'Fairer' Sex? Corruption and Women in Government." Abstract. Policy Research Report on Gender and Development. Working Paper Series, No. 4. The World Bank. http://www.worldbank.org/gender/prr.

Dorff, Elliot N. & Newman, Louise E. (1998). *Contemporary Jewish Theology*. New York: Oxford University Press.

Douglas-Klotz, Neil (1999). *The Hidden Gospel: Decoding the Spiritual Message of the Aramaic Jesus*. Wheaton, IL: Quest Books.

Douglas-Klotz, Neil (2003). *The Genesis Meditations: A Shared Practice of Peace for Christians, Jews and Muslims*. Wheaton, IL: Quest Books.

Edmunds, R.D. (1980). *American Indian Leaders: Studies in Diversity* Lincoln, NE: University of Nebraska Press.

Eisler, Riane (1987). *The Chalice and the Blade. Our History, Our Future*. San Francisco: HarperSanFrancisco.

Eliade, Mircea (1978). *A History of Religious Ideas: Volume 1 From the Stone Age to the Eleusinian Mysteries*. Chicago: University of Chicago Press.

Encyclopædia Britannica (2003). "Muhammad". Encyclopædia Britannica Premium Service. 15 Oct, 2003 http://www.britannica.com/eb/article?eu=108142

Freeland, Cynthia (1994). Nourishing speculation: A feminist reading of Aristotelian science. In *Engendering Origins: Critical feminist readings in Plato and Aristotle*. Edited by Bat-Ami Bar On. Albany: State University of New York Press.

Fuller, Robert C. (2002). *Spiritual, But Not Religious: Understanding Unchurched America*. Oxford University Press.

Gandhi, Mohandas (1957). *Mohandas K. Gandhi: An Autobiography*. Boston: Beacon Press.

Gardner, Peter M. (December 1991). "Forager's Pursuit of Individual Autonomy." *Current Anthropology*, Vol. 23, No. 5. p. 559.

Geary, David C. & Flinn, Mark V. (2002). Sex Differences in Behavioral and Hormonal Response to Social Threat: Commentary on Taylor et al (2000). *Psychological Review*. Vol. 109(4) pp. 745-750.. American Psychological Association.

Geertz, Clifford (1973). *The Interpretation of Cultures: Selected Essays*. New York: Basic Books.

Ghanem, As'ad (2001). *The Palestinian-Arab Minority in Israel, 1948-2000: A Political Study*. New York: State University of New York Press.

Ghazali, Abdus Star (1999). *Islam in the Post –Cold War Era*, launched in the internet June 1999, accessed January 28, 2004. URL: http://www.ghazali.net/book2/Intro1/intro1.html

Ginwala, Frene (1998). Foreword. In *Women in Parliament: Beyond Numbers*. Azza Karan. (Ed). Stockholm, Sweden: International Institute for Democracy and Electoral Assistance.

Goodland, Stephen J. (Ed.) (2001). *The Last Best Hope: A democracy reader*. San Francisco: Jossey-Bass.

Grinde, Donald A. (1994). Review of Gibson, John Arthur. Concerning the (Iroquois) League. *American Indian Culture & Research Journal*, 18:1. pp. 175–177.

Gundersen, Adolf G. (1998) Religion, Politics and the Native American Land Ethic. *Democracy and Nature: International Journal of Inclusive Democracy*, Vol 4. Issue 2/3. pp. 181–203.

Haley, J.L. (1997). *Apaches: A History and Culture Portrait*. Norman, OK: University of Oklahoma Press.

Hall, Manley P. (1944/1972). *The Secret Destiny of America*. Los Angeles, CA: The Philosophical Research Society, Inc.

Hall, Manley Palmer (1951). *The Adepts: In the Western Esoteric Tradition. Part V. America's Assignment with Destiny*. Los Angeles, CA: The Philosophical Research Society, Inc.

Hall, Manley Palmer (1988). *An Encyclopedic Outline of Masonic, Hermetic, Qabbalistic and Rosicrucian Symbolical Philosophy*. Los Angeles, CA: The Philosophical Research Society, Inc.

Hardt, Michael and Negri, Antonio (2002). *Empire*. Cambridge, MA: Harvard University Press.

Hart, Gary (2004). *The Fourth Power: A Grand Strategy for the United States in the Twenty-First Century*. New York: Oxford University Press.

Haught, James A. (1991). Holy Homicide. *The Humanist* on-line. http://www.wvinter.net/~haught/homicide.html

Helminski, Camille Adams (2003). *Women of Sufism: A Hidden Treasure: Writings and Stories of Mystics Poets, Scholars & Saints*. Boston & London: Shambhala Publications.

Heper, Metin (2000). The Ottoman Legacy and Turkish Politics. *Journal of International Affairs*. Volume: 54. Issue: 1, p 63. Columbia University School of International Public Affairs

Holt, Thomas C. (2002). *The Problem of Race in the Twenty First Century*. Cambridge, MA: Harvard University Press. Reviewed by Lee. D.

Baker, *American Anthropologist*, Vol. 106, No.1, March 2004, pp. 168–172.

Hourani, Albert (1962). *Arabic Thought in the Liberal Age, 1798-1939*, Cambridge University Press.

Huntington, Samuel P. (1997). *The Clash of Civilizations and the Remaking of World Order*. New York: Touchtone Book.

Johansen, Bruce E. (1999). *Native American Political Systems and the Evolution of Democracy: An Annotated Bibliography*. Westport, CT: Grenwood Press.

Johnson, Paul (1987). *A History of the Jews*. New York: Harper and Row.

Juergensmeyer, Mark (2000/2003). *Terror in the Mind of God: The Global Rise of Religious Violence*.Berkeley: University of California Press.

Kagan, Robert (2003). *Of Paradise and Power: America and Europe in the New World Order*. New York: Alfred A. Knopf.

Kant, Immanuel (1957). *Perpetual Peace*. New York: Macmillan.

Kaplan, Eran (2005). The National Religious Settlers and Zionist Revisionist Ideology. In *Tikkun: A BimonthlyJewish & Interfaith Critique of Politics, Culture & Society*, Vol. 20, No.5. pp. 29–32, 67–68.

Karam, Azza (Ed.) (1998). *Women in Parliament: Beyond Numbers*. Stockholm, Sweden: International Institute for Democracy and Electoral Assistance.

Khan, Hazrat Inayat (1979). *The Unity of Religious Ideals*. New York: Sufi Order Publications.

Khan, I. (1984). *Notes from the Unstruck Music from the Gayan*. Tucson, AZ: Message Publications.

Kimball, Charles (2002). *When Religion Becomes Evil*. San Francisco: HarperSanFrancisco.

King, K.L., MacRae, G.W., Wilson, R.Mcl. & Parrott, D.M. (1990). The Gospel of Mary. In *The Nag Hammadi Library*. James M. Robinson (Ed.) New York: HarperCollins.

Kolas, Ashild (2003). Class in Tibet: Creating Social Order Before and During the Mao Era. In *Identities: Global Studies in Culture and Power*, 10. New York: Taylor and Francis, Inc. pp. 181-200.

Kramer, Stanley (1963). *The Sumerians: Their History, Culture, and Character*. Chicago: University of Chicago Press.

Kyi, Aung San Suu and Clements, Alan (1997). *The Voice of Hope: Conversations with Alan Clements*. Suffolk: Penguin.

Larousse (1968). *Larousse Encyclopedia of Mythology*. NY: Prometheus Press.

Lauterbach, Jacob Z. (Trans.) (1976). *Mekilta De-Rabbi Ishmael*. Philadelphia: The Jewish Publication Society of America.

Lazare, Daniel (2003). The One-State Solution. *The Nation*, November 2003.

Leahey, Thomas Hardy (1997). *A History of Psychology*. (4th Edition). Upper Saddle River, NJ: Prentice-Hall.

Lesch, Ann M. & Tschirgi, Dan (1998). *Origin and Development of the Arab-Israeli Conflict*. Westport, CT: Greenwood Press.

Lewis, Samuel L. (1975). The Jerusalem Trilogy: Song of the Prophets. Novato, CA: Prophecy Pressworks.

Lings, Martin (1983). *Muhammad: His Life Based on the Earliest Sources.* London: Allen & Unwin.

Lorenz, K. (1967). *On Aggression.* New York: Bantam Books.

Lovenduski, Joni and Karan, Azza (1998). Women in Parliament: Making a Difference. In Karan (1998).

McBade, Joseph (1971). *A Rationalist Encyclopaedia: A Book of Reference on Religion, Philosophy, Ethics and Science.* Gryphon Books.

McGrarth, Robert V. (2003). *A Historical Examination of the Debate Between the Stockholder Model and Social Institution Model of Corporation.* Lesley University Publication (online).

Merton, Thomas (1964). *Gandhi: On non-violence.* New York: New Directions Publishing Corporation.

Metzger, Bruce M. (1992). *The Text of the New Testament: Its Transmission, Corruption, and Restoration.* (3rd Edition). New York: Oxford University Press.

Mijares, Sharon G. (2003). *Modern Psychology and Ancient Wisdom: Psychological Healing Practices from the World.* Binghamton, NY: Haworth Press, Inc.

Mijares, S. (2003a). Tales of the Goddess: Healing Metaphors for Women. In Mijares (2003). pp. 71–95.

Miles, Jack (1995). *God A Biography.* NY: Vintage Books.

Mills, Jane (1989). *Woman Words: A Dictionary of Words about Women.* New York: The Free Press.

Morris, Benny (1999). *Righteous Victims: A History of the Zionist-Arab Conflict, 1881-1999.* New York: Knopf.

Muller, F. Max (1886). *Manu, The Law of Manu,* in *The Sacred Books of the East,* Vol. XXV., ed. F. Max Muller Oxford, UK: Clarendon Press. Also on http://www.people.memphis.edu/~kenichls/1301 Hindu CreationCaste.html

Pagels, Elaine (1995). *The Origin of Satan.* New York: Vintage Books.

Parrinder, G. (Ed.) (1971). *World Religions: From Ancient History to the Present.* New York: Facts on File publications.

Parrot, Douglas M. (1988). The Gospel of Mary. Edited by Douglas M. Parrot. *The Nag Hammadi* Library. James M. Robinson, General Editor. New York: Harper Collins.

Pearce, J.C. (2002). *The Biology of Transcendence.* Rochester, VT: Park Street Press.

Peoples, James and Bailey, Garrick (2000). *Humanity: An Introduction to Cultural Anthropology.* Stanford, CA: Wadsworth.

Phillips, Kevin (2004). *American Dynasty: Aristocracy, Fortune, and the Politics of Deceit in the House of Bush.* New York: Viking.

Purcell, H. (2004). *The Secret Life of Mr. Jinnah.* Produced by Hugh Purcell. Documentary televised on LinkTV. San Francisco, CA. Dish Network, 9400. August 3, 2004.

Rafea, Ali, Aliaa and Aisha (2004). *Islam from Adam to Muhammad and Beyond.* Bath (UK): The Book Foundation.

Rahner, K. & Vorgrimler, H. (1965). *Theological Dictionary*. New York: Herder and Herder.

Ramban (1978). *Ramban (Nachmanides): Writings & Discourses. vol. 1* Translated and annotated with Index by Rabbi Dr. Charles B. Chavel. New York: Shilo Publishing House, Inc.

Roy, Arundhati (2003). *War Talk*. Cambridge, MA: South End Press.

Roy, Arundhati (2004). The New American Century. Opening plenary of the World Social Forum in Mumbai. http://www.thenation. com January 22, 2004.

Rummel, R.J. *Freedom, Democracy, Peace; Power, Democide and War*, Ch. 2. URL: http://www.hawaii.edu/powerkills/DBG.CHAP1.HTM

Russell, Bertrand (1999). *Russell on Religion*. Routledge, UK.

Said, Edward W. (1995). *Orientalism: Western Conception of the Orient,* fourth edition. London & New York: Penguin Books (first published 1978).

Savarkar (1938/39). Savarkar's presidential address to RSS members in Nagpur on December 28, 1938. Indian Annual Register, 1938 (1939), Vol. II, Calcutta.

Schipper, Lewis (1993). *Spinoza's Ethics: The View from Within*. New York: Peter Lang.

Schwartz, Howard (1998), *Reimagining the Bible : The Storytelling of the Rabbis*. NY: Oxford University Press.

Sears, David (1998). *Compassion for Humanity in the Jewish Tradition*. Northvale, NJ: Jason Aronson.

Shah, Idries (1964). *The Sufis*. New York: Anchor Book.

Shvedova, Nadezhda (1998). Obstacles to Women's Participation in Parliament. In Karan (1998).

Stiglitz, Joseph E. (2002). *Globalization and its Discontents*. New York: W.W. Norton and Company.

Stone, Merlin (1976). *When God was a Woman*. NY: Harcourt, Brace & Jovanovich.

Storr, A. (1983). *The Essential Jung*, Collected Works 8. Princeton, NJ: Princeton University Press.

Suskind, Ron (2004). *The Price of Loyalty: George W. Bush, the White House and the Education of Paul O'Neill*. New York: Simon & Schuster.

Swimme, Brian (1996). *The Hidden Heart of the Cosmos: Humanity and the New Story*. Maryknoll, NY: Orbis Books.

Taylor, Alan R. (1991). *The Super-Powers and the Middle East*. New York: Syracuse University Press.

Taylor, S.E., Klein, L.C., Lewis, B.P. et al (2000). Female Responses to Stress: Tend and Befriend, Not Fight or Flight. *Psychological Review*. Vol. 107(3). pp. 411–429. American Psychological Association.

Tolstoy, Leo (1988). *A Confession and Other Religious Writings*. NY: Penguin Publications.

Toynbee, Arnold J. (1946/1974). *A Study of History: Abridgement of Volumes I-VI*, by D.C. Somervell. Oxford: Oxford University Press.

Victoria, Brian Daisan (1997). *Zen at War*. Weatherhill.

Victoria, Brian Daisan (2003). *Zen War Stories*. New York: Routledge Curzen.

Wadud, Amina (1999). *Qur'an and Women: Reading The Sacred Text From a Woman's Perspective*. New York: Oxford University Press.

Watt, Montgomery (1985). *Islamic Philosophy and Theology: An Extended Survey*. Edinburgh University Press.

Webster (1989). *Webster's Encyclopedic Unabridged Dictionary of the English Language*. New York: Gramercy Books.

Webster (2000). *Random House Webster's College Dictionary*. NY: Random House.

Werner, E.T.C. (1994). *Myths and Legends of China*. Mineola, NY: Dover Publications.

Wheeler, Romana Louise (2002), *Walking like an Egyptian: A Modern Guide to the Religion and Philosophy of Ancient Egypt*.

Wilber, Ken (1996). *A Brief History of Everything*. Boston: Shambhala Publications.

Willis, R. (Ed.) (1993). *World Mythology*. NY: Henry Holt and Company.

Wolf, Fred Alan (2000). *Mind Into Matter: A New Alchemy of Science and Spirit*. Needham, MA: Moment Point Press.

World Bank (2001). The International Bank for Reconstruction and Development: The World Bank. (2001). *Engendering Development: Through Gender Equality in Rights, Resources, and Voice*. New York: Oxford University Press.

Index

Wrestling with God: The story of my life
Lloyd Geering

Lloyd Geering, a minister and professor in the presbyterian church in New Zealand, was tried for heresy in 1967. Like bishops Robinson (UK) and Spong (USA), he became an innovative and challenging voice in the emerging debates about God and religion in the second half of the twentieth century. His 1966 article, 'What Does the Resurrection Mean?' (printed in this volume) led to the famed heresy trial. Found innocent, Geering became the foundation professor of religion at Victoria University. In *Wrestling With God* Geering writes movingly of the interior and family life that form the backdrop to his controversial public life.

264 pp., £14.95 / $29.90, 9781845400774 (pbk.)

Grassroots Spirituality
Robert Forman

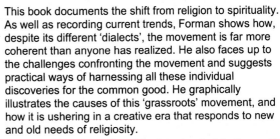

This book documents the shift from religion to spirituality. As well as recording current trends, Forman shows how, despite its different 'dialects', the movement is far more coherent than anyone has realized. He also faces up to the challenges confronting the movement and suggests practical ways of harnessing all these individual discoveries for the common good. He graphically illustrates the causes of this 'grassroots' movement, and how it is ushering in a creative era that responds to new and old needs of religiosity.

'Easy-to-read . . . it is also a key text for those with academic interests.' *Reviews in Theology and Religion*

230 pp., £17.95 / $29.90, 0907845681 (pbk.)

Cognitive Models and Spiritual Maps
Jensine Andresen & Robert Forman (ed.)

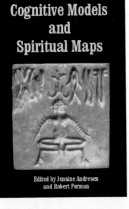

This book throws down a challenge to religious studies, offering a multidisciplinary approach — including developmental psychology, neuropsychology, philosophy of mind and anthropology. Contributors include Jensine Andresen, Arthur Deikman, Stanley Krippner, Phillip Wiebe, Ken Wilber, Christian de Quincey, Brian Lancaster, James Austin, Andrew Newberg, Eugene d'Aquili and Robert Sharf.

'A thoroughly gripping read . . . I cannot do justice to the sophistication of the positions on offer.' *Human Nature Rev.*

'Anyone who is or should be interested in the new cognitive science of religion cannot leave these papers unread.' R.Nauta, *J. Empirical Theology*

288 pp., £17.95 / $29.90, 0907845134 (pbk.)

God In Us: A case for Christian humanism

Anthony Freeman

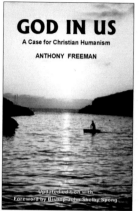

God In Us is a radical representation of the Christian faith for the 21st century. Following the example of the Old Testament prophets and the first-century Christians it overturns received ideas about God. God is not an invisible person 'out there' somewhere, but lives in the human heart and mind as 'the sum of all our values and ideals' guiding and inspiring our lives. Updated edition, with Foreword by Bishop J. Spong. Revd. Anthony Freeman was dismissed from his parish for publishing this book, but he remains a C. of E. priest.

'Brilliantly lucid and to-the-point style.' *Philosophy Now*
'A brave and very well-written book' *The Freethinker*

96 pp., £8.95 / $17.90, 0907845177 (pbk.)

What a Piece of Work: On being human

Helen Oppenheimer

What is special about human beings? Hamlet mused, 'What a piece of work is man! How noble in reason! how like a god!' but went on to speak of 'this quintessence of dust'. Helen Oppenheimer prefers to start with the dust and move to the glory: we really are animals — and from these animals has come Shakespeare. People are indeed 'miserable sinners' — and also magnificent creatures. Lady Oppenheimer does not disguise that she is a Christian theologian whose subject is ethics, but she writes equally for non-Christians. She has published ten books on philosophical theology and Christian ethics.

96 pp., £8.95 / $17.90, 1845400631 (pbk.) June 2006

The Varieties of Religious Experience:
Centenary essays, ed Michel Ferrari

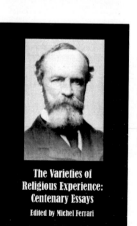

William James published his classic work on the psychology of religion, *The Varieties of Religious Experience*, in 1902. To mark the centenary, leading contemporary scholars reflect on changes in our understanding of the questions James addressed. Contributors include Eugene Taylor, Eleanor Rosch, G. William Barnard, Jens Brockmeier, Keith Oatley, Maja Djikic and Martin Marty.

'This volume signifies something of a resurrection of William James' legacy.' **Jeffrey Mishlove**, *J. Scientific Exploration*

'The essays — lucid and lively — evince the extraordinary range of fundamental issues broached by James.' *THES*

'I couldn't put it down'. **Nicholas Humphrey**

160 pages, £17.95 / $29.90, 0907845266 (pbk.)